THE GREAT BOOK OF
BOSTON
SPORTS LISTS

THE GREAT BOOK OF

BOSTON

SPORTS LISTS

Andy Gresh & Michael Connelly

RUNNING PRESS
PHILADELPHIA · LONDON

Published by Running Press,
A Member of the Perseus Books Group

ISBN 978-0-7624-4285-0
Library of Congress Control Number: 2011925145

E-book ISBN 978-0-7624-4369-7

9   8   7   6   5   4   3   2   1
Digit on the right indicates the number of this printing

Cover and interior designed by Joshua McDonnell
Edited by Greg Jones
Typography: Boton and Helvetica

Running Press Book Publishers
2300 Chestnut Street
Philadelphia, PA 19103-4371

Visit us on the web!
www.runningpress.com
www.cbsbostonsports.com

DEDICATIONS

Andy Gresh:

To my parents, the dumb kid's an AUTHOR NOW! To my brother Steve and my sister (in-law) Sara, all the blessings you deserve in life. You were there for me during the darkest days and I'll never forget it. To my other brothers, Nelson and Charod, you've always believed in me, no matter the situation or goal, and for that I'm forever indebted . . . C.R.E.A.M. I take none of you, and what each of you have done for me, for granted. My success is because of you.

To my little people, Connor and Jack. Someday you'll understand why I'm the way I am. You've both made me see what I was missing in life. And finally, to my Betsey, the greatest gift I've ever been given is your unconditional love. Every move in my life is geared to make you smile, happy, and as fulfilled as I am. In a book of lists, you are #1 with no challengers. You are my end game.

Michael Connelly:

To my beautiful wife Noreen, whose interest in sports has evolved from supportive to loving fan. To my life's joy, my son Ryan, for whom sports has been a wonderful bond between father and son. To my father, John Connelly Jr., who introduced his three sons to the wonder of sports. To my mother, Marilyn Connelly, who sat through sporting events at cold baseball fields and freezing skating rinks without complaint and with much support. To my brothers and sisters, who are not just my siblings but my friends.

CONTENTS

Acknowledgements

Andy Gresh:

Many thanks to Michael Connelly who brought me aboard this project. It was fun to do, and his experience was invaluable, along with that of our guy Greg Jones at Running Press. Greg brought us to completion in such a timely fashion and with ease. It was a pleasure working with you both. I also want to thank the management of CBS radio in Boston and my station, 98.5 The Sports Hub, for giving us the promotional vehicle needed to push this project to another level. In a book of lists, I also want to list the names of others who deserve my thanks including Dan Shaughnessy, Tony Massarotti, Tom Brennan, Mike Gorman, Don Orsillo, Dave Goucher, Gil Santos, Tom Brady, the New England Patriots, Howie Sylvester, Mike Giardi, Taylor Twellman, Gary Tanguay, Art Martone and the staff at CSNNE.com, Trent Tompkins, Eric Sauer, Bill Thompson, Bob and Robin Hall, Joan Whiting, Kevin "Baldo" Miller, Scott Zolak, Jim Louth, Nick Cattles, Rich Schertenleib, Fred Toettcher, Rob Poole, Greg Dickerson, Mike Babchik, Gary Williams of Golf Channel, Scott Masteller, Terry Foxx, Ron St. Pierre. They all contributed in some way. If I missed you, join the line of people who have a problem with me.

Michael Connelly:

I would like to extend my sincere thanks to all the celebrities who submitted lists to the book. To Greg Jones of Running Press Book Publishers, whose belief in the project made the ramblings of two sports nuts a book. To my assistant editor, Robert Doherty, for his guidance and thoughtful suggestions. To my oldest friend, Robert Tracey, whose help was invaluable. To former Princeton goalie, Wally McDonough, who provided his sincere perspective. To Steven Alperin, who has been selfless in his efforts to help maximize the potential of all four of my books. To Charlie Cahill, whose passion for sports is only matched by his help with the book. To Erin McCarran for her assistance in marketing the project. And to my co-author, Andy Gresh: it was a pleasure.

Introduction

We in the Northeast take our sports very seriously. Philadelphia, New York and Boston are maybe the three best sports cities in America. But Boston is clearly the best. We cheer. We boo. We throw stuff. We chastise. We debate. But we also take in the joys of winning and bond over it. And at its core, that's what this book is all about. Whether you use it to start or end a debate is up to you.

Unlike Michael, who's on his fourth book, this is my first book as an author. I come from the world of sports radio, which is immediate reaction to and analysis of what's going on. I have a pretty good gauge on how many people are consuming sports in Boston every day. Almost 20 percent of the people each day who listen to the radio in Boston listen to sports radio. And as crazy as that may sound, I think it's actually way more than that. I don't think the numbers tell the whole story.

For generations, people in Boston have bonded over the Red Sox. In many ways, just like in New York City, the love for baseball is passed down through generations. Many phone calls to sports radio start with, "I've been watching this team for years...." The 2004 season changed Red Sox Nation forever when the Sox won their first World Series since 1918. Sox fans suffered through so many close calls and heartbreaks on the long road to winning that elusive World Series championship after 86 years. Then it happened. I always used to joke on the air that I wanted to own a bunch of funeral homes across New England when the Sox finally won it all, because lots and lots of folks would die. Many who read this book remember exactly where they were, and who they were with, when the Sox "reversed the curse" against the St. Louis Cardinals.

For some, Fenway is a monument that should never be torn down. For most of us, Fenway is where we practice the worship of the Red Sox as if we were going to church on Sunday. Folks across New England have a picture or just the memories of the first time they walked on Yawkey Way and had their first sausage and pepper sandwich.

The old Boston Garden was full of great memories of the Bruins and the Celtics. Red Auerbach waltzed into town in 1950 and turned the Celts into a dynasty—three different times! Whether it was getting Bill Russell or Dave Cowens or exploiting a loophole in the NBA bylaws to draft Larry Bird while he was still in college, Auerbach set a tone and an expectation of winning with the Celtics that has become commonplace. I would love to know how many men in Boston still to this day smoke cigars because Red Auerbach did at the end of every Celtics win. I know because of him, I love Chinese food. And also because I'm fat, but that's beside the point.

After some lean years and time in the "new" Garden, the Celtics have risen again under Danny Ainge. He was given a lot of rope by fans and ownership to fix the team because he's a link to the Celtics' past. He was regarded as the man to lead the team after Auerbach was gone and people like Rick Pitino came in and failed fabulously. Ainge had credibility in this city, which buys you an extra year or two of patience from the fans—even if he took the job with no front-office experience. Bottom line is, people have once again embraced Celtics basketball.

The team that used to get overlooked in "Titletown" was the Bruins—until 2011! The B's won three Game 7s on the way to their first Stanley Cup in 39 years and had a rolling rally parade that was bigger than the celebration for the 2004 Red Sox. Fans came back to the team who rooted for Milt Schmidt, Bobby Orr, Cam Nely, and Ray Bourque.

Orr made hockey mainstream in the Hub in the early 1970s, and its popularity was felt all the way to the construction business as new rinks were built all over New England because kids wanted to play and wear #4. Orr is the biggest icon in Boston sports history, and whenever the B's lost, it brought out some of the most venomous criticism of the team and management. And because the Bruins never went above and beyond when it came to spending money in the 80s and 90s, the team never really challenged for a Stanley Cup. IT drove casual fans away and you were left with a hardcore hockey fan base that was ignored for years and years.

In 2011 the hockey fans of New England were rewarded by Zdeno Chara, Patrice Bergeron, and Brad Marchand with the long-awaited Stanley Cup victory over the Vancouver Canucks and an estimated 1.3 million fans celebrated on a sunny Saturday in June.

Hockey's lineage runs deep; in Boston and it is now back and bigger than ever. Fans can actually call talk radio and discuss the team like the other three pro sports, and coach Claude Julien has his hand stamped to enter the club of championship-winning coaches. Hockey was forgotten for a while, but it's now back in a big way.

Pro football is relatively new to the city of Boston. There are a few reasons for this. It starts with a lack of interest in college football. Doug Flutie made Boston College football relevant in the early 1980s because he was a hometown hero. But in truth, that's the last time BC was making news on the football field that people would pay attention to. And New England college football consists mostly of small college games that are friends and family occasions only.

The pro game in Boston really dates back to the 1960s and the Boston Patriots of the AFL. Gino Cappelletti was the star of those old AFL teams that played in four different stadiums from 1960-69. Contemporary Pats fans have little connection to those teams or that era of football, other than Gino, who still serves as the Patriots radio color analyst.

Since joining the NFL and becoming the New England Patriots, the team has been very inconsistent. There was the Super Bowl run of 1985 that ended with the Pats getting destroyed by the Chicago Bears. But to be completely honest, there are three men who saved the Patriots: Robert Kraft, who kept the team from being moved to St. Louis; Bill Parcells, who set a path for winning and led them to a Super Bowl; and Drew Bledsoe, who was the first overall pick in the 1993 NFL Draft and gave the fans a player to really attach themselves to, a real superstar. For some Pats fans, football started here the day Bill Parcells walked into town.

Kraft and his family invested in a new stadium and with the hiring of Bill Belichick in 2000, we found our new Red Auerbach. Belichick has led the team to four Super Bowls, winning three of them. He is regarded as a genius. He also drafted the new Bobby Orr in Tom Brady.

Every New England kid now wants to be an NFL quarterback who's married to a supermodel. The region has lots of football fields, so the construction impact won't be like the impact Orr had. But some soccer and lacrosse teams will benefit from more flat land being used as athletic fields.

Brady's ability to win in the clutch has turned everyone into a Pats fan and created a new phenomenon: Pink Hat Fans. This phenomenon has been exacerbated by the Red Sox winning their 2004 championship and Fenway Park becoming a place to be seen so you can have cool pictures on your Facebook page. This book will not satisfy those fans.

This book is for the fans who know that Larry Bird was more than just a white guy who wore nut hugger shorts and had a porn mustache. This book is for the fans who will want guys like Tony Eason to never be allowed back into the state of Massachusetts because of his 0-8 performance in Super Bowl XX. This book is for the fans who love "Old Time Hockey." And this book is for the fans who know that the upside down exclamation point thing that the guy in orange holds on the football sidelines is actually a down marker.

A lot of people have contributed to this book. My involvement comes from Michael reaching out to me via Facebook and bringing me aboard. My wife convinced me to look past the fact that he once wrote in his Top 10 column on BostonHerald.com, "Who's Andy Gresh and why do I have to listen to him during Patriots broadcasts?" He and I have joked about how I'm not "Mr. Popular" with some, including some in his house! But if you think about it, it's that passion for sports that makes books like this needed and possible.

I have to thank him for getting me in on this. It's been a lot of fun. Michael's other books—26 Miles to Boston, Rebound! and The President's Team—have been well received and critically acclaimed. Hopefully this one will be as well. He's a great writer.

So whether using it to settle a discussion in a bar, reading it on the toilet or using it as the definitive word in a family sports discussion during the holidays, we hope this book makes all of you think about your life as a Boston sports fan. We hope it also brings back some good memories. Because at the end of the day, we follow sports to suspend our reality and get us away from our workday lives.

We hope you find this book as fun to read as it was to write. Because at the end of the day, we're fans too.—AG

Some players, groups, teams, sentiments, landmarks and events in Boston sports history have so captured the attention of the local community, we've had to invent new terms to identify them. Here are some of the more prominent ones that have entered our sports lexicon over the years.

17. Mosi's Mooses. Mosi Tatupu was one of the most popular athletes in Boston sports history. His rooting section called themselves Mosi's Mooses.

16. Manny Being Manny. For eight years, Manny Ramirez raked like no Red Sox right-handed hitter ever had. He also sat out games, faked hamstring pulls and urinated inside the Green Monster, making his tenure in Boston both heralded and tumultuous. His indignant behavior could only be explained as, "Manny being Manny."

15. Cowboy Up. The 2004 Red Sox were comprised of a bunch of self-proclaimed "idiots" galvanized by their spiritual leader, Kevin Millar. Millar used the phrase "cowboy up" to demonstrate the need for the team to step up in the clutch.

14. The Big Three (II). Teammate of the Celtics' original "Big Three," Danny Ainge was sitting in the same seat as his previous boss, Red Auerbach, when he pulled the strings like the former general manager and assembled a championship team around three future Hall of Famers—Paul Pierce, Ray Allen and Kevin Garnett.

13. Red Sox Nation. Dan Shaughnessy of the *Boston Globe* appropriately termed the world of Red Sox fans, who are spread out across the planet, as Red Sox Nation.

12. The Boston Massacre. When the Yankees came to Fenway Park on September 7, 1978, they were four games behind the Red Sox. When they left four games later, they were tied in the standings after outscoring the Red Sox 42-9.

11. The Gallery Gods. Roger Naples, who had Bruins season tickets for over seven decades, led this group of hearty Bruins fans. They sat in the second balcony of the old Boston Garden. The Gallery Gods were loyal to the core, through good times and bad.

10. Pesky Pole. Longtime Red Sox shortstop and singles hitter Johnny Pesky snuck six of his career's 19 home runs around the right-field pole in Fenway. The pole sat only 302 feet from home plate. In honor of Pesky's well-placed home runs, former Red Sox pitcher Mel Parnell dubbed the yellow marker Pesky Pole.

9. The Kraut Line. Milt Schmidt, Woody Dumart and Bobby Bauer skated on the same line for the Boston Bruins in the 1930s and '40s. They grew up in the same town— Kitchener, Ontario. They lived in the same apartment in Brookline and went off to war together. The three were all of German descent and were thus nicknamed the Kraut Line.

8. Squish the Fish. After 18 straight losses in Miami, the Patriots went to Miami for the AFC Championship Game in January of 1986 with momentum, belief and fate on their side. Patriots fans who traveled by plane from Boston to Florida for the game chanted "Squish the Fish!" Following the Patriots historic 31-14 win, hoarse Pats fans chanted it again the whole way home.

7. Morgan Magic. Local product Joe Morgan took over the reigns of the Boston Red Sox from fired manager John McNamara during the 1988 All-Star break. He instantly lit a spark under the underachieving team. The Red Sox proceeded to win 12 consecutive games, 19 out of 20, and 24 straight at home under Morgan. The team was nine games behind when Walpole's Morgan took over. They finished as AL Eastern Division champions.

6. The Curse of the Bambino. This was the title of a book authored by long-time Boston sportswriter Dan Shaughnessy. The essence of the book was a theory that the Red Sox had been jinxed since selling Babe Ruth to the Yankees in 1919. Most Red Sox fans discounted this notion as foolish. None the less, the phrase took flight.

5. The Green Monster. Boston is a city of great historical significance. The most famous landmark in the entire city is the left-field wall at Fenway Park. Known as the Green Monster, the 37-foot green fence has boldly stood guard over Fenway Park since 1913.

4. The Big Three. Red Auerbach was the master of the NBA deal. Through trades and drafts, he acquired these three Hall of Famers—Larry Bird (6-9), Kevin McHale (6-11) and Robert Parish (7-0). Together, the original Big Three led the Celtics to three world championships.

3. Heartbreak Hill. Over the 26-mile course of the Boston Marathon, there is one stretch of topography that symbolizes the momentous challenge of the route. It is the third and final hill on Commonwealth Avenue. Great Boston sportswriter Lawrence Sweeney once called that last hill "heartbreaking" for its cumulative effect upon a runner. The nickname "Heartbreak Hill" was born.

2. The Big Bad Bruins. They were big and bad—and good. The two-time Stanley Cup champion Bruins of the early 1970s could score, hit, fight and win. They captured the attention of New England, leading to the hockey craze that consumed six states.

1. The Impossible Dream. The Red Sox were coming off eight straight losing seasons when new Boston Manager Dick Williams pledged before the 1967 season that Boston would "win more games than we lose." Led by Yaz and Jim Lonborg, the team's journey to the World Series seemed nothing less than an Impossible Dream.

Note: George Scott was signed by the Red Sox at the age of 18 and made his major league debut for Boston in 1966, appearing in the All-Star Game in his rookie season. The following year, the first baseman hit over .300, won the first of his eight Gold Gloves and finished in the top 10 of MVP voting while playing a major role in the Red Sox Impossible Dream season. Here, "Boomer" shares his favorite memories from 1967—the most magical year in Boston sports history.

11. Dick Williams. He was the perfect manager for that team. He taught us how to win and what it took to win.

10. Great People. All the folks around the 1967 team were great people. Mr. Yawkey was a great owner. Dick O'Connell was a great general manager. Ed Kenney and Neil Mahoney in baseball operations were great, too.

9. Close Team. Some people have called Red Sox teams in the past, "25 players, 25 cabs." Not this team. We really cared for each other. All 25 of us wanted to get in the same cab. We were all so young, like a bunch of high school kids playing the game and pulling for each other.

8. In the Locker Room After the Final Game (October 1, 1967). After we beat the Twins, we all sat in the locker room together and listened to the other games on the radio. Everything had to fall perfectly for us to clinch the pennant, and it did. The Angels beat the Tigers and we celebrated.

7. Billy Rohr's Almost No-Hitter (April 14, 1967). Billy Rohr's first career game and he threw a great one. Billy was the nicest person I ever met in baseball. He had great stuff and showed it that day. Yaz's catch in that game was amazing. The ball was already past him and he somehow dove straight out and caught it.

6. Jim Lonborg Hits Thad Tillotson (June 21, 1967). This didn't necessarily bring us closer because we were already a close team. This showed how tough Jim Lonborg was. He would protect us hitters. He wasn't afraid to pitch inside. He was the best pitcher in baseball in 1967.

5. Jose Tartabull Throws Out Ken Berry (August 27, 1967). The throw home by Jose, who didn't have the strongest arm, and the amazing catch and tag, by Elston Howard to end the big White Sox game is what typified the type of baseball we played that year. If you go up and down the roster, every player did something great to help us win a game.

4. The Pop Up to Petrocelli (October 1, 1967). All year, we played for that moment and when it happened, it defined us as winners. That weekend against the Twins, we faced their top two pitchers in Jim Kaat and 20-game winner Dean Chance. The Twins gave us trouble that year (we were 5-11 against them in 1967 going into that game). We took on their best and beat them.

3. The 10-Game Winning Streak (July 14–23). In the middle of the year, we went on a long winning streak that included six tough road games. Before that we knew we were good. But this confirmed it.

2. Carl Yastrzemski. Yaz exemplified leader. Every hit he had that year was big. You had to be there to believe it. It still is the greatest year by any baseball player. If he came up to the plate and the game was tied or we were behind, he delivered. His year meant so much to the team, the city and baseball.

1. Boston Red Sox Fans. The Boston fans are the best fans in baseball. They always support the team and deserve good teams. I'm glad we gave them one in 1967.

In sports history, many players have produced for short periods of time. The players that appear on this list were able to sustain a level of excellence throughout an entire, remarkable season.

Honorable Mentions. Craig Janney (1986-87) accumulated 81 points in 37 games for Boston College hockey; Damian Constantino (2003) went on a 60-game hitting streak for Salve Regina; Jack Foley (1961-62) averaged 33.3 points a game for Holy Cross basketball; Red Sox shortstop Nomar Garciaparra (2000) hit .372; "Chuckin'" Charlie O'Rourke (1940) led Boston College's "Team of Destiny" to a Sugar Bowl win; Winchester native Joe Bellino (1960) ran, passed, caught, returned and punted his way to the Heisman Trophy at Navy; Joe Dudek of Plymouth State broke walter Payton's college career touchdown record with 25.

21. Ricky Santos (2005). The multi-talented quarterback for UNH threw 39 touchdowns and ran for eight. At the conclusion of the following year, Santos was awarded the Walter Payton Award.

20. Gino Cappelletti (1964). Gino was "Mr. Everything" for the Patriots. He played flanker, defensive back and kicker. In 1964, he caught 47 passes while scoring seven touchdowns and kicking 25 field goals and 36 extra points for a total of 155 points for the season.

19. Ronnie Perry, Sr. (1952). As a sophomore, the Holy Cross Crusader led the school's basketball team to the quarterfinals of the NIT and its baseball team to the College World Series title. (In 1954, he led the basketball team all the way to the NIT championship.)

18. Luis Tiant (1974). "El Tiante" took the ball every fourth day and often twirled a gem. On the season, he was 22-13 with 25 complete games and seven shutouts with a 2.92 ERA.

17. Tim Wakefield (1995). It was his first season with the Red Sox, and from May 27 to August 13, Tim Wakefield's knuckler was unhittable. During this stretch, he was 15-1 with a 1.65 ERA.

16. Harry Agganis (1952). After returning from active service in the Marines, "The Golden Greek" led Boston University in football, setting 15 school records, and in baseball, batting .323. He was drafted in the first round by the Cleveland Browns, but elected to sign with the Red Sox in order to play baseball and stay near home.

15. Roger Clemens (1986). "The Rocket" was young and clean of any "suspicion" in 1986. During the season, Clemens went 24-4 with a 2.48 ERA, earning not only the Cy Young Award, but MVP honors, too.

14. Tim Thomas (2011). In leading the Bruins to the 2011 Stanley Cup, Tim Thomas set an NHL record with a .938 save percentage in the regular season—and he improved that to .940 during the playoffs. He authored two shutouts in Game 7s in these playoffs, including the Cup clincher in Vancouver. For his efforts he was awarded his second Vezina Trophy (NHL's best goaltender) and the Conn Smythe Award (playoff MVP).

13. Tom Brady and 12. Randy Moss (2007). In the most potent single-season for a QB-WR combination in NFL history, MVP Brady set an NFL record with 50 touchdown passes and Moss set another record with 23 TD receptions as they led the Patriots to a 16-0 record for the regular season.

11. Phil Esposito (1970-71). Espo always had great position and his stick on the ice. In his greatest season, he netted 76 goals and distributed 76 assists for the Big Bad Bruins.

10. Jim Rice (1978). Jim Ed's 1978 season was, at the time, one of the most awesome power displays in baseball history. He totaled 406 bases on the season, with 25 doubles, 15 triples and 46 home runs. In addition to his power numbers, #14 hit .315 and was awarded the MVP Award.

9. Larry Bird (1984-85). As with Ted Williams, you could select one of many seasons for Larry Bird. For his 1984-85 campaign, Bird won one of his three MVP awards while averaging 28.7 points, 10 rebounds and 6.6 assists.

8. Doug Flutie (1984). The quarterback no one else wanted delivered Boston College to national prominence. In the senior season of his Hall of Fame career, #22 threw for 3,454 yards and 27 touchdowns, including the famous Hail Mary TD against Miami. For his efforts, Flutie won the Heisman Trophy, the Maxwell Award and the Davey O'Brien Award.

7. Cam Neely (1993-94). The power right wing played on one leg and scored 50 goals in 44 games. The goals came on backhands, one-handed pokes, tips and slap shots. The greatest right wing in NHL history.

6. Ted Williams (1953). Williams served his country for the second time in his career when he went to the Korean War and flew 39 missions. When The Splendid Splinter returned, he started his first game on August 16, 1953, going 2 for 3 with a home run. For the remainder of the season, Williams hit .407 with 13 home runs. The 1941 season may have been his best (.406 with 37 home runs and a 1.287 OPS), but 1953 may have been his most admirable.

5. Pedro Martinez (2000). The greatest Red Sox pitcher of all time submitted a season for the ages in 2000. His record, of 18-6 (12-1 on the road) was not an indicator of his supremacy. The American League Cy Young winner held hitters to a .167 batting average and posted an ERA of 1.74 (0.85 in wins). His WHIP (walks + hits per innings pitched) was 0.737—the best in baseball history. In Pedro's six losses, his team scored an average of 1.16 runs a game.

4. Bill Rodgers (1977-78). During a 365-day period, "Boston Billy" Rodgers won the Boston Marathon, the Fukuoka Marathon and the New York City Marathon (twice!). His dominance would help incite a worldwide running craze and place him on the cover of *Sports Illustrated* twice.

3. Bobby Orr (1969-70). The greatest hockey player ever to skate onto the ice, Orr put the Bruins back on the hockey map in the 1969-70 season, leading the team to its first Stanley Cup in 29 years. The Boston defenseman scored an unthinkable 120 points while earning the Art Ross Trophy (top point scorer), the Conn Smythe Trophy (MVP of Stanley Cup), the James Norris Memorial Trophy (best defenseman) and the Hart Memorial Trophy (MVP).

2. Bill Russell (1956-57). In the period from March 24, 1956, to April 13, l957, Bill Russell won three unique and distinct championships. First, he led the University of San Francisco to 55 straight wins and its second consecutive men's basketball national championship while averaging 21 points and 21 rebounds per game. Next, he led the United States men's basketball team to an Olympic gold medal in Brisbane with a win in the final over Russia 89-55. Then he joined the Celtics for the last 48 games of their NBA season and helped the team win its first championship in April. During the NBA postseason, Russell averaged 13.9 points and 24.4 rebounds.

1. Carl Yastrzemski (1967). From April to October, Yaz carried the Red Sox on his back and into the World Series. In the second-to-last season of the pitcher-dominated "Raised Mound Era," Yaz hit .326 with 44 home runs and 121 RBI to win the Triple Crown and the MVP. But it wasn't just about stats. It was that every time the Red Sox needed a big hit—Yaz came through. During the magical 1967 Impossible Dream season, #8 captured the hearts and attention of all of Boston and finally escaped the shadow of the Sox previous left fielder.

Best Performances by Supporting Players :: MC

These players weren't prominent contributors to the local teams. For the most part, they sat on the sidelines in Boston. But whether it was destiny or the alignment of stars, these athletes answered when called upon in a big moment with a play or performance beyond anyone's expectations.

11. Conner Henry. At best a journeyman guard, Conner Henry played in only 46 games for the Celtics. But his dunk over Charles Barkley on national television in 1987, combined with a debut performance in which he shot 3-4 on three pointers, made him a hit at the Boston Garden.

10. Jeff Stone. When the well-traveled outfielder stepped to the plate in the bottom of the ninth on September 28, 1990, it was Stone's first major league at-bat of the season. The Red Sox were tied with the Blue Jays in the standings and in the game. With two outs and Wade Boggs on third, Stone lined a single into center field off Tom Henke in a walk-off win that pushed the Red Sox to the division title.

9. Fred Coleman. The wide receiver came to the Patriots by way of the XFL. He had two career NFL receptions, one of which played a key role in a 17-16 comeback win over the Jets during the 2001 Super Bowl season.

8. Jose Tartabull. The weak-armed outfielder was positioned in right field for Boston in a critical late-August game against the White Sox in the midst of the Impossible Dream season of 1967. With one out in the ninth inning and the tying run on third base, Tartabull caught a fly ball for the second out and then threw a seed to the plate, where catcher Elston Howard made a great catch and tag to secure the victory. It was only the third assist of the season for Tartabull.

7. J.R. Redmond. Commentator John Madden advised taking a knee, but Tom Brady knew better. The 2002 Super Bowl was tied at 17-17 and the Patriots had the ball on their own 17-yard line with no timeouts and less than two minutes on the clock. The Patriots quarterback led the team down the field with three key throws to running back J.R. Redmond. The last catch included an 11-yard run after the reception in which Redmond also got out of bounds to stop the clock. The rest is history. During the regular season, Redmond had grabbed just 13 receptions.

6. Bobby Kielty. In Game 4 of the 2007 World Series, late-season Red Sox acquisition Bobby Kielty hit a home run in his only at-bat of the Series. Kielty's eighth-inning solo shot provided the winning margin in Boston's 4-3 victory to clinch the Series.

5. Moe Lemay. The left wing was a late-season acquisition. He played in only two regular-season games for the Bruins and then became a playoff sensation. Lemay scored four goals during the Bruins 1988 run to the Stanley Cup Finals, along the way helping the Bruins beat the Canadiens in a playoff series for the first time in 45 years.

4. P.J. Brown. Talked out of retirement by Paul Pierce and Ray Allen, the Celtics forward signed as a free agent late in the 2008 season. In the classic first-round series against the Cleveland Cavaliers, Brown shot 73 percent from the field, hitting the biggest shot of his career late in Game 7. His 10 points and six rebounds in Game 7 helped advance the Celtics to the next round and eventually win the championship.

3. Dave Roberts. In Game 4 of the 2004 ALCS against the Yankees, pinch runner Dave Roberts stood on first base with the Red Sox trailing 4-3 in the ninth inning. Everyone in the park knew he was stealing, and that he did. Roberts proceeded to score on a Bill Mueller single, and the rest is history.

2. Glenn McDonald. A 1974 first-round pick by the Boston Celtics, McDonald did little to distinguish himself before the 1976 NBA Finals against Phoenix. But in the triple-overtime Game 5, which many have labeled as the greatest game in NBA history, four Celtics fouled out, compelling Head Coach Tom Heinsohn to turn to the fresh-legged McDonald. In a 63-second span, McDonald scored six points, leading the Celtics to a 128-126 victory and an eventual NBA championship.

1. Bernie Carbo. With the Red Sox trailing 6-3 in the eighth inning of Game 6 of the 1975 World Series, Bernie Carbo was sent to the plate to pinch hit. With a 2-2 count, Carbo launched the ball into the center-field bleachers to tie the game. Carbo's blast put the Red Sox in position to win the greatest game in World Series history.

These are the leaders who pulled the strings and called the shots for our teams. We sometimes questioned their wisdom. But in the end, we knew that we were lucky to have them leading our teams. Some ruled with an iron fist, while others were players' coaches. Either way, they were successful and helped guide our teams to glory.

Honorable Mentions. University of Maine Baseball Coach John Winkin; Dick Farley of Williams football; Joe Mullaney of Providence basketball; Bill Cleary of Harvard hockey; Doc Rivers, who led the Celtics to the NBA championship in 2008; Joe Cronin, who won over 1,000 games and one pennant with the Red Sox; Jack Bicknell of Boston College football; Jim Calhoun of Northeastern and UConn basketball; Geno Auriemma of UConn women's basketball; the Petronelli Brothers, who trained and managed Marvelous Marvin Hagler; Mary and Evy Scotvold, who coached figure skaters Nancy Kerrigan and Paul Wylie to Olympic medals; Greater Boston Track Club's Bill Squires, who coached Bill Rodgers, Alberto Salazar, Greg Meyer and Dick Beardsley; Barbara Stevens, who led Bentley University's women's basketball team; Reading High Track Coach Hal Croft.

11. Dick Williams (1967-69). He promised that his Red Sox would win more games than they would lose, and he delivered. As the conductor of the Impossible Dream season of 1967, Williams will forever be honored in Boston for that wonderful year.

10. Frank Leahy (1939-40). He led Boston College football to a 20-2 record. In 1940, his Eagles went 11-0, including a Sugar Bowl victory over Tennessee that gave BC a share of the national championship. Following the 1940 season, he left to coach at Notre Dame.

9. Chuck Fairbanks (1973-78). The Patriots coach came to Foxboro Stadium from the University of Oklahoma. During his six years as head coach, he raised the franchise to a level of respectability. His teams reached the post-season twice, with both playoff runs ending in disappointment. In 1976 against the Raiders, the Patriots were robbed of the opportunity to advance. In 1978, the Patriots had Super Bowl aspirations, only to flounder amidst controversy when the owners suspended Fairbanks for interviewing for the University of Colorado job. He was reinstated for the Houston Oilers playoff game, but the Pats lost badly, and then lost Fairbanks.

8. Terry Francona (2004–). "Tito" is the perfect manager for the 21st-century athlete. He manages players, and in turn, they commit their talents to the cause. In 2004 and 2007, he did what no Boston manager could do in the previous nine decades when he led the Red Sox to World Series championships.

7. Jack Parker (1973–) and 6. Jerry York (1994–). The two great college hockey coaches have been connected since their high school days. Parker, who was born in Somerville, starred for Catholic Memorial High School and then Boston University before coaching the Terriers to national titles in 1978, 1995 and 2009. York, who was from Watertown, played at Boston College High School and then at Boston College before coaching his college alma mater to national titles in 2001, 2008 and 2010 (he also won a national title in 1984 as coach of Bowling Green). There is no rivalry like this in all of sports—alumni coaching their schools from the same city to national championships and against one other. And between them, they have over 1650 wins!

5. Don Cherry (1974–79). "Grapes" was the ultimate players' coach. His teams loved him and played hard for him. They were tough and skilled and successful. Cherry was a dapper dresser who loved his dog Blue as much as he loved his players. Cherry did everything but lead his team to a Stanley Cup, losing in the playoffs twice to the Montreal Canadiens. His strong personality eventually clashed with the owner, and his exodus was quick and painful.

4. Bill Parcells (1993–96). The full-page ad in the papers upon his arrival said it all: "Parcells—that's right, Parcells." The Big Tuna came to town and resurrected the Patriots. In his four years, he turned the Pats into a winner, leading them to the 1997 Super Bowl against the Packers. His departure was less than glorious, but he certainly left the team in better shape than he found it.

3. Tom Heinsohn (1969–78). The great power forward was given the Celtics head coaching job by Red Auerbach only because Bill Russell didn't want it. Never truly accepted, all the fiery coach did was lead the Celtics to their all-time best season record (68-14 in 1972-73) and win two NBA championships (in 1974 and 1976).

2. Bill Belichick (2000-). Schooled in the art of football, Belichick came to New England after leaving the Jets. He then built the Patriots into one of the great dynasties in NFL history. During a seven-year period, he led the Patriots to three Super Bowl victories and four AFC Conference championships. With his hooded sweatshirt, he demanded that his team play the right way and, in turn, made the New England community proud. In Bill We Trust!

1. Red Auerbach (1950-66). With rolled-up program in hand and victory cigar ready to be lit, "The Cantankerous One" won nine NBA championships in 10 years as a coach. He then handed the reigns to his favorite player, Bill Russell, and moved up to the front office, where he orchestrated seven more championships. He survived Irv Levin, John Y. Brown and Rick Pitino.

As coaches and leaders, these men failed to inspire or motivate their players. The X's and O's they drew on the chalkboard were misplaced and their teams lost and underachieved. As a coach of one of our prominent local teams, you are a custodian of an institution that we hold dear. When your team fails, the quality of life in the community suffers, and you must be held accountable.

Honorable Mentions. Patriots Coach Clive Rush (5-16); Patriots Coach Joe Mazur (9-21); Boston College Football Coach Dan Henning (16-19-1 and a betting scandal).

10. Rod Rust (1990). It was bad enough that Coach Rust's team embarrassed the community with its 1-15 record. The worst part was the shame that they brought upon the Patriots franchise with the Lisa Olson harassment scandal.

9. Ed Chlebek (1978-80). Chlebek, who came by way of Eastern Michigan, took the helm for the Eagles in 1978 when the Boston College football roster included six future NFL players. But despite this talented collection of players, the team was 0-11 for the season. This record included losses to Holy Cross, UMass, Villanova, Temple, Army, Navy, Air Force and Tulane during BC football's lone winless season.

8. Grady Little (2002-03). In some ways, this is unfair, but life is unfair. Little led the Red Sox to a 188-136 (.580) record as manager. He even got them to Game 7 of the 2003 ALCS against the Yankees. But then came that little matter of him leaving Pedro Martinez in too long that we Bostonians just can't forgive.

7. Pete Carroll (1997-99). Pete was pumped and jacked when he took over the Patriots. In the previous season, Bill Parcells had led the team to a Super Bowl appearance. With Carroll at the controls for the next three years, the team trended downward. The regular-season win totals during Carroll's reign: 10, then 9 and lastly 8. Following the 1999 season, Carroll was relieved of his duties after compiling a 27-21 record.

6. Joe Kerrigan (2001). The pitching coach who was afraid of "high" pitch counts took over the reins of the Red Sox during the 2001 season. He proceeded to alienate both Pedro Martinez and Manny Ramirez, who in turn shut it down for the rest of the season. His 17-26 record was enough of a sampling to convince the Sox front office that Kerrigan belonged in the bullpen.

5. M.L. Carr (1996-97). Yes, he took one for the team by allowing the Celtics to bottom out in order to enhance their draft position. But it was very painful to watch. Coach Carr's record of 48-116 (.293) didn't remind any Celtics fans of the 1960s.

4. Steve Kasper (1996-97). Kasper was one of the great defensive centers in Bruins history. Unfortunately, his success on the ice didn't translate to success behind the bench. His quiet disposition failed to inspire his charges. His attempt to spark the team by benching Cam Neely and Kevin Stevens led to his demise and his ultimate sacking. After two years at the helm, his losing record of 66-78-20 was enough to compel management to go in a different direction.

3. Butch Hobson (1992-94). The Red Sox brain trust showed Morgan Magic the door to make sure it didn't lose hot managing commodity Clell "Butch" Hobson. The new Red Sox manager arrived in Winter Haven and was immediately disrespected by his ace, Roger Clemens, who ran laps with Hobson while wearing earphones so he could ignore his new boss. Hobson compiled a record of 207-232 (.472) during his tumultuous three years as the Boston skipper.

2. Dave Lewis (2007). This was General Manager Peter Chiarelli's first big decision and he whiffed badly. Dave Lewis must have had a great interview with the GM to be able to overcome his Hitler moustache and uninspiring demeanor. The Bruins gave him a four-year contract. Lewis was done after one year with a record of 35-41-9 (.463).

1. Rick Pitino (1998-2001). It wasn't just the losses—it was the arrogance. The coronation at the Boston Garden to announce Pitino's arrival was worthy of Julius Caesar. "Slick Rick" demoted Red Auerbach when he took the position of "President." He mishandled prospects Joe Johnson and Chauncey Billups. He compiled a 102-146 (.411) record as the Celtics coach. Red Auerbach isn't walking through that door, Tommy Heinsohn isn't walking through the door. My favorite line about Pitino that I read, "We thought we were getting Michael Corleone, but instead we got Fredo."

My Top 10 Boston Sports Moments
:: by Senator Scott Brown

Note: Scott Brown won election to the United States Senate from Massachusetts in 2010. He credits sports for giving him direction in life and channeling his drive to succeed. An avid fan, his leading sports passion is basketball. In college, he starred at Tufts University as a long-range shooter for the Jumbos, averaging 10 points a game in the era before the three-point line. Here, he lists his top Boston sports moments for us.

10. Carl Yastrzemski's Last Home Run. This was the end of an era. Yaz's career spanned three decades, 3,308 games and 432 home runs. But he never was able to win a World Series.

9. Ray Allen Breaks the All-Time Three-Point Record. On February 11, 2011, while the Celtics were playing the Lakers, Ray Allen became the all-time NBA leader in total three-point field goals (2,562), breaking Reggie Miller's record.

8. Bruins Beat Vancouver Canucks to Win the 2011 Stanley Cup. It took nearly 40 years, but the Bruins came back to win Lord Stanley's Cup, by shutting out Vancouver 4-0 in Game 7 of the series.

7. Ted Williams' Last At-Bat. Only Teddy Ballgame could have done this— hitting a home run in his last at-bat, in the last game of his career on September 28, 1960. This ended the playing career of arguably the greatest hitter of all time, and a great American.

6. Bill Russell's Jersey Retired a Second Time (1995). Still reeling from the bitter sting of racism, Bill Russell did not allow the public to witness his #6 jersey being retired in 1972. By 1995, he had forgiven the people who had treated him disrespectfully and embraced a new and open City of Boston, the home of the Celtics, the team he loved.

5. Bobby Orr's Goal to Win the 1970 Stanley Cup. We all know the famous picture of Orr jumping through the air after tripping and scoring against the St. Louis Blues. This was Bobby Orr at his greatest. Boston was all about the Bruins that year.

4. Patriots Beat Raiders with Adam Vinatieri Field Goal in "The Snow Bowl." When Adam Vinatieri kicked the game-winning field goal in the middle of a February nor'easter, the Patriots not only won what became known as "The Snow Bowl," but set the stage to win their first Super Bowl two weeks later.

3. Celtics Win Championship in 2008. This was the return of the Boston Celtics as a dominant team. Gone were the heroes of the past—Bird, Parish, McHale, Cousy, Russell, Heinsohn and Havlicek. The new heroes were Garnett, Rondo, Allen and Pierce.

2. Red Sox Beat Yankees in Game 7 of 2004 ALCS. The Curse of the Bambino was finally broken when the Red Sox took the ALCS by beating their archrivals, the Yankees. Not only did the Sox advance to win the World Series, but the legend of Curt Schilling's bloody sock was born.

1. Doug Flutie's Hail Mary Pass in Miami. Without question the most impressive comeback of my lifetime. In the Eagles' November 1984 comeback win, Doug Flutie put Boston College on the map for football and earned himself the Heisman Trophy. Everyone in Massachusetts knows where they were when that play happened.

We have the Freedom Trail and Newbury Street and Fanueil Hall. But there is no place I'd rather be on a perfect night than Fenway Park. It's Boston's greatest jewel.

14. Red Sox Bullpen Cart. I loved as a kid when a team would change pitchers. Joe Mooney, from the grounds crew, would drive a souped-up golf cart topped with a Red Sox hat to pick up the new pitcher in the bullpen.

13. Fenway Frank. They have since changed hot dogs. However, the old-day dog was the best. Sitting at your seat with your hot dog covered with spicy Gulden's Mustard out of the packet.

12. The Green Monster. Every time I go to a game at Fenway, I still get a thrill out of walking up the ramp before a game and seeing the green field and the players taking batting practice and the Green Monster standing tall over Fenway Park. It is probably the most unique element of any sporting stadium in the world. Its scoreboard is old school. The Yawkeys put Morse code pledging their love on it. The ladder affixed to the wall used to be used to get balls out of the screen. Lastly, there's the way Yaz used to take balls off the Green Monster and hold scared runners to singles.

11. "We Want A Hit!" When I was young, all the kids around the park at a matinee game used to chant, "We want a hit!" through the bottom of their popcorn containers.

10. Sherm Feller. The friendly sound of Sherm Feller's greeting: "Ladies and gentlemen, boys and girls—welcome to Fenway Park!"

9. Billboard Sign. Whenever there was a big game and there were no tickets, daring teenagers would climb the billboard sign behind Fenway's center-field wall and watch the game for free.

8. "Sweet Caroline." By the eighth inning, Red Sox Nation is in full voice. Hearing 38,000 sing, "So good, so good, so good!" is pretty cool. (I wish they sang the national anthem that loud.)

7. "Well, I Love That Dirty Water. . . ." Nothing like walking out of Fenway after an exciting win and hearing the song "Dirty Water" by The Standells.

6. Police on Horses. In the 1970s when I went to Fenway, the Boston Police used to ride onto the dirt apron that borders the field after the game.

5. Cask and Flagon and Baseball Tavern. Before a game, both bars are great meeting spots to have a couple of beers, catch up with friends and get excited for the game.

4. Yawkey Way. The Red Sox have done a great job of making each game an event. Yawkey Way is full of activities and energy. You can get your peanuts, pistachios and/or program there.

3. Citgo Sign. As a young kid, I loved watching this sign light up in different patterns in the late innings of a blowout night game. New England sports history.

2. Peanut Guy. Rob Barry is the greatest passer in New England sports history. This kid could hit you in the hands with a bag of peanuts from 30 rows away on the move while being bumped.

1. Ice Cream Sundae Bar. I loved going there to get a Sundae Bar as a snack later in the game after my Fenway Frank and popcorn. Vanilla and chocolate ice cream covered in chocolate (also Cool Dogs and soft ice cream in a little Red Sox helmet).

My Top Kicks for the Patriots :: by Adam Vinatieri

Note: Adam Vinatieri is at his best in the biggest moments. The South Dakota State product always came through in the clutch for the New England Patriots, whether it was kicking a postseason game-winner through a New England snowstorm, or through air thick with tension in the final seconds of an indoor Super Bowl. This future Hall of Famer will go down as the greatest NFL kicker of all time and one the greatest winners in Boston sports history.

6. Longest Field Goal (57 Yards) vs. Chicago Bears on November 10, 2002. The game was played at the University of Illinois in Champaign. For the fact that it was my longest field goal, I have to add it to my list of kicks I'm most proud of.

5. Overtime Winner (40 Yards) vs. Jacksonville Jaguars on September 22, 1996. You always remember your first game-winner. Overtime game at Foxboro—doesn't get better.

4. Divisional Playoffs Winner (46 Yards) vs. Tennessee Titans on January 10, 2004. The wind-chill factor was 14-below zero and the score was tied. The kick sent us into the AFC Championship Game against the Colts.

3. Super Bowl XXXVIII Winner (41 Yards) vs. Carolina Panthers on February 1, 2004. The significance of this kick makes it one of my favorites.

2. Super Bowl XXXVI Winner (48 Yards) vs. St. Louis Rams on February 3, 2002. This kick was special because of what it meant to the team and to the city. Winning your first Super Bowl is like welcoming your first child—it is special. After the kick was good, it was time to celebrate. We were world champs!

1. The "Snow Bowl" Kick (45 Yards) vs. Oakland Raiders on January 19, 2002. The sheer difficulty of the kick makes this field goal the one I'm most proud of. Four-to-five inches of snow on the ground, blizzard conditions, down by three points. Miss it and you go home, hit it and you go to overtime. You couldn't stack the chips any higher.

The intensity of Boston sports is felt on the floor, in the stands, in the media and in the air. It's the passion that makes our sports world so unique and special. Sometimes the fervor that envelops our teams manifests itself in extracurricular acts of physical aggression. Below is a list of such outbursts.

Honorable Mentions. O.J. Simpson vs. Mel Lunsford; Chris Nilan taking a swing at Ken Linesmen leaving the ice; Boston College Basketball Coach Gary Williams vs. player Martin Clark; Jeff Nelson and Karim Garcia against Paul Williams of the Fenway ground crew; George Scott chases Tippy Martinez; Brian Daubach vs. Tampa Bay; Pedro Martinez vs. Ice Williams; Danny Darwin vs. George Bell; Ted Green-Wayne Maki stick fight; Cam Neely and a *Boston Globe* sign against Claude Lemieux.

17. "Rage at the Cage"—Mike Greenwell vs. Mo Vaughn (August 24, 1991). Old school Mike Greenwell didn't take kindly to rookie Mo Vaughn's batting practice etiquette and let him know it. The two teammates mixed it up against the cage while television cameras rolled.

16. Will McDonough vs. Raymond Clayborn (September 9, 1979). There have been a number of incidents involving Boston athletes picking fights with their elders. Manny Ramirez mixed it up with 64-year-old Red Sox traveling secretary Jack McCormick. Jim Rice exchanged "pleasantries" with 62-year-old Sox PR man Bill Crowley, and then later with his 57-year-old manager, Joe Morgan. However, the most noted May/September battle occurred when Patriots defensive back Raymond Clayborn and great *Boston Globe* writer Will McDonough squared off. Clayborn didn't appreciate McDonough standing near his locker and showed his displeasure by poking the writer in the eye. The Southie-bred scribe answered the bullying with three punches that sent Clayborn sprawling into his locker.

15. Danny Ainge vs. Tree Rollins (April 24, 1983). In the midst of the Celtics clinching the first round of the Eastern Conference playoffs, a frustrated Tree Rollins elbowed Danny Ainge. The Boston guard responded by tackling Atlanta's 7-1 center. During the ensuing scrum, Rollins almost bit off Ainge's finger. The headline in the following day's *Boston Herald* read, "Tree Bites Man."

14. Robert Parish Annihilates Bill Laimbeer (May 26, 1987). In Game 5 of the heated Eastern Conference Finals against the Pistons, "The Chief" sought retribution on Detroit thug Bill Laimbeer's head with three solid blows. Earlier in the series, Laimbeer had tripped Larry Bird to the floor. Johnny Most said it best, "They have been called a dirty ballclub and I can see why! This is a typical, typical disgusting display by Rodman, Laimbeer and Isiah Thomas. The yellow gutless ways they do things here. And they tell me, I shouldn't say bad things about Isiah Thomas. And I say, 'why not?'"

13. Pat Sullivan vs. Matt Millen's Helmet (January 5, 1986). For years, the Sullivan family and their team, the Patriots, had been abused by the Oakland Raiders. In 1976, New England was robbed of a playoff win against Oakland. In 1978, the Raiders' Jack Tatum delivered the tragic hit on Patriots wide receiver Darryl Stingley. Then in 1986, in a manifestation of pent-up frustration, Pat Sullivan taunted Raider Howie Long after the Patriots 27-20 upset win over Oakland in the 1986 playoffs. Coming to Long's aid, teammate Matt Millen slammed his helmet off Sullivan's head, splitting it open. The hit sent Sullivan home with stitches and a victory.

12. Jason Varitek vs. Alex Rodriguez (July 24, 2004). A-Rod got brushed on the arm by a pitch thrown by Bronson Arroyo, and he took exception. As the Yankee third baseman walked toward first base, he uttered f-bombs and challenges. Red Sox catcher Jason Varitek took up A-Rod on the offer and made him eat his catcher's mitt. The rest is history. The incident sparked the Red Sox, who won the thrilling game 11-10. The Sox ended the season by going 46-20 and took the momentum into the postseason, where they beat the Yankees in the ALCS and won the World Series.

11. Red Sox vs. Yankees/Pedro vs. Zimmer (October 11, 2003). In Game 3 of the ALCS, Pedro Martinez buzzed Karim Garcia behind his head. The Yankees bench coach, 72-year-old Don Zimmer, took offense to the pitch and charged. Martinez, who threw Zimmer to the ground. Later in the game, Manny Ramirez would not take kindly to a Roger Clemens fastball and set off another bench-clearing affair. The Red Sox would lose the game 4-3, and the series 4-3.

10. McHale Takes Down Rambis (June 6, 1984). After a devastating 137-104 loss in Game 3 of the 1984 NBA Finals, Larry Bird sent a message to his teammates through the press: "We played like sissies . . . the heart wasn't there." Provoked, Kevin McHale answered the challenge in Game 4 when he clotheslined Lakers forward Kurt Rambis. The incident changed the momentum of the series and propelled the Celtics to the championship.

9. Red Sox vs. Yankees (May 20, 1976). When Yankees outfielder Lou Piniella tried to bowl over Carlton Fisk at the plate in the Bronx, the fuse was lit. Fisticuffs broke out, both benches emptied. During the fight, New York third baseman Graig Nettles sought out Red Sox pitcher Bill Lee and put him out for the season. Throughout the fight, Yankees Mickey Rivers and Otto Velez circled the pack, sucker-punching Red Sox in the backs of their heads.

8. John Wensink Challenges Entire Minnesota Bench (December 1, 1977). Never has a sporting team been as disgraced as the Minnesota North Stars were on this day. In a two-bout event, the Bruins' Terry O'Reilly dominated North Stars left wing Steve Jensen with devastating "Taz" lefts. At the same time, Boston's John Wensink punished and bloodied Minnesota's Alex Pirus in the undercard. When Wensink was finished, he wanted the whole Minnesota team. Leaving the linesmen to assist Pirus, Wensink skated directly to the North Stars bench and called out the entire team. Sadly, there were no takers. This caused Wensink to motion his hands toward them in a gesture of disgust before skating off the ice to a raucous salute from the Garden faithful.

7. Red Sox vs. Yankees (June 21, 1967). In a classic Red Sox-Yankees moment, Boston hurler Jim Lonborg protected his teammates by drilling New York pitcher Thad Tillotson, who had beaned Boston's Jim Foy in the head in the top half of the inning. Lonborg's retaliation ignited a bench-clearing brawl that required the intervention of the New York City police force, which included Red Sox shortstop Rico Petrocelli's brother. Going into the game, the Red Sox were one game over .500. From that point forward, they went 60-39, advancing all the way to the World Series in the Impossible Dream season.

6. Derek Sanderson vs. the New York Rangers (April 11, 1970). Early in Game 3 of the quarterfinals of the NHL playoffs, Rangers goalie Ed Giacomin came out of his net to tell "The Turk" Sanderson that Rangers Coach Emile Francis had put a bounty on his head. Soon thereafter, Sanderson was jumped in the corner by several Rangers, including Walt Tkaczuk and Brad Park. The Bruins would go on to win the series, and then the Stanley Cup

5. Larry Bird vs. Julius Erving, Moses Malone and Charles Barkley (November 9, 1984). After 30 minutes of play, Larry Bird had 42 points and Dr. J had just six. Obviously frustrated, Erving knocked Bird down. When the two superstar forwards went back up court, they squared off, nose-to-nose. No punches were thrown until Sixers Charles Barkley and Moses Malone arrived and grabbed Bird from behind. Then the good Doctor took three shots at Bird's face. As Celtic announcer Mike Gorman said, "I thought J had more class than that."

4. The Bruins vs. Madison Square Garden (December 23, 1979). With five seconds left and the Bruins holding a 4-3 lead, Boston goalie Gerry Cheevers stoned Ranger Phil Esposito on a breakaway. Esposito smashed his stick into pieces, sparking a chaotic finish. Despite the horn sounding, players from each team squared off. During the scrum, a New York fan reached over the glass and hit Bruins winger Stan Jonathan in the face and stole his stick. The Bruins responded by climbing the glass and entering the seating area. Terry O'Reilly led the charge, followed by Peter McNab and Mike Milbury. McNab caught one of the culprits and held him down while Milbury ripped off his shoe and beat the fan with it, then threw the shoe onto the ice.

3. Stan Jonathan vs. Pierre Bouchard (May 21, 1978). In Game 4 of the 1978 Stanley Cup Finals, Montreal Canadien Pierre Bouchard, who stood 6-2, picked a fight with the wrong guy—Boston's 5-8 Stan Jonathan. When it was over, linesman John D'Amico was covered in Bouchard's blood. Jonathan hit the Canadien with 11 rights until he freed up his left hand. Then it only took two lefts to put Bouchard face down on the ice.

2. Pat Quinn vs. Boston (April 2, 1969). When you take on Bobby Orr, you take on the city of Boston. Toronto Maple Leafs defenseman Pat Quinn and Bobby Orr had a running feud going into the first game of the playoffs. During the second period with the Bruins leading 6-0, Quinn took a run at Orr with a high elbow, knocking the defenseman unconscious. The Garden erupted. Quinn was taken to the locker room by police escort while the crowd chanted, "We want Quinn! We Want Quinn!"

1. Sam Jones and Stool vs. Wilt Chamberlain (April 1, 1962). In Game 5 of the 1962 Eastern Division Finals, the Boston-Philadelphia rivalry escalated from competitive to combustible. After an altercation between Sam Jones and Wilt Chamberlain, the Celtic guard ran for a stool to ward off the giant. "I wasn't about to fight that son of a gun on fair terms," explained Jones. During the fight, the benches emptied. In the midst of the chaos, Philly's Guy Rodgers suckered Celtic Carl Braun and split his lip. Infuriated, Braun chased Rodgers. This compelled Rodgers to pick up the same stool Jones had brandished at Chamberlain, then hide behind the Boston police. (Braun would say later, "I tried to get back at him, but the cops were too fast.") Seconds later, Celtic tough guy Jim Loscutoff went after Rodgers, but the guard again ran for cover. Throughout the skirmish, incited fans rushed the court to help the Celtics. Only two of the hundreds that charged the floor were arrested. The Celtics won the game, the series and later the championship.

My Favorite Sports Memories Growing Up
:: by Micky Ward

Note: A line in the Dropkick Murphys song about Micky Ward, "Warrior's Code," sums up the Lowell boxer: "The spirit of a Warrior, the champion's heart." There may have never been an athlete in New England who competed with more heart and courage than Micky Ward. His boxing career included winning the WBU Light Welterweight title and his trilogy of amazing fights against Arturo Gatti. Ward's life served as the inspiration for *The Fighter*, an Oscar-winning film released in 2010. Micky's list below represents some of his favorite memories from growing up and watching sports in New England.

5. Patriots Secondary of the Late 1970s. When I was younger and played football, I played safety. So when I watched the Patriots, I was a big fan of their secondary—Mike Haynes, Ray Clayborn and especially Tim Fox. I used to love when Fox would come up and bang receivers. I liked that.

4. One of My Favorite Red Sox Players. When I was a kid, I was a fan of Yaz, Fred Lynn, Jim Rice and Carlton Fisk. But one player who I really liked watching was Butch Hobson. I could really relate to him. He threw from the side, played third and wore #4. When I was playing Little League and Senior League, I threw from the side, played third and wore #4, too.

3. My Favorite Patriots Growing Up. I loved watching the Patriots in the '70s and '80s. The old school players that stood out were Sam "Bam" Cunningham, Randy Vataha, Steve Grogan, John Hannah, Mosi Tatupu and Andre Tippett. They were some of my favorites.

2. The Bruins in the 1970s. They won two Stanley Cups led by the great Bobby Orr. I've had the pleasure to meet #4 and I can tell you—he's a better person than he is a player.

1. Celtics Championships (1981, 1984 and 1986). I loved watching the Celtics in the '80s. Larry Bird, Kevin McHale and Robert Parish, that was the original Big Three! They brought the Celtics back to greatness.

Picking just seven guys from the storied history of the Boston Bruins was extremely difficult. The defensemen were easy, but if you don't look closely, you could pass over some damn good forwards. We've been blessed with some of the greats of the game.

Goalie—Gerry Cheevers. Won two Stanley Cups in Boston and was at his best in the playoffs. He had a 33-game undefeated streak in 1972 and set AHL and WHA records for goaltending as well. If he didn't bolt for the WHA in 1972, his place in Bruins history would be more prominent. But when it came down to nut-cuttin' time, he was the best in this team's history. A 53-34 record in the playoffs is damn good.

Defenseman—Bobby Orr. He revolutionized the position and the game. He IS hockey in Boston and would have an ownership stake in the Bruins if Alan Eagelson hadn't screwed him out of it. We'll never see a 40-goal season from a defenseman again, and Orr scored 40 effortlessly. Paul Coffey could score, but he couldn't set up others the way Orr did. This guy deserves that statue in front of the Garden.

Defenseman—Ray Bourque. Career leader for scoring as a defenseman, in part because he played for so long. He went on to win a Stanley Cup with the Colorado Avalanche, and when he brought it back to Boston, 25,000 people showed up to see Bourque with another team's Stanley Cup! Unheard of! It shows the connection fans had to him as a person.

Center—Phil Esposito. With 459 goals in just over eight seasons, including a 76-goal campaign in 1970-71, Espo dominated here in the Hub and had multiple 60-goal seasons. His numbers just make your jaw drop. One of the best natural goal scorers of all time, he won a Hart Trophy in 1969 and was a part of two Stanley Cup winners in Boston.

Winger—Milt Schmidt. Won the Stanley Cup as a player in 1939 and 1941 and was the GM when the Bruins won the Cup again in 1970 and 1972. At the time of his retirement in 1955, he was the third leading scorer in NHL history and second in assists. He was the 1951 MVP in a season where he only scored 21 goals and 50 points. To me, that's a testament to the kind of player he was and the respect he commanded.

Winger—Johnny Bucyk. "The Chief" actually started his NHL career with the Detroit Red Wings, but flourished when he came to Boston. In 21 seasons as a Bruin, he scored 20 or more goals 16 times with a peak of 51 in the 1970-71 season. He's still a part of the Bruins organization today as the director of road services. Player, broadcaster, front office man—he's a Bruins lifer and the organization is better for it.

Coach—Tom Johnson. No obvious choice here. You also have Art Ross, Don Cherry and Harry Sinden. I went with Johnson because of his winning percentage and the fact that he has the 1972 Stanley Cup on his coaching resume. He oversaw an era in Bruins history that every B's fan wants to recreate. A .738 winning percentage is nothing to sneeze at. And while he didn't have a long coaching career, his success can't be ignored.

The New England region has been lucky to have some of the best sports announcers in the business. And most have stuck around long enough for us to grow attached to their voices and their distinct broadcasting styles. I rate these guys as the 10 all-time best. And to those doing the jobs today, no offense if you didn't make the cut . . . yet!

10. Don Gillis. The legendary sports director for Channel 5 from 1962-83, Gillis also hosted *Candlepin Bowling* until 1996. He pioneered the 11 p.m. sportscast and was a Boston institution. Gillis did color commentary at times for Bruins and Celtics games and was a Red Sox pregame and postgame host.

9. Johnny Bucyk. "The Chief" served as color analyst for the Boston Bruins for 15 years. After a 23-year playing career that gained him induction into the Hockey Hall of Fame, he walked into the booth, continuing a love affair with fans in Boston. Bucyk now works for the B's front office and is a great ambassador for the organization.

8. Mike Gorman. For 30 years now, Celtics fans have been pretty lucky to listen to this guy. As good a college and pro basketball play-by-play man as you'll find anywhere, Gorman can call a UConn women's game or a Celtics playoff battle and quickly suck you into either. He knows to let the pictures do the talking and add just the right amount of narrative. And his genuine self comes across on the air, as he really is one of the good guys in broadcasting.

7. Bob Wilson. He walked away before the 1994 lockout season after parts of four decades as a B's color analyst, but is mainly known as the radio voice of the Bruins. He missed the 1970 Cup win, but will always be remembered by Boston fans for calling so many of the other great games in B's history.

6. Gino Cappelletti. An AFL MVP in the early 1960s, Gino made the transition to coach, then Patriots color analyst—a job he has held for going on 27 years now. He has first-name recognition. I know working on the Patriots Radio Network for seven years now, all you have to say is "Gino" and people know whom you're talking about. A Patriots Hall of Famer who is a pleasure to be around. I don't know anyone who doesn't like him.

5. Fred Cusick. If you include his time in radio, Cusick was involved with the Bruins for over 40 years. He's a Hockey Hall of Famer who also did some football work in the early 1960s when the Pats were in the AFL. "SCORREEEEE" will be his forever.

4. Ned Martin. Voice of the Red Sox from 1961-92, he also did Ivy League football, Patriots football back in their AFL days and baseball on national radio. Martin worked with 11 different partners on baseball and also called some of the biggest moments in Red Sox history. All you have to do is know your Red Sox eras and you can figure out how many big moments he broadcast. He spoke with intelligence, mixing in quotes from poets and philosophers. A true legend.

3. Curt Gowdy. He was the voice of the Red Sox for 15 years before leaving for national broadcast glory in 1965. Gowdy called just about every sport at the national level and is a broadcasting legend, both here and across the country. If you grew up in the 1970s and '80s like me, you may not have known he had worked in Boston. But Gowdy left his mark on the Boston sports scene before becoming a national legend.

2. Gil Santos. The longtime Patriots radio voice has called over 700 Pats games! Just an amazing number. If it happened in Patriots history, Gil has probably called it. Throw in Penn State and Boston College football, Boston Celtics games on TV, and Providence College basketball and his status as a legend is cemented. He's a lock to go into the Patriots Hall of Fame and I'm lucky and proud to call him my colleague and friend.

1. Johnny Most. The greatest calls in basketball history belong to Johnny. No play-by-play man today would be able to get away with what Most pulled off. He would mix in commentary and take cheap shots at the opponents while calling the play. He hardly ever criticized the Green and he was as much an institution as the players. He sits alone and unchallenged atop this list.

Top 10 Moments of My Broadcast Career
:: by Gil Santos

Note: Since the 1960s, Gil Santos has been a part of the history of Boston sports. Whether calling games on television or as the longtime voice of the Patriots Radio Network, he's seen a lot. Luckily, he put down the Top 10 moments of his legendary career for this book.

10. Boston College Beats Heavily Favored Texas, 14–13, at Alumni Stadium Under the Lights (September 11, 1976). Texas comes into the game as two-touchdown favorites. But Eagles running back Neal Green goes 78 yards for a BC touchdown on the first play from scrimmage and BC never trails en route to a HUGE win for the program at that time. The win was clinched when Texas PK Russell Erxleben missed a 50-yard FG—just wide right—on the final play of game. Many of the Texas players went onto the NFL, including Raymond Clayborn, who was the Pats first-round pick.

9. Celtics vs. Atlanta Hawks in New Orleans (March 12, 1986). Larry Bird sets a Celtics single-game scoring record by dropping 60 points on the Hawks. He was blazing hot—everything he threw up went in and we televised it live back to New England. The show Bird put on was so incredible that even the Hawks players gave him a standing ovation at the end of the game. When I interviewed him on live TV, Bird said he told Kevin McHale, who had set a Celtics record by scoring 56 points in a game on March 3, that he would break his record before the month of March ended . . . and he did.

8. Patriots vs. Minnesota Vikings at Foxboro Stadium (November 13, 1994). This was Drew Bledsoe's coming out party in just his second season in the NFL. The Pats were getting hammered 20-0 in the first half. A last-second field goal made it 20-3 at the half. Bledsoe then came out in the second half and threw two TD passes and got the Pats into FG range to send it to overtime at 20-20. Bledsoe then threw his third TD pass to FB Kevin Turner in OT to nail down a 26-20 win.

GRESH NOTE: It was my radio partner, Scott Zolak, who told Charlie Weis and Bill Parcells to let the kid chuck it to get the win. They listened and owned the game.

7. Patriots at Pittsburgh Steelers, AFC Championship Game (January 27, 2002). The Steelers were two-touchdown favorites and I opened the broadcast by saying, "Despite the fact that all the experts are saying the Patriots are going to get blown out today, they have decided to show up anyway and play the game." I truly felt the Pats would win because they had been playing so well over the second half of the season. The Pats lost Tom Brady to a knee injury in the first half and Drew Bledsoe came off the bench to throw a TD pass to David Patten that put them ahead. Then the Pats got a touchdown on a blocked FG attempt that they returned for a score to end up with a 24-17 win and a trip to the Super Bowl.

6. Patriots at Pittsburgh Steelers, AFC Championship Game (January 23, 2005). The Pats started fast in this one, as Tom Brady hit Deion Branch for a 60-yard TD pass in the first quarter. Pittsburgh was never in the game, as Brady went 14 for 21 with two touchdown passes for a then career-best QB rating of 130.5 for the game. His passing enabled the Pats to torch the Steelers, with Corey Dillon leading New England's ground attack in an eventual 41-27 win that wasn't even as close as that score would indicate.

5. Patriots vs. Philadelphia Eagles, Super Bowl XXXIX in Jacksonville, Florida (February 6, 2005). The one thing that sticks out in my mind was the tremendous amount of Philly fans who were in Jacksonville for the game. Turns out, some Philly radio station offered to fly any fans who wanted to go there just to be on hand for the Eagles big Super Bowl win. WRONG!! Thousands of people who didn't have tickets went just to raise hell. But it was the "silent minority" Patriots fans who celebrated the 24-21 win that was settled when Rodney Harrison intercepted a Donovan McNabb pass late in the fourth quarter to wrap it up. The final score did not truly indicate how much the Pats controlled the game on both sides of the ball.

4. Patriots vs. Tennessee Titans, AFC Playoffs Divisional Round (January 10, 2004). Hard to forget this night game because it was two degrees at kickoff. The schedule maker should have been forced to sit outside with the fans so he could suffer as they did. It was so cold I was having trouble forming my words on play-by-play because my lips were numb. But we survived, thanks to the Patriots 17-14 win. Tom Brady threw an early TD pass to David Givens that got the Pats off to a 7-0 lead en route to the win, which wasn't clinched until a Steve McNair pass on fourth down went incomplete in the closing seconds. Very tough win for the Pats in brutally cold conditions.

3. Patriots vs. Carolina Panthers, Super Bowl XXXVIII in Houston, Texas (February 1, 2004). New England had played the Texans in Houston in November when the Pats won in OT for their seventh win in a row. After the game, we told any and all Houston folks who would listen that we'd be back in January for the Super Bowl. That's how confident I felt about the Pats that season. They went 14-2, winning their final 12 regular-season games, then beat the Panthers 32-29 in the Super Bowl. Weird game, as the Pats defense smothered Carolina early and their quarterback Jake Delhomme looked lost. Problem was, the Pats offense kept punting, as little things kept halting scoring drives and the first quarter ended at 0-0. Then in the second quarter, nobody could get a stop. It was 14-10 at the half, then 21-10 Pats, and I felt like it was over. But I was very wrong. Carolina scored back-to-back TDs in the fourth quarter to go ahead 22-21. Back came the Pats on a Brady-to-Vrabel TD pass and a Kevin Faulk run for a two-point conversion as the Pats went up 29-22. Carolina didn't quit and a Ricky Proehl TD reception tied it at 29-29. That's when the biggest play of the game came as John Kasay's kickoff went out of bounds and the Pats had the ball at their own 40 to start the winning drive, which ended on Adam Vinatieri's 41-yard field goal for the 32-29 win. Very exciting game.

2. "The Snow Bowl," Patriots vs. Oakland Raiders, AFC Playoffs Divisional Round (January 19, 2002). I remember listening to the weather forecast all day long and it was calling for snow to start around 4 p.m. and continue through the night for this playoff game. Sure enough, I pull into my parking space at the old Foxboro Stadium at exactly 4 p.m. and the first snowflakes start to fall. By game time, it was a winter wonderland. Heavy snow covered the field in white and I had to guess at what yard markers the ball was on. Making it worse, the Pats were losing 13-3 and time was running out. Then came the famous "Tuck Rule" play. It looked like Brady had fumbled when he was sacked and Oakland recovered. However, being inside two minutes until the end of the game, referee Walt Coleman was summoned to review the play. The replay showed Brady's arm coming forward as he was hit, making it an incomplete pass and the Pats held onto the ball. You know what happened next, Brady scored on a six-yard TD run to make it 13-10. He then drove the Pats into FG range for Vinatieri's 46-yarder that tied it at 13-13. It went to overtime, where "Tom Terrific" completed all eight of his passes in setting up Adam's game-winner. The final was 16-13 and that win convinced me the Pats were destined to win the Super Bowl.

1. What Else? Patriots vs. St. Louis Rams, Super Bowl XXXVI in New Orleans, Louisiana (February 3, 2002). Seems everyone except the Patriots figured Pittsburgh would be in the Super Bowl and they had to scramble in New Orleans to replace all the Steelers stuff they had in place with Patriots gear. The Pats had not allowed any team to score more than 17 points for eight consecutive games, including two playoff games. It was that, along with my belief that Brady was indeed real and something special, that had me very confident the Pats would win. Ty Law's interception return for a TD gave the Pats a 7-3 lead and they never trailed again. At halftime, with the Pats up 14-3, all of us in the broadcast booth and out in the press room who were with the Patriots just looked at each other and put a finger to our lips so as not to say anything that might jinx what appeared to be happening. When the Rams tied the game at 17-17 with 1:17 to go, I still felt Brady would get them in position to win. Of course, that's what he did, calmly getting them to the spot that let Adam Vinatieri kick the game-winning 48-yard FG as time expired to make the Patriots World Champions. All of us in our booth, me included, had tears streaming down our faces as we took in that great moment. Without question, the biggest, most exciting and satisfying moment of my 50-year broadcasting career.

I must say, I thought this would be the toughest list to do, but in the end it was pretty easy. The Celts have Hall of Famers, and then guys who are in the Hall of Fame of Hall of Famers—the kinds of guys who get the secret passcode to a special wing of the Hall. The high-end talent this team has had is amazing.

Center Bill Russell. Was there anybody else? An 11-time NBA Champion. A five-time MVP. A 12-time All-Star. On every NBA anniversary team imaginable. His ability to block shots and play defense was contagious in a way we've rarely ever seen. He also broke down racial walls not only in the city of Boston, but also in the NBA as the league's first black coach. I say this on the radio all the time, there are winners and there are champions. Russell defines a champion.

Forward Dave Cowens. OK, so I'm taking some creative liberties here. Cowens was primarily regarded as a small center (6-9). But he did play some power forward, so to me, he's a forward because he deserves to be on this starting five. He averaged over 17 points and 13 rebounds a game during his NBA career. He was known for his balls-out play and his personality quirks. He once took a leave of absence to be a cab driver because he was burned out. He coached both in the NBA and WNBA and won an MVP as a player. One of the all-time greats.

Forward Larry Bird. The best "hick" in NBA history. He may be an overrated defender to some, but when it came to scoring and passing the basketball, there were few like him. He also averaged 10 rebounds a game for his career and was a world-class trash talker. He took pride in being the best white guy in what was perceived as a black man's league. To me, the best one-on-one rivalry in NBA history, and possibly sports history, is Bird vs. Magic Johnson.

Guard John Havlicek. An eight-time NBA champion, 13-time NBA All-Star and the man whose steal in the 1965 East Finals led legendary C's broadcaster Johnny Most to proclaim, "Havlicek stole the ball" (one of the best calls in NBA history). He was also a football player good enough to get drafted by the Cleveland Browns. And after a short stint with the Browns, he chose basketball. He took the football mentality to the court with him as he was named to the league's All-Defensive Team five times. A real blood-and-guts guy.

Guard Bob Cousy. You know you've got stroke when you're the only guy who could get away with calling Red Auerbach by his given name: Arnold. Cousy was a six-time NBA champion and is a fixture in New England basketball. He went to Holy Cross and coached at Boston College, leading them to an Elite Eight appearance in the NCAA tournament and an NIT Finals. He's still used as a measuring stick for comparing point guards in today's NBA. And he's a true gentleman, to boot.

Coach/GM/Grand Poobah Red Auerbach. What didn't this man do for this franchise? He established the winning mentality that still exists today in Boston. He didn't care what fans thought, he didn't care what ownership thought (especially John Brown). He just did what he felt was right for the organization. He stared racism in the face by naming Bill Russell head coach and changed the league forever. No one will ever win as many titles as an NBA coach and general manager as Red did.

Historical points of reference between teams help to create a link to past performances, thus bonding one game to another, one season to another, one era to another. Long memories held by players, owners and fans help to sustain the intensity of such matchups, creating a cumulative extension from game to game and playoff series to playoff series.

10. Williams vs. Amherst Football. The two schools from the Berkshires have been archrivals for almost two centuries. The Amherst Lord Jeffs and the Williams Ephs are the protagonists in the Biggest Little Game in America!

9. Boston College vs. Notre Dame Football. When the two Catholic schools line up against one another, they treat each other in a very unchristian manner. In the 1940s, Notre Dame stole Boston College's greatest football coach, Frank Leahy. In 1992, Lou Holtz called for a fake punt late in a game that his team won 54-7. One year later, David Gordon's last-minute field goal for Boston College allowed the Eagles to gain revenge by beating the Irish and ruining their national championship aspirations.

8. Boston College vs. Boston University Hockey. The two schools both reside on Commonwealth Avenue and share the same goal of hockey supremacy. Year after year, they battle in Hockey East, the Beanpot and the NCAA, with no quarter given.

7. Harvard vs. Yale. These two Ivy League Schools are rivals in the sports arenas, in the admissions offices, in endowment balances and in the business world. The two institutions have waged war for three centuries.

6. Patriots vs. New York Jets. The border war started when Bill Parcells left the Patriots to take over the New York Jets. He took running back Curtis Martin with him one year later and the rivalry intensified. Soon thereafter, Bill Belichick turned down the opportunity to coach the NYJ. Belichick built a dynasty in New England and became a target of Jets coaches Eric Mangini and, later, Rex Ryan.

5. Celtics vs. St. Louis Hawks. The Celtics traded two Hall of Famers, Cliff Hagan and Ed Macauley, to the Hawks for the greatest team player of all time, Bill Russell. The two teams then met four times in five years for the NBA title, with the Celtics winning three of the four. The rivalry would get so heated that Red Auerbach once punched Hawks owner Ben Kerner in the mouth because of the height of a hoop.

4. Bruins vs. Montreal Canadiens. For years, the Canadiens dominated the Bruins. From 1946 through 1987, the teams met in 18 playoff series, and the Canadiens won all of them. They got every draft pick, call and bounce of the puck. For years, Boston's pro hockey team had an inferiority complex, but it never dampened its will to win—especially against the Canadiens. The Bruins finally got some payback in the first round of the 2011 playoffs. After dropping the first two games at home, the B's battled back and won Game 7 in Boston, setting them on course to winning their first Stanley Cup in nearly four decades.

3. Celtics vs. Los Angeles Lakers. The Celtics and Lakers have met in the NBA Finals 12 times. The Celtics won the first seven series and nine of the dozen. Players like Chamberlain, Baylor, West, Kareem, Magic and Kobe have done battle with Russell, Sam Jones, Bird, Pierce and Garnett in the NBA's most prolific rivalry.

2. Celtics vs. Philadelphia 76ers (and Philadelphia Warriors). From the days of Wilt Chamberlain and the Philadelphia Warriors, to the parquet battles against Moses Malone and Andrew Toney, the Boston-Philly pro basketball rivalry is one of the most intense in sports history. The 1981 Eastern Conference Finals series, which the Celtics won in seven games, is still considered by many as the greatest series in Boston sports history.

1. Red Sox vs. New York Yankees. It's like no other rivalry in all of sports. The passion whenever the Red Sox meet the Yankees is palpable. Brawls, knockdowns, promises and threats are all part of this maniacal match-up. Fenway Park and Yankee Stadium serve as the stages for the Shakespearian play that takes place on the field between these two protagonists, year after year.

These players were determined to be the best at their trade, and in most cases, their personal rivals made them even better as they felt compelled to raise their game to assure their dominance upon their peer. Sometimes the rivalries were infused with mutual respect; others were built on hatred.

10. Roger Clemens vs. Dave Stewart. This was a rivalry because they were prominent All-Star right-handers at the same time. The only difference was that Roger "threw up" on himself when facing Stewart, and Stewart was an ace.

9. Bobby Orr vs. Brad Park. The Bruin and New York Ranger defensemen were the best in the game in the early to mid 1970s. The two would battle each other in the playoffs and the Stanley Cup. Orr and his Bruins would come out on top more times than not.

8. Carlton Fisk vs. Thurman Munson. The rival catchers from Boston and New York couldn't be more different except for their competitive spirit. Fisk was the prototypical catcher, while Munson was Blutarsky with a mask. They genuinely disliked each other, but that brought out the best in each of them.

7. Micky Ward vs. Aturo Gatti. These two combatants were stars in one of the great boxing trilogies in the history of the sport. The first fight of the trio was one of the great fights of all time, and Round 9 was one of the great rounds of all time. Two warriors respecting the sport, their trade and each other.

6. Nomar vs. Jeter. The two rival shortstops were destined for the Hall of Fame. They both were gifted with talents never seen before at the position. Then one sat in the dugout while the other dove into the crowd. The argument of who was better was forever decided.

5. Larry Bird vs Julius Erving. Julius Erving was everything as an athlete Larry Bird wasn't. He could jump and run and dunk and finger roll. Nonetheless, Bird dominated the good Doctor at every turn (unless Moses Malone and Charles Barkley were holding him from behind).

4. Tom Brady vs. Peyton Manning. I'll give Peyton the nod in the category of commercials and *Saturday Night Live* skits. But other than that, Tom Brady has proven to be a better quarterback when it matters in the postseason. I present three rings to one ring as Exhibit A.

3. Larry Bird vs. Magic Johnson. Rivals from their days in college, Bird and Magic would stare each other down in four separate championships (one NCAA; three NBA Finals). Magic would get the better of Bird, but the two together would catapult the NBA from a depreciating asset into a global juggernaut.

2. Ted Williams vs. Joe DiMaggio. The debate of "who was better" has been waged since the days of big band music. In the end, DiMaggio has the rings (10) and Ted Williams is the greatest hitter of all time (six batting titles). There was a rumor that they were almost traded for each other. It would have been fascinating to see DiMaggio with the Green Monster and Williams with the short porch in right field of Yankee Stadium.

1. Bill Russell vs. Wilt Chamberlain. One center won championships. The other won scoring titles. One was the greatest team-winner of all time. The other was the greatest individual center of all time. One measured his success by the number of rings he earned. The other measured success by the number of carnal conquests he made.

These individuals went out of their way to injure or instigate trouble against Boston athletes. Their resumes are full of examples of dirty play and notorious behavior. They cheapened the game through their ugly play and diluted the quality of their sports.

Honorable Mentions. Bobby Wade; Craig Nettles; Dennis Rodman; Wayne Maki; Isiah Thomas; Chuck Person; Joba Chamberlain; Eddie Shack.

14. Chris Nilan. The West Roxbury/Catholic Memorial/Northeastern product went up to Montreal and became a pugnacious instigator. His butt end to Rick Middleton's mouth should have been a 15-game suspension.

13. Mickey Rivers. Who could forget how the crow-footed Yankee center fielder sucker punched Red Sox in the backs of their heads during the 1976 brawl between the two teams?

12. Keith Magnuson. The Chicago Blackhawks defenseman did everything possible to get Bobby Orr off the ice. He picked fights and hit him late. Magnuson was no match for Orr. However, Magnuson's constant harassment cheated fans of Orr's brilliance because Orr spent so much time in the penalty box due to having to defend himself.

11. Pat Quinn. The Maple Leaf went head hunting for Bobby Orr and found his target. Quinn knocked out the Bruin defenseman with a high shot to his head. Quinn had to be escorted by police as the Boston Garden crowd called for his head.

10. Ralph Sampson. The 7-4 center out of Virginia was blessed with an amazing skill set for his size. But when he was drafted by the Houston Rockets, he became an underachiever and a sullen, angry player. This chip on his shoulder manifested itself most dramatically in the 1986 playoffs when Sampson picked a fight that included a kick against Celtic guard Jerry Sichting, who stood a foot shorter than the underperforming Sampson.

9. Matt Walsh. The former Patriots employee felt compelled to inject himself into the Spygate controversy. He was quickly befriended by U.S. Senator Arlen Specter, whose usual duties in Washington D.C. were postponed to make way for his attempts to justify the Super Bowl loss of his constituents, the Philadelphia Eagles, and their vomiting quarterback.

8. Rick Mahorn and 7. Jeff Ruland. Celtics announcer Johnny Most nicknamed the Washington Bullets dastardly duo "McFilthy and McNasty." Both names could be applied to either villain, and they both committed plenty of crimes against the Celtics.

6. Dale Hunter. The Washington Capital player's late hit on Craig Janney as the Bruin was celebrating a goal in the 1990 playoffs, was one of the worst cheap shots in NHL history. Hunter was not suspended for any games. Janney was concussed.

5. Matt Cooke. The punk skates around the ice looking to cheap shot opponents. His head shot on Marc Savard literally ended a human being's career. He should have been banned for life for the end result of his dirty work.

4. Claude Lemieux. The instigator loved to use his stick as a weapon. When the victim of his blade work wanted to handle the disagreement like a man, Lemieux would turtle into his shell. After taking a stick to his face from Lemieux, the Bruins' Cam Neely didn't care that Lemieux assumed the position—he made him kiss the *Boston Globe* sign on the Garden boards.

3. Bill Laimbeer. This Herman Munster lookalike was a cheap-shot artist. The Detroit Piston center played the game 15 feet from the hoop in an effort to mask his lack of athletic ability. He played the game the wrong way and the league allowed him to. His clothesline of Larry Bird should have been an automatic suspension. But as usual, he escaped punishment. I loved watching Laimbeer get ignored when he tried to shake hands before games with Larry Bird.

2. Jack Tatum. It wasn't just his tragic hit on Darryl Stingley. Tatum was an animal who tried to injure people and end their careers. In Stingley's case, he succeeded. He was never suspended for the hit, nor did he ever apologize for it.

1. Ulf Samuelsson. His premeditated dirty plays against Bruin great Cam Neely took a toll on the right winger's legs. Samuelsson virtually ended the Hall of Famer's career. He robbed us fans of years of enjoyment. We could no longer watch the greatest power right winger in NHL history.

I know a list on this topic has been put together by the Patriots and some panel of theirs. But we need an objective, comprehensive list of 27 players by position, plus coaches. Well, the head coach and QB were easy, but the other spots are up for debate. So much so, that a few introductory notes of explanation are necessary to explain some of my choices:

Why No Mike Vrabel? Even though Buoniconti was only here a few years, he is a Pro Football Hall of Famer and played great while he was here in the Patriots AFL days. He's on the Worst Trades list in this book, so you know how I feel about that transaction. Vrabel was a HUGE part of the Belichick run in the 2000s, but he gets nudged out...just barely.

Why Bill Belichick as defensive coordinator? I almost went with Parcells as head coach, ONLY because he rang in the Kraft era and gave the franchise credibility for the first time in its history. But I'm not that stupid. And whether it's his first run here or the current run, BB should be the permanent Defensive Coordinator of the NEP. Plus, they gave up a first-round pick for the guy. Best value in Pats history!!

Why Curtis Martin over Jim Nance? Martin is the only bell-cow back the Pats have ever had. He was a 350-carry-a-year guy and even though he went to the Jets, he's still on this list. We knew what the Pats would be missing when he left and the only other guy in team history like Curtis was Corey Dillon, and that was really for only one season. So off I went with Martin.

Why Randy Moss over Troy Brown? The 52-game production of Moss is the best run in Pats history for a WR. I took the three full seasons of Moss and the three best full seasons of Troy and compared them:

—Troy Brown. 282 receptions, 3,033 yards, 12 touchdowns;

—Randy Moss. 250 receptions, 3,765 yards, 47 touchdowns.

No further evidence, your honor.

OFFENSE

Quarterback. Tom Brady.

Running Back. Curtis Martin.

Running Back. Sam Cunningham.

Wide Receiver. Stanley Morgan.

Wide Receiver. Randy Moss.

Tight End. Ben Coates.

Tackle. Bruce Armstrong.

Tackle. Matt Light.

Guard. John Hannah.

Guard. Logan Mankins.

Center. Dan Koppen.

COACHES

Head Coach. Bill Belichick.

Offensive Coordinator. Charlie Weis.

Defensive Coordinator. Bill Belichick.

DEFENSE

Defensive Lineman. Richard Seymour.

Defensive Lineman. Julius Adams.

Defensive Lineman. Houston Antwine.

Defensive Lineman. Vince Wilfork.

Linebacker. Andre Tippett.

Linebacker. Tedy Bruschi.

Linebacker. Nick Buoniconti.

Linebacker. Steve Nelson.

Cornerback. Mike Haynes.

Cornerback. Ty Law.

Safety. Fred Marion.

Safety. Rodney Harrison.

SPECIALISTS

Kicker. Adam Vinatieri.

Punter. Rich Camarillo.

Longsnapper. Lonnie Paxton.

Returner. Troy Brown.

Top Dozen Sports Guys
I Want to Have a Beer With :: AG

I don't know a sports fan on the planet who doesn't sit there watching a postgame press conference or an interview and say, "I'd like to have a belt with that dude. Some alcohol, along with my sparkling personality, will loosen them up and get them to start telling the truth." When asked who he'd like to have a beer with, Tom Brady chose Joe Montana and Steve Young. "They were my two football idols growing up and I dreamed about being a pro QB because of them." Here is my list of sports figures I'd like to tie one on with, from Boston and beyond.

12. Joe Paterno. I always wanted the chance to play for Penn State. And Happy Valley is one of the greatest places I've ever been. JoePa finds a way to get kids to play for an old man who almost crapped himself on the sidelines at Ohio State. Some people in the Midwest wouldn't have made the dash for the hopper because they'd be so happy to be there.

11. Manny Ramirez. Who wouldn't want to get some truth serum into this guy and let him go. To me, he's complex and that intrigues me to no end. Plus, I'd love to hear from THAT guy about the Boston media and what it was like being the King of Boston. Which he was for a time.

10. Hulk Hogan. I don't wanna hear from anyone who buys and reads this book that Hulk isn't an athlete. What he does is not a sport, but it is athletic, so bite me. I've read his book and I'm sure he has more stories about Andre the Giant and "Rowdy" Roddy Piper that he couldn't put in the memoir. Those are the ones I want to hear!

9. Randy Moss. I was a Moss guy when he came into the NFL from Marshall. Pats fans found out that a big-time outside threat helped in the 2010 playoffs. His story is compelling. He's got some issues. And he's going to the Pro Football Hall of Fame. I'd take just an hour to chronicle his 2010 season.

8. Bill Russell. The era in which he played is a major part of our country's history. He suffered some of the things that befell Jackie Robinson and his story is amazing and inspiring. Plus, he saw the inner workings of Red Auerbach as a player and as a coach. I want to know why Boston got the racist tag and how he feels about the city now.

7. Terry Bradshaw. I grew up in Pittsburgh and this guy never gets his due as one of the best of all time. No one ever mentions him in the Montana conversation because the famous "Steel Curtain" defense gets most of the credit for the Steelers glory years of the 1970s. But his Super Bowl performances were stellar and he's maybe the most underrated QB in NFL history. His personal story is interesting, but I want to hear about Art Rooney, Chuck Noll and Pittsburgh back then.

6. Jimmie Johnson. Not the football coach, the NASCAR driver. I'm driven by success. For me personally, one of the reasons I wanted to do this book is because it's a sign of career success. This guy has won five straight NASCAR championships. At that level of racing, it's utterly amazing. I love to talk to winners because they tell you something you don't know and have a unique perspective on life, work and accomplishment. And even though most don't like NASCAR, I like winning and dominance. Everybody has to respect that.

5. Doc Rivers. He manages multi-multi-million dollar spoiled brats and gets them to be selfless, play defense and turns them into winners. And he played in an era where there wasn't all this money for these players and he has seen the league evolve. He could provide some amazing insight.

4. Mike Tyson. I want to know how it was to act in *The Hangover*. And maybe what it was like to be a 20-year-old and the king of boxing. His movie, *Tyson*, was nice, but there's so much more to chronicle. And yes, I'd sing "In the Air Tonight" with him, but I wouldn't take the punch.

3. Bill Parcells. I've always loved this guy. I'm lucky to work with a former player of his who is a Parcells loyalist and has told me a ton of stories about the guy. Just watch *Sound FX* on NFL Network and convince me he's not compelling and you wouldn't want to know what makes him tick. Funny, smart, witty and a winner.

2. Tiger Woods. Unless I got the guy so drunk, he couldn't see, I don't think I could get him to talk. But damn do I want to try. And I want details—ALL THE DETAILS. I may ask a question or two about golf. But I've got to know about some of the other things in life THAT guy has experienced.

1. Barry Bonds. He was my favorite player regardless of the uniform he played in. And he is, for better or worse, baseball's all-time home run king. He knew what he did and I want to see how honest he'd be about things. And with all the money our federal government has sunk into prosecuting him, I'd love to know how they tried to squeeze him to flip or talk.

There is something exciting about a draft. It allows fans to fantasize about the potential of the current team with the additions of talented, young newcomers. Over the years, those responsible for our teams' drafts have sometimes heightened our expectations for coming seasons with their picks, and other times have made us scratch our heads in disbelief. This list presents the highlights of what turned out to be our local teams' best draft classes.

17. Boston Bruins, Class of 1982. First Round (first overall) Gord Kluzak; Second Round (39th overall) Lyndon Byers; Third Round (60th overall) Dave Reid; Sixth Round (123rd overall) Bob Sweeney.

16. Boston Bruins, Class of 1980. First Round (18th overall) Barry Pederson; Third Round (60th overall) Tom Fergus; Fourth Round (81st overall) Steve Kasper; Ninth Round (186th overall) Michael Thelven.

15. Boston Red Sox, Class of 1973. First Round (17th overall) Ted Cox; Second Round (41st overall) Fred Lynn; Eighth Round (185th overall) Butch Hobson.

14. New England Patriots, Class of 2003. First Round (13th overall) Ty Warren; Second Round (36th overall) Eugene Wilson; Fourth Round (120th overall) Asante Samuel; Fifth Round (164th overall) Dan Koppen; Seventh Round (239th overall) Tully Banta-Cain.

13. Boston Red Sox, Class of 1989. First Round (23rd overall) Mo Vaughn; First Round (29th overall) Kevin Morton; Fourth Round (110th overall) Jeff Bagwell; Sixth Round (163rd overall) Paul Quantrill.

12. New England Patriots, Class of 1977. First Round (fifth overall) Stanley Morgan; First Round (16th overall) Raymond Clayborn; Second Round (44th overall) Horace Ivory; Second Round (52nd overall) Don Hasslebeck.

11. New England Patriots, Class of 1976. First Round (fifth overall) Michael Haynes; First Round (12th overall) Pete Brock; First Round (21st overall) Tim Fox.

10. New England Patriots, Class of 1996. First Round (seventh overall) Terry Glenn; Second Round (36th overall) Lawyer Milloy; Third Round (86th overall) Tedy Bruschi; Fourth Round (101st overall) Heath Irwin.

9. Boston Celtics, Class of 1953. First Round (fifth overall) Frank Ramsey; Third Round Cliff Hagan.

8. New England Patriots, Class of 1993. First Round (first overall) Drew Bledsoe; Second Round (31st overall) Chris Slade; Second Round (51st overall) Todd Rucci; Second Round (56th overall) Vincent Brisby; Fourth Round (110th overall) Corwin Brown; Eighth Round (198th overall) Troy Brown.

7. Boston Red Sox, Class of 1976. First Round (22nd overall) Bruce Hurst; Second Round (46th overall) Glenn Hoffman; Fifth Round (118th overall) Mike Smithson; Seventh Round (166th overall) Wade Boggs; Ninth Round (214th overall) Gary Allenson; 12th Round (286th overall) Reid Nichols.

6. Boston Celtics, Class of 1978. First Round (sixth overall) Larry Bird—the fact that Red Auerbach utilized the junior-eligible loophole made this an amazing steal.

5. New England Patriots, Class of 1995. First Round (23rd overall) Ty Law; Second Round (57th overall) Ted Johnson; Third Round (74th overall) Curtis Martin; Third Round (88th overall) Jimmy Hitchcock; Fourth Round (112th overall) Dave Wohlabaugh.

4. Boston Celtics, Class of 1980. First Round (third overall) Kevin McHale and Robert Parish (via trade).

3. Boston Bruins, Class of 1979. First Round (eighth overall) Ray Bourque; First Round (15th overall) Brad McCrimmon; Third Round (57th overall) Keith Crowder; Sixth Round (120th overall) Mike Krushelnyski.

2. New England Patriots, Class of 1973. First Round (fourth overall) John Hannah; First Round (11th overall) Sam Cunningham; First Round (19th overall) Darryl Stingley; 14th Round (342nd overall) Ray Hamilton.

1. Boston Celtics, Class of 1956. Territorial pick—Tom Heinsohn; First Round (second overall) Bill Russell (draft rights gained via trade with St. Louis Hawks); Second Round K.C. Jones.

The later rounds of drafts tend to get dismissed as exercises in futility by many fans and journalists. But savvy personnel evaluators can sometimes unearth gems long after the first-round picks have finished being interviewed and gone home. Here are the biggest, brightest late-round draft gems found by area sports teams, ranked in order of the rounds they were selected in.

21. Jim Nance, 19th Round (151st Overall) in 1965.

20. David Eckstein, 17th Round (581st Overall) in 1997.

19. Dennis "Oil Can" Boyd, 16th Round (413th Overall) in 1980.

18. Sam Hunt, 15th Round (374th Overall) in 1974.

17. Ray Hamilton, 14th Round (342nd Overall) in 1973.

16. Gene Conley, 10th Round (90th Overall) in 1952.

15. Rick Weitzman, 10th Round (110th Overall) in 1967.

14. Kevin Youkilis, Eighth Round (243rd Overall) in 2001.

13. Ronnie Lippett, Eighth Round (214th Overall) in 1983.

12. Jody Reed, Eighth Round (198th Overall) in 1986.

11. Troy Brown, Eighth Round (198th Overall) in 1993.

10. David Givens, Seventh Round (253rd Overall) in 2002.

9. Craig James, Seventh Round (187th Overall) in 1983.

8. P.J. Axelsson, Seventh Round (177th Overall) in 1995.

7. Tom Brady, Sixth Round (199th Overall) in 2000.

6. Dan Koppen, Fifth Round (164th Overall) in 2003.

5. Ben Coates, Fifth Round (124th Overall) in 1991.

4. Steve Grogan, Fifth Round (116th Overall) in 1975.

3. Fred Marion, Fifth Round (112th Overall) in 1982.

2. Dwight Evans, Fifth Round (109th Overall) in 1969.

1. Stan Jonathan, Fifth Round (86th Overall) in 1975.

When putting this list together, a friend of mine from CSNNE.com asked me, "What do you do with Ted Williams, Yaz, Manny Ramirez and Jim Rice? One of them has to be left out." "He's right," I said. "Oh shit." But I figured it out in the end.

LF Ted Williams. The best hitter in baseball history. Still, I had to think twice about starting him in left field because I had to also find spots for Yaz and Manny Ramirez. But I came back to Williams. He's the best hitter of a great Hall of Fame bunch.

CF Fred Lynn. Even though he was only in Boston for six years, he won a Rookie of the Year and MVP in the same season here. The career wasn't long, but it was stellar. Dom DiMaggio got huge consideration along with Reggie Smith, but the awards push Lynn over the top.

RF Dwight Evans. This isn't close. He was one of the classiest and best Red Sox in history. He was a stellar fielder who won eight Gold Gloves and a consistent hitter who played 20 seasons in the majors and belted at least 20 home runs in 11 of them. I didn't even research other Sox RFs for this list.

3B Wade Boggs. Maybe the best Fenway hitter ever and that includes Ted Williams. Another baseball Hall of Famer, Boggs had more than 200 hits, 100 runs and 40 doubles in six consecutive seasons. He's in the 3,000 hit club and even though he sold his soul at the end of his career to the Tampa Bay Rays, he'll always be remembered as a Red Sox.

SS Johnny Pesky. We need to remember that Pesky broke in as a 22-year-old who finished third in the MVP voting with a .331 average and over 200 hits and 100 runs scored. He then lost three years while serving in WWII. He came back as a 26-year-old and had two more seasons with over 200 hits and averages of .324 and .335. Then he started to decline, but slowly. He played a total of 10 seasons with a career .307 average. Sorry, Nomar fans—Johnny's the right choice. LET'S PLAY BALLLLLLL!!!

2B Bobby Doerr. The nine-time All-Star drove in more than 100 runs six times. From 1940-50, he never hit less than 15 homers in a season and was a good fielder. Maybe the easiest choice of all these positions.

1B Carl Yastrzemski. Arguably the second best hitter in Red Sox history, Yaz moved to first base towards the end of his career. He played 760 games there, but, just like a manager, I had to find a way to get him on this team. I don't think anyone will argue with me.

C Carlton Fisk. It was between "Pudge" and Jason Varitek. Fisk wins because he was a superior hitter to "Tek" and comparable defensively. His career average was only .269, but he hit 376 homers and drove in 1,330 runs. He's in the Hall of Fame and is one of the best catchers ever.

DH Manny Ramirez. Yes, over David Ortiz. "Papi" may have owned this position, but at the end of the day, Man-Ram is a better hitter. He's a career .313 hitter with over 550 home runs and I felt he was more deserving. Manny has hit at a higher level than Ortiz for a longer period of time. Imagine a 3-4-5 of Yaz, Ted and Manny!

Starting Pitcher Pedro Martinez. The best starting pitcher I've ever seen. His 1999 and 2000 seasons are among the best any starter has ever had in baseball and alone either season would stand out on any pitcher's resume. But the fact they were back-to-back just makes it that much more amazing. For 1999, he had a 23-4 record and 2.07 ERA; in 2000 he went 18-6 with a 1.74 ERA. IN THE STERIOD ERA!!! There have been a lot of great pitchers in Sox history, but Petey's the best.

Closer Jonathan Papelbon. Now this is a little tough because the save has only been a statistic in baseball since 1969, so some great relief pitchers are going to be forgotten. "Pap" is the prototypical closer. He's high-velocity, high-intensity and is quick to forget when he's had a bad night. He's a 35-40 save guy every year and gives any manager the easy option at the end of the game. He's got the ninth locked up, so just get him in position to close out the game. And some think he's a good dancer. I don't.

Manager Terry Francona. He has two World Series wins. But compared to Bill Belichick and Doc Rivers, "Tito" gets taken for granted sometimes. His ability to deal with the everyday grind of baseball and dealing with some of the spoiled brats that play it nowadays make him the obvious choice here. He handles the media great. He never throws a player under the bus while he's playing for him. And he's well-respected in the game. Easy choice.

Note: When Bobby Orr played, kids wanted to rush the puck. When Larry Bird played, kids wanted to throw lookaway passes. When Fred Lynn played, kids wanted to make diving catches and mimic his beautiful swing. His talents were transcendent. Lynn played center field with grace and swung with ease. His 1975 rookie season, for which he won both Rookie of the Year and Most Valuable Player honors, was historic.

The man also knows his restaurants, and offered us a list of his favorites. Or as he puts it: "I thought that I would do something a little bit different for my Top 10 and list my favorite restaurants from when I was playing ball. Only one of them, Belisle's, is no longer around. As you can see, it's a pretty varied lot. This is a part of the game that I miss. The order is tough for me as these are very different places, but here it goes."

11. In-N-Out Burger, California. Burgers only. Double-Double with cheese, grill the onions, fries, shake and out the door.

10. Gino's East, Chicago. If you are a fan of deep-dish pizza, then this is your place. Two or three pieces is about it. Carved my name on a beam in the Seventies. Wonder if it's still there.

9. Bo Brooks, Baltimore. Blue crabs anyone? Had them by the bushel. Had to be careful, as you would always have cuts on your fingers after eating these guys...pitchers beware.

8. P.J. Clarke's, New York City. Best bacon cheeseburgers on the planet. Plenty of atmosphere and the place was hopping after games.

7. Stroud's, Kansas City. Pan-fried chicken like your grandma used to make. Loved their fried chicken livers, too.

6. Charley's on Newbury Street, Boston. Great place to go after a game to unwind. Super beers on tap and food to match.

5. Shuckers at The Fairmont Olympic Hotel, Seattle. Best fresh oyster menu in the league. Killer seafood chowder with hot bread. Can't go wrong with anything on the menu.

4. Mader's, Milwaukee. If I was in town for three games, I made sure that I hit each one of these restaurants. Most of the locals went to Mader's for their German food.

3. Karl Ratzsch's, Milwaukee. Super German food. Beer served in steins as long as your arm.

2. Belisle's, Just Outside of Anaheim, California. This place featured huge portions of food, all of it homemade. Couldn't eat it all. Best of all, it was open 24 hours, so we could get there after games.

1. The Lark, Just Outside of Detroit. European country inn style restaurant. A cozy place with great food and ambience.

Top 10 Boston Marathoners :: by Bill Rodgers

Note: Bill Rodgers is the greatest marathoner in the history of the event. In his career, he won 22 marathons, including four victories in both the prestigious Boston and New York Marathons. His dominance compelled *Sports Illustrated* to select him for two covers and helped ignite the running boom across the U.S. in the 1970s. Known as "Boston Billy," Rodgers will go down as one the region's all-time greatest athletes. Here, he lists the Top 10 runners (with one notable and humble exception) in the history of the Boston Marathon.

10. Fatuma Roba. Three-time women's winner (1997-99) from Ethiopia.

9. Cosmas Ndeti. Three-time winner (1993-95) from Kenya.

8. Ibrahim Hussein. Three-time winner (1988, 1991-92) from Kenya. He was the first African runner to win in Boston, opening the door to decades of dominance by runners from the African continent, most of them Kenyans.

7. Rosa Mota. Three-time women's winner (1987-88 and 1990) from Portugal.

6. Gerard Cote. Four-time winner (1940, 1943-44 and 1948) from Quebec, Canada. He was an intense competitor who would infuriate opponents.

5. Robert Kipkoech Cheruiyot. Four-time winner (2003, 2006-08) from Kenya who broke the course record in 2006 with a time of 2:07:14.

4. Catherine Ndereba. Four-time women's winner (2000-01, 2004-05) from Kenya.

3. Joan Benoit Samuelson. Two-time winner (1979 and 1983) who lived in Maine and attended Bowdoin College. Both wins established new course records. Her 1983 time (2:22:43) also established a new world record. She won her first Boston Marathon wearing a Red Sox cap.

2. Johnny Kelley. Two-time winner (1935 and 1945) from Medford, Massachusetts who ran the race 61 times, the last time in 1992 at age 84.

1. Clarence DeMar. Seven-time winner (1911, 1922-24, 1927-28 and 1930) of the Boston Marathon. Known as "Mr. DeMarathon," he set four course records in his seven wins. He lived in Melrose, Massachusetts and was a Boston sports star.

Characters Who Have Enriched Our Sports World :: MC

As important as the players, coaches and the sporting event itself are the people who add flavor and atmosphere to the game, race or match. The below list is a sampling of characters who have contributed to the overall experience of Boston sports as we know it. Some have contributed for decades, some for just a few seasons or games, some for even less time than that. But in a wide variety of ways, they all left their unique imprint on the sports scene in our town.

Honorable Mentions. Rob Barry (no Fenway vendor could throw a bag of peanuts like him); Ed Canto (a.k.a. "The Sausage King"); Billy Dunn (police officer in the Red Sox bullpen).

10. Sherm Feller. "Ladies and gentlemen, boys and girls, welcome to Fenway Park."

9. Mark Henderson. Working at Schaefer Stadium in the midst of a December 1982 blizzard as part of a work release program from prison, Mark Henderson played a pivotal role in a Patriots victory over the Miami Dolphins. Assigned to man the sideline John Deere tractor plow, he was prompted in the fourth quarter by Patriots Coach Ron Meyer to clear a path for kicker John Smith to attempt a field goal. The kick was good and the Patriots went on to win 3-0. Dolphins Coach Don Shula seethed and Henderson was presented with a game ball.

8. Busty Heart. No one could turn heads at a Celtics game like this bodacious blond.

7. George the Peanut Guy. "Peanuts, cashews, paaa-stachioos!" There was no better sound when walking into Fenway Park than the sing-song bark of George as he stood by his peanut cart on Yawkey Way, selling his merchandise in the little brown bags.

6. Rudolph "Spider" Edwards. For 33 years, "Spider" swept the Boston Garden's parquet floor with style and cool. Upon his retirement, his broom was auctioned off for charity, netting $1,600.

5. Rene Rancourt. You can't have a big Bruins game without the man in the tux and cummerbund belting out the national anthem in full voice while standing on the rolled-out carpet, every high note bringing loyal Bruins fans to a full froth. Only when he has set the stage will Rene signal the crowd with a double fist pump that it's time to play hockey.

4. The Brown Family. Since the Boston Marathon began in 1897, a member of the Brown family has served as the starter of the race. The family has also made countless contributions to the Boston Garden and to the Celtics.

3. Joe Mooney. The Red Sox groundskeeper was cantankerous, belligerent and grumpy. But as long as you weren't on the receiving end of his grunts and demands, then you could truly appreciate his work. There may be no greater sight than the panorama of the green grass of the ball field as you walk up the ramp prior to a Red Sox game with a Fenway Frank in hand and your heart aflutter.

2. Jock Semple. The Scotsman had both a temper and a passion for the Boston Marathon. For six decades, he protected the race as if it was family. Yes, he was memorialized by the infamous pictures of him trying to expel "illegal" runner Kathy Switzer (because she was female) from the race. However, it was his years as caretaker of Boston's gem that he will be remembered for most.

1. John Kiley. The organist is the answer to the trivia question: who played for the Red Sox, Bruins, Celtics and Patriots (at Fenway Park). It wouldn't be a sporting event without the melodic sounds of John Kiley wafting across the court, ice or field.

We asked the fans via our book's Facebook page and listeners to 98.5 The Sports Hub to tell us about their favorite gin joints and flapjack houses. Here's what they came up with.

16. Nick Cabral. Absolutely can't leave out Halftime Pizza across the street from the Garden. Good food and decorative Bruins and Celtics memorabilia all over the restaurant.

15. Dave Lapoint. Home Plate in Taunton. Not really a dive, but it's great. Excellent food, load of TVs, UFC fights, a cool Green Monster replica seating area and their general manager Frank . . . Frank is awesome.

GRESH NOTE: Hopefully, Frank hooks you up for life.

14. Ben Mitchell. The Breakfast Club Diner in Allston is amazing. This place has unbelievable diner food. The best steak and cheese omelette north of Philly!

13. Kevin Steele. Eagles Deli on Beacon Street in Chestnut Hill. And Tex Barry's Hot Dogs in Taunton. Those two are musts.

12. Dennis Boyer. The Red Arrow in Manchester, New Hampshire. Grab a seat at the counter as long as you don't mind the fact that there are 20 people standing right behind you waiting for a spot to open up. Best breakfast: Crab Cakes Benedict.

11. Kevin Kelly. It's gotta be Suppa's in Lowell right next to the UMass-Lowell campus. Great fatty food to get you through the day and open late.

GRESH NOTE: Isn't there always that real hole-in-the-wall place in every college town? At the University of Rhode Island, we had Kingston Pizza. Eat there and you'll smell like the place for a week.

10. Jason Whitford. Oneyville Hot Weiners in Providence. This place is a hole in the wall, but serves up the best hot weiners, coffee milk and fries after a sporting event. A true hidden gem.

9. Marc Cappello. Casey's Diner in Natick. Best hot dogs on the planet— period.

GRESH NOTE: As long as the Flutie brothers' band isn't playing, I'm in.

8. Glen Spardello. Red Wing Diner, right near Gillette, best fried clams.

7. Hank Johnson. The Foxy Lady in Providence, RI. Not only do you get eggs...but legs! The rule of thumb is to go where fat guys eat. There is no one fatter than Mo Vaughn and he was a regular.

6. Dolly Jo McPherson. The Friendly Toast in Portstmouth, New Hampshire. The decor is insane, prices are good and yummy portions are huge. Egg in a Hole—my favorite.

5. Jason Morley. The Fours on Canal Street. The Tony C. and Bobby Riggs sandwiches are both delicious and the Reggie Jackson picture by the restrooms is legendary.

4. Mark Lenehan. Lynwood Cafe in Randolph. Legendary bar pizza and an old-school feel to it from the second you walk inside.

3. Michael Welch. Real Boston fans go to Sullivan's Tap. Pabst bottles and Cheetos out of the vending machine.

2. Sandy Drain. Picasso's Pizza and Pub in Warwick, Rhode Island. Since there's no happy hour, they have the hungry hour. Best chicken parm sandwich in the state.

1. Andy Gresh. Luxe Burger Bar in downtown Providence. Near the Capital Grille, which makes it even better. Great food, stiff drinks, cheap.

Too Much Hype :: MC

These players and coaches came to Boston with the promise of future greatness. Sadly, they never realized the potential that was advertised. Though desperate fans yearned for deliverance and their next superstar, these dozen just turned out to be cases of misplaced hype.

Honorable Mentions. Kevin Morton; Bobby Sprowl; Frankie Rodriquez.

12. Gerald Green. The Celtics made the high school star the 18th overall pick of the 2005 NBA draft. He could jump, but that was about it. Green was eventually dumped to Minnesota in the Kevin Garnett trade.

11. Craig Hansen. The poor kid was drafted in the first round in 2005, and four months later he was on the mound in the pennant race. It was too much, too early, and the former St. John's closer never recovered. In three uneven seasons for the Red Sox, the reliever compiled a record of 3-5 with a 6.15 ERA.

10. Donnie Sadler. For years, the Red Sox were a boring station-to-station team. The only time a Boston runner seemed to go from first to third was to hand his helmet to the third base coach at the end of an inning. When whispers of a lightning-fast Donnie Sadler started creeping up Route 95 from Pawtucket in the late 1990s, Boston craved the speed. In the end, Sadler stole just nine bases in three seasons with the Sox and hit .242.

9. Michael Bishop. The most popular player on any team is the backup quarterback. Michael Bishop came to New England as a flashy athlete from Kansas State who had been a Heisman finalist. People begged for Bishop to play. For his career in New England, he was 3 for 9 passing for 80 yards.

8. Sam Horn. Anyone who can hit the ball out of the park in McCoy Stadium will certainly demand the attention of Red Sox Nation. In 1987, Horn hit 30 home runs in 333 at-bats at Pawtucket. When he arrived at Fenway, his power didn't translate to the big leagues. In three seasons with the big club, the big lefty hit 16 home runs and had a .223 batting average.

7. Butch Hobson. The one-time Red Sox folk hero was the organization's Triple A manager in Pawtucket. Then in the winter of 1994, the Red Sox were so desperate to keep him from going to the Yankees that they terminated popular New Englander Joe Morgan and brought in the good ol' boy from Alabama. Over Hobson's three years as Sox manager, he posted a 207-232 record and was ignored by his ace, Roger Clemens.

6. Frank Shorter. The U.S. marathon star and 1972 Olympic gold medalist came to Boston with big hopes and left the city a broken man, complaining about the race.

5. Kenneth Sims. The big defensive lineman out of Texas was taken by the Patriots with the first overall pick in the 1982 draft. He was more talk than action. In eight years, the Longhorn never made a Pro Bowl. However, he did break his leg on an illegal leg whip.

4. Hart Lee Dykes. The wide receiver from Oklahoma State was drafted by New England in the first round with the 16th overall pick. He got more attention for hanging out with Irving Fryar and gun fights than for his play on the field. In two years, he caught 83 passes and was never heard from again.

3. Brian Rose and Carl Pavano. Both pitchers ascended through the ranks of the Red Sox farm system and were projected as the future co-aces of the staff. Combined, they won 11 games for the big club before being shipped off.

2. Daisuke Matsuzaka. There might not be another player in Boston sports history who arrived amid more buzz than "Dice K." The Red Sox outbid the Yankees (yes, "outbid") to gain the Japanese pitcher's services. He arrived at Fenway with his favorite gyro ball and reports of deep pitch counts. What the Red Sox got instead was a five-inning starter who nibbled at corners and took forever to throw the ball.

1. Rick Pitino. The slickster who was born to sell used cars was wooed to Boston by Paul Gaston. Pitino threw a bash for himself at the Garden to introduce his royal highness to Boston. He also stole Red Auerbach's position of president and then proceeded to lead the Celtics to a 102-146 record over his three wildly unsuccessful years here. I wonder if he feels bad for such "indiscretions."

Hollywood sits a long way, both culturally and geographically, from Boston. But that hasn't kept movie producers from including our sports scene in their films. Here are 10 examples of area sports teams and players showing up in movies over the last few decades, along with a star rating for each film.

10. *Celtic Pride* (Zero Stars). Should have been named for the Clippers.

9. *Fever Pitch* (Two Stars). A love triangle between Jimmy Fallon, Drew Barrymore and the Red Sox. Still can't believe they were allowed on the field during the World Series celebration.

8. *Summer Catch* (Two Stars). The main character pitches in the Cape Cod League. Could have been three stars, if he didn't leave the mound with a no-hitter.

7. *Blue Chips* (Two Stars). Bob Cousy plays himself; Shaq tries to play somebody besides himself.

6. *The Town* (Three Stars). Ben Affleck co-stars with a Bruins jacket.

5. *Love Story* (Three Stars). Ryan O'Neal plays a Harvard hockey player who gets body checked by Ali McGraw.

4. *The Friends of Eddie Coyle* (Three Stars). Peter Boyle takes Robert Mitchum to a Bruins game at the Boston Garden, then shoots him on the way home.

3. *Field of Dreams* (Three Stars). James Earl Jones takes Kevin Costner to a Red Sox game at Fenway, but doesn't shoot him on the way home. Could have rated higher, but Kevin Costner's movie wife was horrendous.

2. *Dumb and Dumber* (Three Stars). Cam Neely as Sea Bass. So stupid, so funny.

1. *Good Will Hunting* (Four Stars). Footage of Carlton Fisk's Game 6 home run serves as the perfect cutaway during a meditation on finding true love.

Biggest Ovations :: MC

These were the moments when Boston fans had a chance to salute the players, the cause, the effort. Standing ovations, whistles, or shouts of exultation were our way of saying, "We appreciate you" and "Thanks."

14. Mariano Rivera on Opening Day (April 11, 2005). In the Opening Day ceremonies of 2005, the Red Sox raised their championship flag and handed out rings. Later, during the ceremonial pregame introductions, the crowd offered its biggest ovation for Yankees closer Mariano Rivera, whose two blown saves the previous October paved the way for Boston's World Series run. Rivera was good-natured and tipped his cap to the crowd.

13. The Women of Wellesley College (Third Monday of April). Each year around the halfway point of the Boston Marathon, the runners are treated to the yells, cries and beckons of support from the women of Wellesley College. The enthusiastic reception helps inspire many runners to reach this point of the race, then carry on into Boston.

12. Canadian National Anthem Cheered at Garden (April 15, 2004). Prior to Game 3 of the NHL Playoff Quarterfinals between the Bruins and the Canadiens, the Montreal Bell Centre crowd booed "The Star-Spangled Banner." When the series returned to Boston, the Bruins fans cheered throughout the playing of "Oh, Canada." Former Bruins Coach and Canadian hockey analyst Don Cherry had predicted, "Boston won't boo our national anthem because they have too much class. . . . Greatest people in the world, Boston."

11. Joe Torre's First Game Back (May 18, 1999). Two months after surgery for prostate cancer, New York Yankees Manager Joe Torre returned to the dugout for a game at Fenway Park. When he came out to present the lineup cards, he was greeted by a two-minute standing ovation by Red Sox Nation. Torre would later comment, "I don't want to say I was surprised, but very touched."

10. Phil Esposito's Number Retirement (December 3, 1987). The most prolific goal scorer in Boston Bruins history had his #7 retired. During the ceremony, Bruins defenseman Ray Bourque, who also wore #7, presented Esposito with a game shirt and then peeled off his shirt to reveal his new #77. This gesture brought down the house.

9. Larry Bird's First Time at Boston Garden (April 8, 1979). Larry Bird, whose draft rights were held by the Boston Celtics, had just finished leading Indiana State on an amazing run to the finals of the NCAA tournament. He attended the last game of the Celtics dismal, 29-53 season with his agent, Bob Wolff. When Bird entered the Boston Garden and made his way to his Loge seat, the crowd erupted into a prolonged standing ovation and called him "Savior." It was the first of many standing ovations the future Hall of Famer would receive at the Boston Garden.

8. Jordan Leandre Runs the Bases (August 17, 2007). After singing the national anthem on Jimmy Fund Day, seven-year-old Jordan Leandre, who was recovering from Ewing's sarcoma, ran around the bases at Fenway. It compelled fans to both cheer and cry at the same time.

7. Carl Yastrzemski's Last Game (October 2, 1983). One last time, Yaz stood in the batter's box at Fenway Park. In the stands, 33,491 Red Sox fans thanked the Hall of Famer for 1967, playing the Green Monster and treating them to decades of excellence. During his speech prior to the game, an emotional Yastrzemski said, "I saw a sign that said, 'Say it ain't so Yaz.' I wish it wasn't."

6. Bob Cousy Retirement (March 17, 1963). The "Houdini of the Hardwood" was honored for his years of great play in the final game of the 1963 regular season. The game would become known as "The Boston Tear Party" after an emotional Cousy struggled to speak. During one stretch of prolonged silence and sobbing, a fan yelled from the seats, "We love ya', Cous!" The crowd erupted.

5. John Havlicek's Last Game (April 9, 1978). The crowd cheered for 10 minutes before the game even started. Hondo played in 1,269 games with his last being a classic. In the greatest retirement game ever, Havlicek led the Celtics with 29 points in a 131-114 shellacking of the Buffalo Braves.

4. Bobby Orr's Number Raised (January 9, 1979). Boston reminded Bobby Orr how much they loved him when his number was raised to the Garden rafters. The six-minute-plus ovation caused Orr's wife, Peggy, to cry and the exhibition game between the Bruins and the Soviet Wings to be delayed. Orr was only 31 years old when he was so honored.

3. The Last Skate (September 26, 1995). On the final night of the Boston Garden, Bruins past and present circled the ice while the notes of "Auld Lang Syne" floated through the Garden. The image of a smiling Bobby Orr skating with #4 on his back was only second to the sight of Normand Leveille, who was stricken with an aneurysm years before, skating with the help of Ray Bourque. There wasn't a dry eye in the house.

2. Darryl Stingley's Monday Night (September 3, 1979). One year after suffering a horrific, paralyzing injury, Patriots wide receiver Darryl Stingley returned to Shaefer Stadium as the guest of honor for the season opener against the Super Bowl champion Pittsburgh Steelers on Labor Day night. When Stingley was announced to the crowd, the ovation lasted seven minutes. This show of appreciation delayed the game as fans and players alike cheered loud and long.

1. Boston Garden Salutes The Kraut Line (February 10, 1942). The Bruins most famous threesome, the Kraut Line—comprised of Milt Schmidt, Bobby Bauer and Woody Dumart—played their last game before reporting to active duty in the Royal Canadian Air Force. During the game, the trio led the Bruins with 10 points in their 8-1 romp over the Montreal Canadiens. After the game, both teams lined up to salute the three Bruins before they went off to fight in World War II. During the ceremony, Schmidt, Bauer and Dumart were presented with checks for a full season's pay, plus bonus. Then in a final gesture of appreciation, the three were carried off the ice on the shoulders of the Bruins and Canadiens while the crowd of 10,420 roared in admiration for their sacrifice for the cause.

We invest our souls in our local teams. We live and die with every win and loss. This investment is validated when we witness moments of extraordinary greatness. These moments have been stamped on our brains and give us the impetus to sustain our support for our teams. We remember where we were and the people we were with when they happened. These plays propelled our teams to greatness and provided us with enduring joy.

Honorable Mentions. OT goal by Krys Kolanos to win the men's hockey national championship in 2001 for Boston College; Ed Krayer's goal in 1989 to win the men's hockey national championship for Harvard; Northeastern's Wayne Turner gives his school its first Beanpot championship in 1980; Harvard's Frank Champi to Pete Varney for a two-point conversion to "beat" Yale 38-38 in 1968; Adam Vinatieri's two field goals in "The Snow Bowl" against the Oakland Raiders.

13. David Gordon Kicks Eagles Past Notre Dame (November 20, 1993). Notre Dame was on its way to the football national title when the Fighting Irish got upset by Boston College in South Bend. The key play was David Gordon's last-second, 41-yard field goal (on a great hold by Glenn Foley off a high and inside snap). The kick seemed to be hooking wide, but somehow backed up through the posts.

12. Brad Park's Overtime Thriller (April 24, 1983). Earlier in the day at the Boston Garden, Tree Rollins of the Atlanta Hawks fought with the Celtics' Danny Ainge and nearly bit off his finger. That night, the Bruins won an overtime thriller against the Buffalo Sabres on Brad Park's rocket slap shot off a loose rebound that sent the Bruins to the conference finals.

11. Don Nelson's Back-Rim-and-In (May 5, 1969). Late in the fourth quarter of Game 7 of the NBA Finals at the L.A. Forum, the Celtics lead of 15 points had been reduced to one point. John Havlicek had possession in the corner, but lost control of the ball. The ball ended up in the hands of teammate Don Nelson, who quickly released a jump shot from the free throw line. The ball hit the back of the rim, bounced high in the air and fell through the hoop. The Celtics improbable championship was secured.

10. Dave Henderson's Home Run (October 12, 1986). "To left field and deep, Downing goes back, and it is gone—unbelievable!" Dave Henderson's home run, with two outs and two strikes in the ninth inning of a potential elimination game of the 1986 ALCS against the Angels, brought the Red Sox back from the abyss and put them back on the road to the World Series.

9. Tim Thomas stones Downie. With 10 minutes remaining in Game 5 of the Eastern Conference Finals, the Bruins were leading the Tampa Bay Lightning 2-1 when Tim Thomas made the greatest save in Bruins history. Tampa forward Steve Downie had the puck on his stick and shot at an open net only to have the Bruins' goaltender dive across the goal crease and steal a certain goal from the Bolt by fully extending his stick and blocking the puck, preserving the Bruins' victory.

8. Mike Eruzione's Winner Against the Soviet Union (February 22, 1980). Winthrop native and former Boston University hockey star Mike Eruzione scored the winner in the third period to secure the United States' "Miracle on Ice" victory over the mighty Soviets.

7. "Havlicek Steals the Ball!" There have actually been three separate steals of monumental consequence in the Celtics history: John Havlicek's steal of 76ers guard Hal Greer's pass to secure the 1965 Eastern Conference Finals; Gerald Henderson's steal from the Lakers in Game 2 of the 1984 Finals; and Larry Bird's steal from Isiah Thomas of the Pistons to force Game 7 of the 1987 Eastern Conference Finals. But none was more monumental (or memorable) than Havlicek's.

6. Doug Flutie's Hail Mary Pass (November 23, 1984). On the day after Thanksgiving Day in 1984, the University of Miami and Boston College squared off in the greatest college football game ever. In the end, it came down to a 48-yard touchdown heave by Doug Flutie to wide receiver Gerard Phelan on the last play of the game to snatch a stunning 47-45 victory for the Eagles.

5. Carlton Fisk's Home Run (October 21, 1975). The image of Fisk waving the ball fair in the 12th inning of Game 6 of the World Series against Cincinnati's "Big Red Machine" capped off what many called the greatest baseball game ever—a contest that also featured a dramatic over-the-head catch by Sox right fielder Dwight Evans and a three-run homer by Boston's Bernie Carbo.

4. Larry Bird's Bank Shot (May 3, 1981). The Celtics were down 3-1 to long-time rival Philadelphia in the Eastern Conference Finals. Boston scratched back with a dramatic win in Game 6 in Philadelphia to even the series. Then in Game 7 at the Boston Garden, Larry Bird's last-second bank shot propelled the Celtics to victory in one of the great series in Boston sports history.

3. David Ortiz's Walk Off (October 17, 2004). Year after year and decade after decade, Boston had been the victim of Yankee superiority. With the Red Sox down 3-0 in the ALCS, Boston first baseman Kevin Millar warned anyone who would listen, "Don't let the Red Sox win Game 4." Thanks to Dave Roberts' stolen base, Bill Mueller's hit and David Ortiz's mammoth home run early the following morning, the Red Sox were on the path to redemption.

2. Bobby Orr's Goal (May 10, 1970). It was the goal. It was the imagery. It was a Stanley Cup victory. Bobby Orr flying through the air in exultation as Boston soared with him. The victory over the St. Louis Blues gave Boston its first Stanley Cup in 29 years.

1. Adam Vinatieri's Field Goal (February 3, 2002). It was more than a Super Bowl victory. For all of New England, it was a moment that provided us sports affirmation. For years, Boston teams had found a way to lose. This time, it was different. Led by a genius coach, a wonder-boy quarterback and a kicker with ice water in his veins, the 14-point underdog Patriots found a way to win over the Rams with Vinatieri's walk-off, 47-yard field goal.

My Top 10 Moments as a Red Sox Broadcaster

:: by Don Orsillo

Note: Don Orsillo fulfilled his lifelong dream in 2001 when he became the Boston Red Sox play-by-play man on NESN. The Melrose native worked his way up to the broadcast bigs by interning for Sox radio man Joe Castiglione while at Northeastern University and then announcing in the minor leagues for a decade that included calling Pawtucket Red Sox games on the radio from 1996-2000. He's a wonderful guy who hasn't changed a bit since he made it to the show. Here's his list of his favorite moments in the NESN chair.

Honorable Mentions. The returns of Trot Nixon, Nomar Garciaparra and Dave Roberts to Fenway in other uniforms; Mike Lowell hitting a home run in his first at-bat upon returning to the Sox lineup after thumb surgery and a proposed trade to Texas; trade deadline day in 2004 when Nomar was traded; Curt Schilling's 200th win.

10. Curt Schilling's Almost No-Hitter in Oakland. This was as fun as doing a no-hitter. Schilling got two outs in the ninth inning before Shannon Stewart broke up the no-no after Schilling shook off Jason Varitek. With all that Curt accomplished, he had never thrown a no-hitter and almost did that day. Almost.

9. David Ortiz Hitting Home Runs 51, 52, 53 and 54. His pursuit of Jimmie Foxx's single-season HR record for the Red Sox was a great chase that started early in the season. I remember that as the HRs piled up, you just knew he was going to do it.

8. Manny Ramirez's 500th Home Run. Having called his 300th and 400th previously with an eye towards his 500th, it was amazing when it happened. Camden Yards was pretty cool, but I imagine home at Fenway would have been even better.

7. Clay Buchholtz's No-Hitter. This was totally out of nowhere and really was as dominant a performance as I have ever seen. There were good hitters in the Orioles lineup and he just dominated all night. The electricity was off the charts in the park. The fact that it was so early in his career added to the drama.

6. John Lester's No-Hitter vs. the Kansas City Royals. I think because it was storybook. He had beaten cancer. He was the winner in the clinching game of the 2007 World Series, and here he was throwing a no-hitter. He had been through so much and then this.

5. Being on the Field in Colorado Interviewing Players After the 2007 World Series. Same drill, but different and special in its own way. And yes, I have dirt from Coors Field.

4. Being on the Field in St. Louis Interviewing Players After the 2004 World Series. It seems like a long time ago now, but we literally talked with the entire roster that night in St. Louis. Since we do not get to broadcast the playoffs on NESN, we do a pregame and postgame show. I have dirt from Busch Stadium, too.

3. On the Yankee Stadium Mound After Game 7 of the 2004 ALCS. After Tim Wakefield allowed the series-winning, walk-off home run to Aaron Boone in Game 7 of the 2003 ALCS, he walked off the mound wondering if he would be the goat and had it on his mind for a year. After the incredible comeback from down 3-0 to the Yankees was complete in Game 7, I interviewed him on the mound from where he had thrown the home run pitch to Boone a year earlier. It was emotional and something I will never forget.

2. Opening Day 2005. Some of my greatest memories as a Red Sox announcer are not doing play-by-play. In fact, one of my all-time favorites was hosting the ring ceremony after the 2004 World Championship on the field. The Opening Day ceremony is always special to emcee, but nothing will ever be better than the introduction of the first Red Sox champs in 86 years.

1. My First Game as the Full-Time NESN Voice of the Red Sox. Hideo Nomo's no-hitter in Baltimore. I was a September call-up in 2000 from the Pawtucket Red Sox and broadcast three Red Sox games on Fox 25 before I was hired to become the full-time Sox announcer on NESN in 2001. After 10 years in the minors, calling my first MLB game with the new job and have it be a no-hitter was just icing on the cake.

Moments of Mischief, Tomfoolery and Malarkey
:: MC

In a sports-crazed town like Boston, fans are often as interested in the events that occur outside the arena as the ones that take place inside it. Sometimes the headlines these athletes make off the field, diamond or ice are more interesting than their play on them. The list below presents non-playing moments in Boston sports history that captured the attention of the masses.

Honorable Mentions. John Graham traffic cop; Paxton Crawford falls out of bed; Wade Boggs falls out of truck and wife drives over him; Wade Boggs attacked and wills himself to become invisible; Patriots post-1986 Super Bowl drug scandal; Irving Fryar does enough to warrant his own list.

12. Larry Bird's Bar Fight (May 16, 1985). During the Eastern Conference Finals against Philadelphia, Boston's star forward reportedly got into a bar fight and injured his shooting hand or arm. The Celtics took out the 76ers, but went on to lose to the Lakers in the NBA Finals. Bird shot 52 percent from the field and 43 percent from three-point land during the regular season. During the postseason he shot just 46 percent from the field and 28 percent from three-point land.

11. "Oil Can" Boyd Meets Siskel and Ebert (Spring Training 1987). While in Winter Haven, Florida for spring training, the Red Sox pitcher was tardy in returning videos of a pornographic nature to the local video store. Police came to the Sox locker room to discuss the issue with Boyd. When the titles of the films were released, Boston media member Chuck Waseleski dubbed the incident, "The Can Film Festival."

10. Patriots Coach Clive Rush Shocked (January 30, 1969). Coach Rush's original press conference was delayed when his plane and train were postponed due to weather conditions. Eventually, the former New York Jets offensive coordinator reached Boston and was introduced to the local media at a makeshift press conference held at Logan Airport. During the Q&A, Rush came in contact with live wires and was shocked. Patriots fans were shocked by his coaching, as his team compiled a record of 5-16 before Rush was fired.

9. Dave Cowens Takes Leave of Absence (November 8, 1976). Just months after the Celtics had won the NBA title, their center had lost his passion to play the game. Cowens, maybe the most genuine and sincere athlete ever to play in Boston, decided it was best to take an unpaid basketball sabbatical. He felt it was wrong to cheat the fans or franchise. During his leave, he drove a cab and took a job as an executive at New England Harness Raceway. On January 14, he returned to the team. During his 29-game leave, the team posted a 15-14 record.

8. Drew Bledsoe and Max Lane Stage Dive (November 13, 1997). It's not every concert at the Paradise that features an All-Pro quarterback and one of his offensive linemen diving off the stage into the crowd. This is just what happened at the Everclear concert in Boston. During the dive, a woman was injured. Reportedly, the players, band and nightclub ended up paying over a million dollars to the victim.

7. Mo Vaughn Flips Truck (January 19, 1998). Driving home from his frequent haunt, The Foxy Lady, the Red Sox first baseman hit an unoccupied car, causing his truck to flip. He was arrested for the 2:15 a.m. incident after he failed field sobriety tests. His courtroom defense for his incoherent actions was an amalgamation of a knee injury, obesity and too many breakfasts at the gentleman's club. He was acquitted.

6. Gene Conley Goes AWOL (July 27, 1962). In a start at Yankee Stadium, the 6-8 tall pitcher gave up eight runs in less than three innings while earning his 10th loss of the season. After the game, the team bus was delayed by New York City traffic. Frustrated and impatient, Conley decided to exit the bus along with infielder Pumpsie Green. Conley jumped in a cab and told the driver, "I want to go to Bethlehem." Conley was taken to El Al Israel Airlines. The Red Sox pitcher bought a ticket to fly to Israel, but was denied passage because he lacked a passport. Green, who had no interest in going to Israel, reported back to the team after missing a game and was fined. Conley reported back to the Red Sox five days later and was fined heavily.

5. Zeke Mowatt Greets Lisa Olson (September 17, 1990). *Boston Herald* reporter Lisa Olson was in the Patriots locker room when tight end Zeke Mowatt positioned his nudeness in the vicinity of her face. Olson would later accuse the Patriots of "mind rape." Patriots owner Victor Kiam reportedly responded by calling Olson a "classic bitch." Patriots fans harassed her and slashed her tires. She eventually left Boston for Australia. The team later purportedly settled a civil law suit Olson had filed.

4. Ty Law Imports Cousin's Bag (December 18, 2000). Scared to fly in the snow, cornerback Ty Law and some other Patriots players begged Coach Bill Belichick to allow them to skip the team flight out of Buffalo. Belichick acquiesced. That night, Ty Law decided to go to Canada to visit a "nightclub." On the way back across the border, customs agents searched the car Law was in and found the drug Ecstasy in a bag. Law paid the fine, but would later claim it was "his cousin's bag."

3. Roger Clemens at Bayou Mama's (January 19, 1991). Roger Clemens was a patron with his brother Gary at the Houston bar called Bayou Mama's. During their stay, a disagreement arose between a Houston policeman and Gary Clemens. When the policeman tried to arrest his brother, Roger reportedly jumped on the cop's back and tried to choke him. Four policemen later, "The Rocket" and his brother were taken into custody.

2. Irving Fryar's Halftime Drive (November 23, 1986). In the first half against the Buffalo Bills, Irving Fryar separated his shoulder and was not allowed to return to the game. At halftime, he left the stadium in his Mercedes Benz, traveling at a high rate of speed. Two miles down the road, the wide receiver slammed his car into a tree and suffered bruises, abrasions and a concussion when his head hit the windshield. He was admitted to Mass General Hospital and released after three days. He did have one catch for 10 yards on the day.

1. Celtic Pride (September 1960). In an effort to promote professional basketball to the Midwest, the Celtics were invited to play in an exhibition game in Marion, Indiana. Prior to the game, the Celtic players were presented with the keys to the city by Marion's mayor. Following the game, the team went to eat dinner at a local restaurant. But African-Americans Bill Russell and K.C. Jones were refused admittance. The Celtics immediately piled into two cabs and drove to the mayor's house and handed him back the keys to the city.

My 10 Favorite Bike Rides in the World
:: by Zdeno Chara

Note: Zdeno Chara became the 18th captain of the Boston Bruins after signing a big-money free agent contract with the club in 2006, and played a huge role in bringing the Stanley Cup back to Boston in 2011. At 6-9, the native of Slovakia is the tallest player in the history of the NHL. A five-time NHL All-Star, Chara won the Norris Trophy as the league's top defenseman in 2009. During his time away from the ice, the hard-shooting defenseman is an avid cyclist known as one of the fittest athletes in all of sports. He listed his 10 favorite places in the world to take a long bike ride below, with the book's authors providing a brief description of each spot.

10. Gatineau Park, Ottawa, Ontario. Known to locals as the Gatineaus, this 363 square kilometer park is only 10 minutes outside of Ottawa.

9. Boston Charles River, Boston, Massachusetts. The beautiful Charles River separates Boston and Cambridge and features riverside paths for cycling, walking and running.

8. Dubrava Vlci Vrch, Slovakia. A plush section of Slovakia to ride in surrounded by oak tree forestry.

7. Inovec, Slovakia. This mountainous area is almost 3,500 feet above sea level.

6. High Tatra's, Slovakia. This popular ski area serves as a cycling and hiking destination in the summer.

5. Beskydy, Czech Republic. The largest land preserve in the Czech Republic is filled with beautiful forests and pastures.

4. Passo di Monte Giove, Italy. This ride travels through a mountainous pass in the Rhaetian Alps. The path is surrounded by forest.

3. Col du Galibier, France. First used as a climb of the Tour de France in 1911, this ascent in southern France goes to over 2,500 meters. In the winter, the route is impassable.

2. L'Alpe d'Huez, France. This mountainous stretch of the Tour de France is located in the French Alps in the central part of the country. For the last quarter-century, it has often served as a stage finish for the race.

1. Mont Ventoux, France. Connected to the Alps, this mountain in southern France is known as the "Giant of the Provence." With its sadistic crosswinds, it is considered the most arduous climb in the Tour de France.

With free agency now a reality in all four major team sports, fan interest doesn't end with the end of a season. Boston teams are blessed with big-market cash flow that allows our GMs to go on offseason shopping sprees for players from other teams and Boston fans to hold countless discussions on the best free agents available. The following free agent acquisitions have had the biggest positive impact in Boston.

12. Bill Campbell (November 6, 1976). The closer came from the Minnesota Twins as the Red Sox first real free-agent signing. "Soupy" had a stellar, All-Star year in 1977, saving 31 games and winning 13.

11. M.L. Carr (July 24, 1979). The rambunctious forward with energy and talent was wooed to Boston from Detroit. Red Auerbach turned a good deal into a great deal when he offered Bob McAdoo as compensation and got a first-round pick in exchange. The Celtic GM wizard then turned that pick into Kevin McHale and Robert Parish.

10. Zdeno Chara (July 2006). For years, the Bruins have been known to be tight with money. But in the summer of 2006, they signed Ottawa Senator defenseman Zdeno Chara to a max contract. He won the Norris Trophy as the league's best defenseman for the 2008-09 season, and led the Bruins to the Stanley Cup in 2011.

9. Johnny Damon (December 21, 2001). Signed as a free agent from the Oakland A's, Damon was a star in Boston. He hit leadoff, played a good center field (yes he threw like a girl) and stole bases. One of the resident "Idiots" on the team, he was part of the puzzle that finally brought a World Series title to Boston.

8. Tim Wakefield (April 26, 1995). The Red Sox took a flyer on the knuckle-balling Pirates castaway, and 15 fine seasons later, you hear Boston fans mention Wakefield in the same sentence as Cy Young and Roger Clemens.

7. Tom Gordon (December 21, 1995). The starter with a great curve ball was brought over from Kansas City. The Red Sox converted him into a closer. They never should have let him go. With hat pulled down over his eyes, "Flash" proved to be a great signing. In 1998, he saved 46 games and made the All-Star team.

6. Keith Foulke (January 7, 2004). I still don't know how he got people out with a change-up that dared hitters on the inside half, but he did. His run in the 2004 playoffs was prolific. He pitched in 11 games and 14 innings while giving up only one run. He should have been named World Series MVP. Was he indignant at times? Yes, but he wasn't paid to be pleasant. He was paid to get big outs, and he did.

5. Tim Thomas (2005). Bruins General Manager Mike O'Connell lifted Tim Thomas from the Finnish team the Jokerit Sports Club with a one-year contract worth $450,000. Thomas would go on to win two Vezina Trophies (2009 and 2011) and the Conn Smythe Award in 2011 as the playoff MVP while leading the Bruins to their first Stanley Cup since 1972.

4. Rodney Harrison (2003). The hard-hitting safety was the type of player you loved when he was on your team and hated when he played on the other team. He brought toughness, a chip on his shoulder and a thirst to win to Foxboro. He was a major piece of the 2003 and 2004 Super Bowl teams.

3. Mike Vrabel (2001). Scott Pioli and/or Bill Belichick recognized the potential of the sparingly used Steeler linebacker and made him into a big piece of the Patriots dynasty puzzle. He was a leader, could cover backs out of the backfield, rush the quarterback (see his Super Bowl hit on Kurt Warner) and was the team's best tight end since Ben Coates.

2. Manny Ramirez (December 9, 2000). Even if you include all the "Manny being Manny" moments, you can't dismiss the fact that he was still one of the greatest righty hitters in the history of the game. Too often, he disrespected the game. However, his ability to hit (274 home runs /.312 average) ultimately allowed Boston to win. For that reason, and that reason alone, a desperate Red Sox Nation looked the other way.

1. Red Sox Signings of January 2003. In one winter month, the Red Sox made themselves into a perennial contender. During January of 2003, the Red Sox signed David Ortiz—the greatest free agent signing in Boston sports history. They also signed Bill Mueller, an infielder who played the game the right way, won a batting title and authored one of the biggest hits in Red Sox history when he knocked in Dave Roberts in Game 4 of the 2004 ALCS. And the Sox also signed reliever and bullpen leader Mike Timlin, who brought experience, fortitude and his camouflage t-shirts to the late innings of big games. Last but not least, they purchased the team's spiritual leader Kevin Millar from the Florida Marlins.

Sometimes having too much money is a bad thing. The big checking account lets a team take risks on free agents it wouldn't ordinarily take. These big-money Boston signings didn't produce here in a fashion commensurate with their compensation.

Honorable Mentions. Paul Coffey; Reche Caldwell; Scott Secules; Matt Clement.

12. Not Our Type of Guys. Zeke Mowatt brought disgrace to the organization with his sexual harassment of reporter Lisa Olson. Jeff Russell hated Boston and was overheard saying that Boston parents teach their children to hate. Mark Blount was a Celtics center who didn't care enough to earn his money.

11. Robinson Checo (December 6, 1996). The wonder pitcher was supposed to be the great find of Red Sox management. He pitched in Japan, and should have stayed there. During his career, he won one game for the Red Sox in return for his handsome million-dollar salary.

10. Mike Torrez (November 23, 1977). The simple fact that he gave up the infamous home run to Bucky "Fucking" Dent in the 1978 division playoff game is enough reason to put him on this list. He finished his career with the Red Sox with a 60-54 record and a 4.51 ERA.

9. Edgar Renteria (January 19, 1994). His resume had "World Series hero" on it. But when he came to Boston and the American League, his game didn't translate. He appeared overweight and spent more time complaining about the bounces on the Fenway infield than properly fielding ground balls. In the end, the Red Sox paid him to play for someone else.

8. Julio Lugo (December 5, 2006). The frail shortstop had one good year (hmmm). This led Red Sox management to take those best-case-scenario stats and project them over the life of a contract. Unfortunately, that one good year turned out to be an aberration.

7. Dominique Wilkins (July 25, 1994). His days of high-flying dunks were behind him. When the Atlanta Hawks great came to Boston, his game had deteriorated, as had his shot selection. For $2.8 million, he shot 42 percent from the field. His paycheck ate up salary cap room and hamstrung the Celtics.

6. Red Sox Signings of December 1990. The Red Sox went Christmas shopping in 1990 and wrapped up Jack Clark and Matt Young. Clark was a star in the National League, but his best days were behind him. Matt Young threw well against the Red Sox and management allowed that brief sampling to affect their judgment and open their checkbook. Young was 2-0 against Boston the season before he became a Red Sox pitcher, but 6-18 against everyone else. Then he went 3-11 in two seasons as a Red Sox pitcher.

5. Martin Lapointe (July 2, 2001). I appreciate that the Bruins spent money on him. However, he was far from a superstar when they signed him. Rumors of a tiff between Boston management and Detroit management may have led to impulsive shopping by the Bruins, who spent superstar money to grab a complimentary player from Detroit in Lapointe. In three years with the Bruins, he earned $16 million while averaging 13 goals and posting a plus/minus of -24 over his last two seasons.

4. J.D. Drew (February 14, 2007). He was the toy in the window that the Red Sox had to have. But Drew is a soft player with Hall of Fame skills who too often didn't answer the call when needed most. For $70 million, we got a .270 hitter who averages 18 HRs and 140 games a year. Not quite old school.

3. Adalius Thomas (March 2, 2007). He came to New England from the vaunted defense of the Baltimore Ravens. He was a big man who was supposed to be able to run with running backs in pass patterns and rush the quarterback. In the end, this $10-million-a-year linebacker was average at best and cut from the team.

2. Jose Offerman (November 16, 1998). He was supposed to fill the shoes of Mo Vaughn. Instead he gave the Red Sox four years of declining play. Boston handed him $25 million. In return, Offerman hit .268 and stole 31 bases while being thrown out 28 times.

1. Pervis Ellison (August 1, 1994). The center was brought to Boston by Rick Pitino, and we know what the Slickster's track record in evaluating talent was for the Celtics. Ellison was paid eight figures for six years and in return spent more time on the bench in street clothes than on the floor earning his paycheck. The Celtics learned the hard way why Ellison's former Sacramento teammate Danny Ainge referred to him as "Out of Service Pervis." Over his time with the Celtics, he averaged 4.7 points and 4.9 rebounds.

My 10 Best Assignments for the *Boston Globe*
:: by Leigh Montville

Note: Leigh Montville has been a columnist at the *Boston Globe*, a senior writer at *Sports Illustrated* and the author of several sports books, including the best-sellers, *Ted Williams: The Biography of an American Hero* and *The Big Bam*. He is considered by many as the finest sportswriter in Boston print history.

"I was a sportswriter/columnist at the *Globe* from 1968 to 1989," Montville recalls. "People always told me during this time that I had a great job and they 'would do what you do for nothing.' With the advent of the Internet and the decline of the newspaper business, they now do.

"This is a top-of-the-head list and surely 10 replacements could be found in a hurry."

10. Spring Training, Winter Haven. There was a small-town, small-time vibration here that has been lost forever. The smell of oranges was mixed with Boston accents and sunshine and the sound of wooden bats hitting baseballs. Lunch was served at a place called Andy's Igloo.

9. Harvard Beats Yale 29-29. There was a reason they made a movie of this game. Rent the movie. Look for me. I'm standing in the middle of the field on the 40-yard line as the final points are scored. OK, I'm standing in a big crowd. The year is 1968.

8. Too Many Men on the Ice. Any visit to the Montreal Forum was amazing. This visit in Game 7 of the Stanley Cup semifinals in 1979 was amazing for bad reasons. Too many men on the ice. Here comes Guy Lafleur, hair streaming in the wind, to tie the game with 74 seconds left. Too many, too many, too many men on the ice.

7. Squish the Fish. This was the giant step to legitimacy in the 1985 AFC Final. The Patriots ended an 18-game losing streak in Miami, 31-14, to qualify for their first Super Bowl. Left the press box in the Orange Bowl early this time. Stood on the sidelines as John Hannah, Andre Tippett and all of them danced during the two-minute warning to "Walk of Life" by Dire Straits. Why do I remember that?

6. Hail Mary Game. Everybody else left the press box early near the end of this November 18, 1984 game against the University of Miami because it was a long walk to the Boston College dressing room at the Orange Bowl. I said I was staying in the press box 'til the end. Because "you never know."

5. 1975 World Series, Game 6. Fisk hits the ball out. Most dramatic moment in Boston sports? Start the argument. I am on the side of the affirmative.

4. 1986 World Series. Met up with a friend and his son in between the eighth and ninth innings of Game 6 at Shea Stadium. Friend was a Yankees fan. Congratulated me on the Red Sox finally winning the Series. Yes, he did.

3. 1969 NBA Finals. I was 26 years old. I had never seen a palm tree or the Pacific Ocean. Not to mention Russell vs. Chamberlain. No, wait a minute. I had seen Russell vs. Chamberlain.

2. All Things Marvin. Watched Marvin Hagler work his way from small halls around the Route 128 loop to the world stage, battle after battle. Stood in the middle of a riot at Wembley Arena in London when he beat Alan Minter for the middleweight title. Pretty good.

1. 1980 Winter Olympics. The Boston component to the U.S. hockey gold medal story made this the best Boston sports story of all time. The *Boston Globe* had so many people on the case, the newspaper rented a house in downtown Lake Placid. This would not happen today.

All week, we go to work or school and try to survive. We measure the quality of our lives, not by our grades or salary so much as by the level of success of our local sports teams. We are emotionally invested in the home teams, and thus we rise or fall with them. Sure we take sports too seriously, but why not? It's a huge part of our lives. What makes the below list even more painful is that all the opponents on it who beat us, went on to win their respective championships (and that in most of these contests, our guys had the lead and then lost it).

Honorable Mentions. Boston College loses to West Virginia in 1993 on a late fumble, costing BC a Sugar Bowl invite; Boston College loses 1998 hockey national championship to Michigan at the Fleet Center; 2011 Patriots lose in playoffs to big-mouth Jets; Desmond Howard and Packers beat Patriots in 1997 Super Bowl; Patriots relinquish lead vs. Colts in 2007 AFC Championship Game; Red Sox lose in 1948 playoff game to Indians.

12. Red Sox vs. St. Louis Cardinals, World Series, Game 7 (October 15, 1946). The continuing controversy over this loss in the 1946 World Series proves that we Boston fans have a difficult time getting over losses. Why Red Sox shortstop Johnny Pesky held onto the ball, allowing Enos Slaughter to score the winning run from first on a single, is still debated in this city—65 YEARS LATER!

11. Bruins vs. Edmonton Oilers, Stanley Cup Finals, Game 1 (May 15, 1990). Some losses, you just don't recover from, and this was one of them. In the first game of the Stanley Cup Finals, the Bruins fell to the mighty Oilers 3-2 in triple overtime. The winning goal was scored by fourth-liner Petr Klima, who logged all of one shift prior to coming on to score the winner. The Bruins outshot the Oilers 52-31 for the game, but the difference could have been 53-31 if not for Glen Wesley's missed attempt on an empty net in the first overtime.

10. Red Sox vs. Cincinnati Reds, World Series, Game 7 (October 22, 1975). Boston led 3-0 in the sixth inning when Bill Lee threw an ill-advised eephus pitch to Tony Perez. The Reds first baseman proceeded to put the ball onto the Mass Turnpike. Joe Morgan's RBI single in the ninth inning, off little-used Red Sox pitcher Jim Burton, would end the Red Sox dream of their first World Series title in 57 years.

9. Marvin Hagler vs. Sugar Ray Leonard, Middleweight Championship Fight (April 6, 1987). The fight might have been lost before it started when the Hagler camp allowed a bigger ring. It was a frustrating bout. Hagler seemed too patient against a fighter who knew how to score with style, despite having little substance to his punches. In the end, Leonard threw more punches, costing Hagler his belt and putting an end to his career.

8. Bruins vs. Philadelphia Flyers, Stanley Cup Finals, Game 6 (May 19, 1974). The 1974 Stanley Cup Finals featured the Big Bad Bruins vs. the Broad Street Bullies. It was an epic showdown in which former Bruins goalie Bernie Parent frustrated Boston, who had the top four scorers in the NHL (Phil Esposito, Bobby Orr, Ken Hodge and Wayne Cashman). Parent shut out the Bruins 1-0 in Game 6 to clinch the Cup. The lone goal was scored by former Boston prospect Rick MacLeish.

7. Celtics vs. Los Angeles Lakers, NBA Finals, Game 4 (June 4, 1987). Everyone remembers Magic's "baby hook." But it shouldn't be forgotten that the Celtics had an 18-point lead at one point. The game came down to two key plays—a Robert Parish turnover and Kevin McHale's fumble of a rebound that gave the ball back to the Lakers for Magic's crushing basket.

6. Patriots vs. Oakland Raiders, NFL Playoffs (December 18, 1976). The Patriots were playing the big, bad Raiders in Oakland for the right to advance to the conference championship. In the fourth quarter, New England squandered a 21-10 lead and allowed the Raiders to score two late touchdowns for a comeback victory. The last touchdown drive was mainly sustained by a "suspicious" roughing the passer penalty called by referee Ben Dreith on Ray "Sugar Bear" Hamilton. Raiders quarterback Ken Stabler scored from the one-yard line with 10 seconds remaining to seal the devastating loss.

5. Bruins vs. Montreal Canadiens, Conference Finals, Game 7 (May 10, 1979). With a one-goal lead late in Game 7 in the Montreal Forum, the Bruins were penalized for too many men on the ice. The Habs took advantage of the power play. With just over a minute left, Bruins-killer Guy Lafleur scored on a slap shot to tie the game. The Canadiens would, of course, go on to break our hearts, yet again, when Yvon Lambert put in the game-winner in overtime.

4. Red Sox vs. New York Yankees, AL East Division Playoff Game (October 2, 1978). Our hearts are broken by a 310-foot home run and by Lou "Jethro Bodine" Piniella blindly sticking his glove out in right field. It was two teams with 99 wins battling for the right to advance to the American League Championship Series. When it was over, the only thing we had left was the promise of a long winter. Bucky "Fucking" Dent!

3. Red Sox vs. New York Mets, World Series, Game 6 (October 25, 1986). "There's a slow roller towards first. . . ." Poor Bill Buckner, it's not your fault. It's not your fault. No, it's not your fault. Roger Clemens had a one-run lead going into the eighth and decided to watch the rest of the game from the dugout, deferring to Calvin Schiraldi. The rest is history.

2. Red Sox vs. New York Yankees, American League Championship Series, Game 7 (October 16, 2003). Note to Grady: when Pedro points to the sky coming off the mound, he's done. Note to Grady: don't use velocity as a benchmark of whether or not your pitcher is done—it's location. Note to Grady: if you do send Pedro back out, allow him one base runner, not four. Note to Grady: don't bring a home run pitcher like Tim Wakefield into a sudden-death game to make freakin' Aaron Boone a New York hero! Ugh!

1. Patriots vs. New York Giants, Super Bowl XLII (February 3, 2008). This was a once-in-a-lifetime sports opportunity—a chance for a perfect season. It would validate the Patriots as the greatest football team ever, while providing us Boston fans a badge of superiority. Sadly, in the end, the offensive line couldn't protect the quarterback. A guy named Asante couldn't hold onto an interception. Some random guy who was out of the league a year later caught a ball against his helmet. And Ellis Hobbs fell for the out-and-up.

Some athletes are just wired differently. While many players recoil when the game or event reaches its critical point, others have the internal hardware to rise to the occasion, the magnitude of the moment enhancing their abilities. These are the athletes you want with the ball in their possession and an opportunity to impact the game when it counts most.

Honorable Mentions. Doug Flutie; Troy Brown; Gerry Cheevers; Keith Foulke; Jim Lonborg.

13. Justin Leonard. With America's 1999 Ryder Cup dreams melting away at The Country Club in Brookline, Justin Leonard exploded to lead the most improbable of comebacks. With seven holes to play, Leonard was down by four holes. Then he began his charge, winning five of the next six holes. Leonard capped off his torrid run with an incredible 45-footer over a brutal ridge to win it on the 17th green. The Europeans are still whining.

12. Derek Lowe. The tall righty was a wonderful talent who could start, close or set up. His career in Boston was uneven, and thus he was branded with the reputation of someone who did too much partying and not enough work to fulfill his potential. But in the postseason, Lowe raised his game to meet expectations. In the 2003 playoffs against the Oakland A's, his two strike outs—by way of nasty two-seamers—clinched the series and left the bases loaded. He followed that moment with his overall performance in the 2004 postseason, where he recorded wins in all three series clinchers.

11. Sam Jones. A vital piece of the Celtics dynasty run from the late 1950s to the late '60s, the shooting guard was at his best in the playoffs. In Game 4 of the 1969 NBA Finals against the Lakers, his buzzer beater coming around the picket fence became his career's signature play. Following Boston's improbable championship in 1969, Jones retired with 10 rings.

10. Dave Henderson. "Hendu" came to Boston by way of Seattle and stayed for only 111 games. However, for the short time that he was here, he made quite an impact. His home run against the Angels in Game 5 of the 1986 ALCS with two outs in the ninth inning that saved the Red Sox from elimination is now part of Boston sports folklore. He followed that with a clutch World Series home run to put the Red Sox ahead in the top of the 10th in the infamous Game 6 against the Mets. If the Red Sox had held that lead and won the World Series, there would be a lot of kids named Hendu walking around Boston.

9. Tim Thomas. In four elimination games during the 2011 playoffs, the Bruins' goalie was 4-0 while stopping 131 of 136 shots. In the Stanley Cup Finals, he gave up eight goals in seven games.

8. Curt Schilling. One of the great postseason pitchers in the history of baseball, Schilling will forever be known for his courageous "bloody sock" win against the Yankees in 2004. During his tenure with the Red Sox, he was 6-1 in the postseason as part of a career postseason record of 11-2.

7. Luis Tiant. If you needed a big game pitched, then "El Tiante" was your man. His whirling, spinning, twirling windup kept hitters guessing. In the last nine days of the dramatic 1978 season, "Louiee" was 3-0. In the 1975 postseason for the Red Sox, he was 3-0—one of the wins coming over the Reds in his amazing 158-pitch performance in Game 4 of the World Series.

6. David Ortiz. "Big Papi" came to Boston as a free agent after being released by the Twins. He will leave the city as one of the most beloved athletes in Boston sports history. In the 2004 postseason, Ortiz had walk-off hits in three consecutive Red Sox wins, including his monumental home run in the 12th inning of Game 4 against the Yankees. For his career, the smiling Dominican has 12 postseason home runs, 10 regular-season walk-off home runs and was a major component of two World Series championship Red Sox teams.

5. John Havlicek. Hondo was a member of eight Celtics championship teams. He always seemed to find a way to positively impact a game's outcome. In the 1965 Eastern Conference Finals, he "stole the ball." In 1974, he was the postseason MVP when he averaged 27.1 points a game. In Game 6 of the 1974 NBA Finals, Havlicek hit one of the great shots in Celtics history—a running baseline jumper over Kareem Abdul-Jabbar in overtime. In his final championship campaign in 1976, foot problems nearly crippled him. However, he still played 58 minutes in the triple-overtime classic of Game 5 against the Phoenix Suns, which included his running bank shot at the end of the second overtime.

4. Carl Yastrzemski. In September and October of 1967, Yaz hit .413 with 12 home runs and 31 RBI. Yes, he did make the last outs in 1975 and 1978, but his mythical performance in 1967 granted Yaz a free pass for the rest of his days.

3. Adam Vinatieri. I know. I know. He's just a kicker. However, he's not an ordinary kicker (e.g. he ran down Herschel Walker from behind on a kickoff return). Vinatieri's 45-yard field goal—through the snow, to tie the Raiders in Foxboro in 2002 and send the AFC Championship Game into overtime—is the greatest kick in football history. His game-winners in Super Bowls XXXVI and XXXVIII, combined with his playoff game-winners against Oakland and Tennessee, are proof enough. This guy was the essence of clutch.

1b. Tom Brady. No NFL quarterback has been better in the clutch than this sixth-round draft pick out of Michigan. He's 8-1 in overtime. He is the greatest two-minute quarterback of all time. He has won three Super Bowls. Now that's performing in the clutch.

1a. Larry Bird. Bird's bank shot to beat the Philadelphia 76ers in Game 7 of the 1981 Eastern Conference Finals is one of the biggest shots in Celtics history. From the moment he arrived from Terra Haute, he found a way to win. Whether he was shooting the last ball in a three-point shooting contest or a playoff game, Bird was simply amazing. Tangible evidence of his greatness under pressure includes: the "Duel Against Dominique," coming out of the locker room hurt against Indiana, getting his revenge against Magic Johnson and his steal against Detroit. It was all part of the brilliant mosaic of Bird's ability to rise to the occasion.

Top Massachusetts High School Basketball Players :: by Skip Karam

Note: Skip Karam coached basketball for Durfee High School for 37 seasons. His teams won 659 games and made it to the postseason tournament 32 times while winning five state championships. The Massachusetts Basketball Coaches Hall of Fame inductee lists his state's greatest high school basketball players in no particular order.

13. Travis Best. Best attended Springfield Central High School where he was named Massachusetts Player of the Year three times. He once scored 81 points in a game—the second-highest total in Massachusetts history. Best was a 1991 McDonald's All-American.

12. Dana Barros. The 1985 graduate of Xaverian High School averaged 40 points as a senior and carried his team to the Eastern Massachusetts Semifinals. He scored over 50 points in a game three times. He went on to star at Boston College and in the NBA.

11. Ron Perry, Jr. The greatest pure shooter in Massachusetts history, Perry was a two-time All-American. He scored 2,481 points for the Catholic Memorial Knights from 1972-76. Imagine what he would have done with a three-point line.

10. Chris Herren. The best player of the 1990s. Chris Herren scored 2,073 points for Durfee from 1990-94.

9. Mike Herren. The Hilltopper led Durfee to two straight state championships in the 1980s before heading to Boston College.

8. Ernie Fleming. The Durfee great led his team to the 1966 Tech Tourney Championship in the Boston Garden and was named Tournament MVP. Went on to play at Gardner-Webb Junior College with Artis Gilmore.

7. Patrick Ewing. The Cambridge Rindge and Latin center was the most dominant big man in state history. He led his high school to three straight state championships and a 77-1 record.

6. Bob Bigelow. In two years for Winchester High School, Bigelow scored 1,000 points and was named to the Top 50 in the USA list. He went on to play for the University of Pennsylvania and was picked in the first round of the 1975 NBA draft by the Kansas City Kings.

5. Jimmy Walker. The Roxbury guard starred at Boston Tech in the early 1960s. He went on to star at Providence College and then in the NBA.

4. Terry Driscoll. The 6-7 power forward dominated for Boston College High School in the 1960s before taking his game to Boston College and then the NBA.

3. Ronnie Lee. The Lexington High School standout led his team to a 51-0 record and two state championships under Coach Rollie Massimino. While at Lexington, he also set the state record in the javelin throw at 234 feet. He went on to the University of Oregon and then to the NBA in 1976.

2. Wilfred Morrison. The Massachusetts high school star went on to play for Boston College in the 1970s.

1. Jack Foley. Known simply as Jack "The Shot," the Worcester native played for Assumption High School, averaging 41 points a game. He went on to star at Holy Cross in the early 1960s and play in the NBA.

Great Massachusetts High School Baseball Players :: by Peter Moscariello and Frank Carey

Note: Reading High School Baseball Manager Peter Moscariello has won over 500 games and 12 Middlesex championships, while Frank Carey of North Reading has won over 600 games. Below, they offer a list, in no particular order, of great Massachusetts high school baseball players who went on to play professionally.

36. Manny Delcarmen, West Roxbury High School.

35. Jeff Allison, Peabody High School.

34. John Doherty, Reading High School.

33. Skip Lockwood, Catholic Memorial High School.

32. Walt Hriniak, Natick High School.

31. Pie Traynor, Somerville High School.

30. John Tudor, Peabody High School.

29. Mark Belanger, Pittsfield High School.

28. Tony Conigliaro, St. Mary's High School.

27. Billy Conigliaro, Swampscott High School.

26. Richie Hebner, Norwood High School.

25. Kevin McGlinchy, Malden High School.

24. Paul Carey, Boston College High School.

23. Brian Rose, Dartmouth High School.

22. Rich Gedman, St. Peter Marian High School.

21. Bill Monbouquette, Medford High School.

20. Harry Agganis, Lynn Classical High School.

19. Mark Sweeney, Holliston High School.

18. Greg Gagne, Somerset High School.

17. Jerry Remy, Somerset High School.

16. Turk Wendell, Wahconah High School.

15. Jeff Reardon, Wahconah High School.

14. Christian Howard, Lynn Vocational High School.

13. Mike Remlinger, Plymouth Carver High School.

12. Rich Dube, Bridgewater Raynham High School.

11. Matt Murray, Boston High School.

10. Pete Varney, Deerfield Academy.

9. Joe Vitiello, Stoneham High School.

8. Jeff Juden, Salem High School.

7. Gary DiSarcina, Billerica High School.

6. Tom Glavine, Billerica High School.

5. Pete Smith, Burlington High School.

4. Ken Hill, Lynn English High School.

3. Mike Pagliarulo, Medford High School.

2. Matt Wohlers, Holyoke High School.

1. Carlos Pena, Haverhill High School.

Top Massachusetts High School Hockey Players
:: by Bill Hanson

Note: Bill Hanson is the greatest high school coach in the history of Massachusetts. Coach Hanson has served as the head hockey coach at Catholic Memorial High School in West Roxbury for 35 years and has won 17 state titles. He knows maybe better than anyone that Massachusetts has produced some of the country's finest ice hockey players. For us, he lists the best of the best of them from the 1950s through the 1990s, in no particular order within their respective decades.

1950s

4. Ralph DeLeo. Boston Tech, tried out with Bruins.

3. Bob and Bill Cleary. Belmont Hill, Harvard, 1960 Olympics.

2. Jim Logue. Malden Catholic, Boston College, 1960 Olympics.

1. Jack Kirrane. Brookline, 1960 Olympics.

1960s

5. Richie Hebner. Norwood, MLB.

4. John Cunniff. Don Bosco, Boston College, 1968 Olympics.

3. Kevin Ahern. Catholic Memorial, Boston College, 1972 Olympics.

2. Bob Kullen. Milton High, Bowdoin, 1972 Olympics, UNH head coach.

1. Dick McGlynn. Catholic Memorial, Boston College, 1972 Olympics.

1970s

6. Robbie Ftorek. Needham, NHL.

5. Mike Fidler. Charlestown, Malden Catholic, Boston University, NHL.

4. Kevin Coughlin. South Boston, Michigan State.

3. Fred Ahern. Tech, South Boston, Bowdoin, NHL.

2. Rod Langway. Randolph, UNH, NHL.

1. Tommy Glavine. Billerica, MLB.

1980s

12. Bob Carpenter. St. John's Prep, NHL.

11. Tom Barrasso. Acton Boxborough, NHL.

10. Bob Sweeney. Acton Boxborough, Boston College, NHL.

9. Marty McInnis. Milton Academy, Boston College, NHL.

8. Paul Stanton. Catholic Memorial, Wisconsin, NHL.

7. Bill Guerin. Wilbraham High, Boston College, NHL, 1998, 2002 and 2006 Olympics.

6. Ted Donato. Catholic Memorial, Harvard, NHL, 1992 Olympics, Harvard head coach.

5. Jeremy Roenick. Thayer Academy, NHL, 1998 and 2002 Olympics.

4. Tony Amonte. Thayer Academy, NHL, 1998 and 2002 Olympics.

3. Shawn McEachern. Matignon, Boston University, NHL, 1992 Olympics.

2. Keith Tkachuk. Malden Catholic, Boston University, NHL, 1992, 1998, 2002 and 2006 Olympics.

1. Kevin Stevens. Silver Lake, Boston College, NHL.

1990s

8. Jim Carey. Catholic Memorial, Wisconsin, NHL.

7. Chris O'Sullivan. Catholic Memorial, NHL.

6. Mike Grier. St. Sebastian's, Boston University, NHL.

5. Shawn Bates. Medford, Boston University, NHL.

4. Tom Poti. St. Peter-Marian, Boston University, NHL.

3. David Hines. Andover, Boston College.

2. Rick DiPietro. Winthrop, St. Sebastian's, Boston University, NHL.

1. Brian Boyle. Hingham, St. Sebastian's, NHL.

These 10 got the headlines in the newspapers, fans screaming for their auto-graphs and attention from the cameras. But their game performances never equaled the level of fawning they received. Making this list doesn't imply they were terrible players, it just suggests that they received a disproportionate level of admiration and/or money in relation to their actual contributions as players.

10. Sam "Bam" Cunningham. The USC running back was the Patriots first-round pick in 1973. He arrived at Schaefer Stadium with a reputation for tough running and a penchant for diving over defenses into the end zone. During his nine years for New England, he was a steady back. However, he only once ran for over 825 yards in a season and averaged less than 4.0 yards a carry for his career. I must admit, his inclusion on this list is greatly influenced by the mem-ory of him running out of bounds in the infamous 1976 playoff loss against Oakland, thus giving the ball back to Oakland for their painful comeback drive.

9. Rick Burleson. "The Rooster" was intense and had a gun from the hole, but in reality he was just a slightly above-average shortstop. Over his seven years with Boston, he averaged 23 errors per season, a .274 batting average and a .326 on-base percentage. In his 4,491 plate appearances as a Red Sox, he hit just 38 home runs (or one for every 118 at-bats), while averaging just nine stolen bases a season.

8. Chris Slade. When I think of Chris Slade, the first image that comes to mind is Slade rushing off the edge and the opposing team's offensive tackle just pushing him behind the quarterback, taking him out of the play. I'm sure teams must have planned to allow him to rush up field and either run through the hole or just have their quarterback step up in the pocket. In his career, he did tally 51 sacks, but I don't remember one that impacted a game.

7. Russ Francis. He was called "All World" by Howard Cosell, but the musta-chioed tight end was more appearance than results. During his six seasons (1975-80) with the Patriots, Francis averaged 32 receptions and four touch-downs a year. He looked great in his uniform, but often seemed more interested in surfing than blocking. He had all the tools. He could run, catch and smile. Unfortunately his production didn't match the rhetoric.

6. Jim Rice. Jim Ed Rice came to Boston as one-half of "The Gold Dust Twins" with Fred Lynn. Over his 16 seasons with the Red Sox, the city of Boston wanted to love Jim Rice, but he wouldn't let the city in. I understand that coming to Boston in the 1970s as an African-American from South Carolina had to be difficult, but in the end he misread the city. He never engaged Boston or got to know us. His persona took a further hit when he reportedly mixed it up with not only the Red Sox 62-year-old Public Relations Director Bill Crowley over a parking spot, but also with his manager—the beloved 57-year-old Joe Morgan—when the skipper pinch hit Spike Owen for him in Rice's declining days. As a player, his power could be awesome (he hit a home run over Fenway's center-field American flag), but it seemed to wane in big moments. Performing in the clutch never seemed to be his strong point, nor was staying out of double plays, which he hit into at an historic rate. From 1982-85, Jim Ed hit into 131 double plays, or one for every 18 at-bats.

5. Josh Beckett. He came to Boston as a Yankee killer, but has ended up being killed by the Yankees for the most part. The righty flamethrower has shown flashes of Hall of Fame talent, but his propensity to serve up home-run balls (116 in 143 starts, as of this writing) and default to his fastball in big situations has made the ace predictable and hittable. In 22 career regular-season starts against the Yankees, the "tough Texan" has an ERA of 6.26, which includes a home run allowed every five innings. Yes, in 2007 he was spectacular. But if you back that year out of his Red Sox stats, he is a below-average pitcher with a 4.29 ERA.

4. Robert Parish. "The Chief" had the great honor of playing alongside two of the greatest forwards in NBA history (Larry Bird and Kevin McHale). He came from Golden State, where he was part of a losing team and had to be broken by Boston Coach Bill Fitch, who yelled, annoyed and embarrassed the stoic center until he would finally run free throw line to free throw line. Yes, he was a component of three championship teams, but he was also the beneficiary of open looks and playing against an opponent's worst big defender. In addition, I must add that his negative comments about Boston—with regards to race and the disposition of its citizens—only added to my opinion of his true place in Boston sports.

3. Joe Thornton. The first overall pick in the 1997 NHL Draft, the rangy center was brought along slowly by his old-school coach, Pat Burns. He eventually developed into a quality center, but was prone to getting lost in the game. It seemed all too often the team captain was hiding behind the net or along the side board waiting for someone else to make a play. The curly haired center's laid-back personality was not a good fit in Boston. Thornton, who admittedly would "take nights off," got truly lost in the playoffs, recording only 18 points in 35 games in the postseason with the Bruins. In 2005, he was traded following a particularly disgraceful performance in the playoffs (zero points in seven games). When he arrived in San Jose, he was suddenly motivated and earned MVP honors. In the end, it will be his smiling/laughing handshake with the Canadiens after being eliminated from the playoffs that I'll remember.

2. Richard Seymour. Richard Seymour apologists loved to say that his greatest contribution to the team was occupying two offensive linemen, thus allowing the linebackers to flow to the running back. That's a pile of bullshit. Not only did teams only assign one blocker to keep #94 out of the backfield, but often it would be a tight end (watch the film). Sure, Seymour possessed Hall of Fame skills, but far too often he was "just another guy" on the football field. In 2006, after holding out, he became the highest-paid player in the NFL. In return for his substantial compensation, he contributed a paltry 24 tackles and four sacks. Yes, he also deflected 10 passes. However, that was a function of Seymour so often being pushed back by a lineman into passing lanes where no quarterback would expect an "All-Pro" to be hanging out. In the end, he talked a lot but didn't deliver. In my mind, a player who is paid that much should not only impact games, but take them over. Seymour seldom did.

1. Roger Clemens. The simple fact that he didn't demand the ball in the 10th inning of Game 6 is all I need to know about his true makeup. Great Boston sportswriter Will McDonough gave #21 the perfect nickname—"The Texas Con Man." Sure Roger Clemens did a masterful job of building the perception of an intense warrior. To most, he was a flamethrowing, tough Texan that knocked batters off the plate and needed a mouth guard because he was so intense. However when it was all said and done, where was he when he was most needed? For you Roger fans, yes I'll grant you that from 1986 to September 1992, he was a great regular-season pitcher. But if you look from September 12, 1992 to September 7, 1996, he was 38-40 with a 3.86 ERA— hardly Hall of Fame-like, wouldn't you agree? Yes, his 20-strikeout performance against Seattle was prolific (I dismiss the second 20-strikeout game against Detroit because I don't know if that was all him . . . if you know what I mean). But a great pitcher or even a good pitcher will be ultimately measured by how he performs in the postseason. And Roger didn't perform in the postseason. In nine postseason starts for the Red Sox, "The Rocket" won an anemic ONE game, while registering a 3.91 ERA. And need I mention the name Dave Stewart?

Underrated Boston Athletes :: MC

For various reasons, the players on this list are underappreciated in this city, despite their quality contributions to the Boston sports world. Do they belong with those who sit in the Boston pantheon of greatness? No, but they certainly deserve more from us than we gave them. We never minimized their efforts, but then again, we never trumpeted them either.

Honorable Mentions. Don Calhoun; Kevin Faulk; Bill Mueller; Marv Cook; Fred Marion; Gilles Gilbert; Don Marcotte; Craig Janney; Mo Lewis.

13. Bill Lee. The "Spaceman" was better known for his antics than for his playing accomplishments. But Lee was actually one of the finest left-handed pitchers in Red Sox history. From 1973-75, he won 51 games and completed 51 games. He was a true pitcher, keeping batters off balance with an above-average curve ball (except the one he threw to Tony Perez) and his ability to mix speeds. His lifestyle rubbed old-school manager Don Zimmer the wrong way, compelling Sox management to deport the lefthander from Red Sox Nation to Montreal. But before being jettisoned from Fenway, Lee pitched for a decade in Boston, throwing over 1,500 innings, winning 94 games for the Red Sox and recording a 3.64 ERA.

12. Gregg Sheppard. The 5-8 center from Saskatchewan was a true Bruin. He played hard on both ends of the ice. While his main job was shutting down the opponent's best scorer, he could also score. Sheppard tallied 30 goals in a season three times and had a total of 155 scores in his Bruins career, 16 of which came shorthanded. And despite playing against the other team's first line every night, he recorded a plus/minus of +149 during his time as a Bruin from 1972-78.

11. Donald Blackmon. This Patriots outside linebacker served as the bookend to Hall of Famer Andre Tippett. Blackmon was fast and a great tackler who controlled the run. His play allowed Tippett to run free to the quarterback and net the more sensational sacks and thus garner the attention. Blackmon's career ended prematurely due to back issues, but he was a mainstay during the mid-1980s on the greatest linebacker group in Patriots history, along with Steve Nelson, Larry McGrew and Tippett.

10. Peter McNab. I know, I know—he didn't take the body (though he did hold the fan down in Madison Square Garden while teammate Mike Milbury hit him with the shoe). So the Gallery Gods called him "Mary McNab." But he was paid to score. In his first six seasons with the Bruins (1977-83), he averaged 38 goals and, despite his soft reputation, he only missed 17 games during his seven full seasons with the team. He ranks ninth all-time in Bruins history for goals with 263.

9. Paul Silas. Between Dave Cowens and Paul Silas, the Celtics controlled the boards and thus the ball during Silas' tenure in Boston from 1972-76. In his four seasons as a Celtic, Silas averaged a double-double (11.52 points-12.32 rebounds). His 12.32 per game rebounding average is third highest in Celtic history behind only Cowens and Bill Russell. Silas was relentless on the offensive boards, accumulating 4.5 offensive rebounds a game in the 1975-76 season. When management wouldn't pay him the money that he had earned, Silas moved on with two championship rings—leaving behind a very disgruntled Cowens, who never looked at management the same way again.

8. Ken Hodge. Coming to the Bruins from the Blackhawks in 1967 as a complementary piece in the Esposito trade, Hodge remained in the shadow of #7 (and of #4) throughout his time in Boston. But with his working the corners and putting the puck in the net, there was no question that Hodge was a major component of the Big Bad Bruins and their two Stanley Cup wins. He scored 50 goals in the 1973-74 season, 11 of them game-winners. He ranks seventh all-time on the Bruins scoring list with 674 points (1.03 a game) and recorded a plus/minus of +289 for his career.

7. Mike Greenwell. Here is a guy who was everything Boston loves in an athlete: he played hard and produced. But for some reason, his place in the city's sports lore doesn't match his game on the field. Although he had the propensity to run down his center fielder, he improved every year in left field and became proficient at playing the Green Monster. At the plate, he batted .3028 for his career—the exact same average as Pete Rose. In 1988, he was robbed of the Most Valuable Player award by a drug-enhanced Jose Canseco. In the end, Greenwell always did Boston proud and honored the long legacy of great Boston Red Sox left fielders during his time at Fenway.

6. Tony Collins. I know he got caught up in the haze of the 1980s, but his actions on the field spoke for themselves. Over his career, he compiled 8,203 total yards while scoring 44 touchdowns for the Patriots. In 1983, he ran for over 1,000 yards and caught 77 passes out of the backfield in 1986. He was a major part of the team that "Squished the Fish" and brought the Patriots back to prominence.

5. Cedric Maxwell. In 1977, a downtrodden Celtics team drafted the gangly forward out of UNC Charlotte with the 12th pick of the first round. In the 1981 NBA Finals against the Houston Rockets, Maxwell demonstrated his ability to perform in the clutch when he led his team to victory, earning a flag for the team and the championship MVP trophy for himself. His innate ability to rise to the occasion was again realized prior to Game 7 of the 1984 NBA Finals when he invited his teammates to "climb on my back boys" and then proceeded to lead the Green to a championship win against the Lakers by scoring 24 points, grabbing eight rebounds and dishing eight assists. But despite these heroics, Maxwell's ultimate contribution went relatively unheralded while the team's other starting forward, Larry Bird, received the basketball world's attention. For his Celtics career, Maxwell shot .559 from the field and collected over 1,600 offensive rebounds while defending the other team's best scorer every night.

4. Adam Oates. Traded to Boston from St. Louis in 1991, Oates passed and scored at such a prolific rate that his name sits besides such Bruin greats as Orr and Esposito on several scoring lists. In the 1992-93 season, he recorded 142 points (45 goals/97 assists)—an average of 1.69 points a game. His partnership with Cam Neely was one of the most fearsome in NHL history. He sits third on Boston's all-time points per game list with 1.36.

3. Clarence DeMar. The seven-time winner of the Boston Marathon goes down as probably the most forgotten Boston sports superstar. A fiery competitor, DeMar was known to take punches at fans or competitors who stood in his way. His count of seven championships would undoubtedly be higher if he hadn't stopped running for five of his prime years on the recommendation of a cardiologist who detected a heart abnormality. When the doctor later died of heart failure, DeMar remarked, "He must have been listening to his own heart." Clarence won his first marathon in 1911 and his last in 1930. At the age of 70 and riddled with cancer, doctors found him running in place in his hospital room. He died later that day.

2. Tom Heinsohn. This city took its lead from Red Auerbach and the Celtic Czar never gave Tommy his due. When Heinsohn was a star at Holy Cross, Auerbach ridiculed his weight. Even when rebounding and hitting hook shots from the corner, he was victimized by the sharp tongue of his coach and mentor. In the last game of his Hall of Fame career, Auerbach left him on the bench, thus robbing Heinsohn of the opportunity to be honored by the Celtics crowd for his many contributions. He then became the Celtics head coach and despite guiding an undermanned Boston team to championships in 1974 and '76 and setting a team record for wins in a season, his old coach and then-general manager fired him in the middle of the 1977-78 season. After 10 championships and more than a half-century of contributions to the team, his place in Boston's collective heart was finally secured. A Tommy Point for Tommy!

1. Stanley Morgan. A first-round draft pick in 1977 out of the University of Tennessee, Morgan was nicknamed "Stanley Steamer." During his pro career, Morgan would compile Patriots records in touchdowns (68), receptions (534) and receiving yards (10,352). Of his 68 touchdowns, 39 were of 30 or more yards. For his career, he averaged 19.4 yards a catch. He caught his first NFL touchdown pass in 1977 from Steve Grogan against the Jets and would catch his last for the Pats in 1989 from Grogan. In between, he caught TD passes from Andy Johnson, Tom Ramsey, Doug Flutie and Tony Eason. A four-time Pro Bowler, Morgan's career should speak for itself. But because of his quiet ways, his contributions in New England remain undervalued. But just consider Morgan's career numbers compared to Hall of Famer Lynn Swann's:

Morgan—557 receptions/10,716 yards/73 touchdowns/19.2 yards per reception.

Swann—336 receptions/5,462 yards/52 touchdowns/16.3 yards per reception.

The best of the best. Trying to whittle down this list was tough. (We've been lucky to have some damn good GMs around here.) I started with 17 deals, but chose these for the final list.

10. Patriots Trade Fourth-Round Pick to the Oakland Raiders for Randy Moss (2007). Believe it or not, this pick was a leftover from the trade of Deion Branch to Seattle the previous year. Moss produced a touchdown per game during his time with the Pats and elevated Tom Brady to another level. In his first year in New England, the Pats came within two minutes of a perfect season, and Moss was a big part of that.

9. Red Sox Trade Casey Fossum, Brandon Lyon, Jorge De La Rosa and Michael Goss to the Arizona Diamondbacks for Curt Schilling (2004). People may not have liked his personality and that there wasn't a camera he wouldn't talk into. But Curt Schilling was a stud in Boston. His performance in the "Bloody Sock Game" in the 2004 ALCS against the Yankees was the stuff movies are made of. And other than Lyon in Detroit, none of these guys did a damn thing in the bigs.

8. Bruins Trade Barry Pederson to the Vancouver Canucks for Cam Neely and a 1987 First-Round Pick—Which Turned Into Glen Wesley (1986). Cam Neely averaged less than 53 games per season during his time with the Bruins. But he could score, hit, skate and fight. He's a cult hero in Boston and is now President of the B's. He represents what Bruins hockey was built on.

7. Red Sox Trade Heathcliff Slocumb to the Seattle Mariners for Derek Lowe and Jason Varitek (1997). Lowe did everything from start games to close them and was more than capable at all of it. He tossed a no-hitter at Fenway and went 3-0 during the Red Sox postseason drive to the 2004 World Series title before heading to the Dodgers and the massive amount of ladies in SoCal. Varitek became the captain of the Sox and a team leader. He was an above-average hitting catcher and a great game caller. When you land a guy with over 100 wins and 50 saves to go with a catcher for a decade in exchange for a pitcher who posted a 12-21 record after you dealt him, THAT'S a steal.

6. Celtics Trade the Fifth Overall Pick in the NBA Draft, Plus Wally Szczerbiak and Delonte West to the Seattle Sonics for Ray Allen (2007). This deal goes in over the subsequent deal for Kevin Garnett because if the Celtics didn't get Ray Ray, KG never would have agreed to leave Minnesota. Allen became the NBA's all-time leader in three pointers and has ably defended everyone from Kobe Bryant to Dwayne Wade. A Hall of Famer for sure.

5. Bruins Trade Pit Martin, Jack Norris and Gilles Marotte to the Chicago Blackhawks for Phil Esposito, Ken Hodge and Fred Stanfield (1967). When you look back on deals like this, you realize that Harry Sinden was really good in his time. Esposito transformed the franchise back into prominence and Hodge was a good, solid player.

4. Red Sox Trade Carl Pavano and Tony Armas, Jr. to the Montreal Expos for Pedro Martinez (1997). This trade meant more than just an increase of on-field production. It welcomed the Dominican population to Fenway and helped the franchise ease the legacy of years and years of racism under Tom Yawkey. Pedro established himself as the best pitcher in baseball during his seven years in Boston, picking up consecutive Cy Young Awards and cementing his status as a first ballot Hall of Famer.

3. Celtics Trade Ed Macauley and the Draft Rights to Cliff Hagan to the St. Louis Hawks for the Second Overall Pick in the NBA Draft (1956). And with that pick, Red Auerbach made a side deal with the Rochester Royals (who held the first overall pick) so he could draft Bill Russell. That started a dynasty in sports that will never be approached again. One of the many brilliant trades Red made.

2. Celtics Trade the First and 13th Overall Picks in the NBA Draft to the Golden State Warriors for Robert Parish and the Third Overall Pick—Which Turned Into Kevin McHale (1980). This may be the most lopsided trade in NBA history. It started yet another Celtics dynasty, elevating the franchise's rivalry with the Lakers and causing the NBA's popularity to skyrocket. Auerbach was amazing. I don't know why people traded with him.

1. Patriots Trade First-Round Pick to the New York Jets for Bill Belichick (2000). I never thought in all my days that a trade for a coach would be the best ever. But Robert Kraft gave BB total control and it turned into three Super Bowl titles and a perfect regular season. Both of them knew what they were doing.

Worst Trades in Boston Sports History (That Didn't Include Babe Ruth) :: AG

These trades have been debated forever and now, excluding the Sox trading Babe Ruth, I once and for all rank them behind *No, No, Nanette*.

15. Red Sox Trade Jaime Moyer to the Seattle Mariners for Darren Bragg (1996). Moyer was supposed to mostly work out of the bullpen for the Sox, but started 10 games, appeared in 23 and went 7-1. He ended up going 145-87 during his time with Seattle. Bragg had a nice .264 average with 20 homers, 136 RBI and 21 steals. Good for a season. Too bad that those were the totals for his three-year Red Sox career.

14. Red Sox Trade Dave Henderson to the San Francisco Giants for Randy Kutcher (1987). The Red Sox acquired Hendu for the 1986 stretch run and he hit .400 in the World Series against the Mets. He was exchanged for Randy Kutcher midway through the 1987 season in part to make room for Ellis Burks. Burks never realized his full potential and hit just 94 homers in six seasons for Boston while Henderson hit 109 in six seasons in Oakland and one year with Kansas City. Kutcher's numbers were so bad with the Sox, I refuse to list them.

13. Celtics Trade Antoine Walker and Tony Delk to the Dallas Mavericks for Raef LaFrentz, Chris Mills, Jiri Welsch and a 2004 First-Round Draft Pick (2003). I know the honk Celtics fans will bitch to me on the radio that after 127 permutations of this trade, we ended up with Rajon Rondo and others by 2007. But Walker leaving before he could win over Danny Ainge was a mistake—confirmed when Ainge traded for Twan' to bring him back for a playoff run just two years later. "Raef LaSofty" will go down as one of the biggest sissies in Celts' history. Mills was a salary cap number and Jiri Welsch was traded for a first-round pick that turned into Rondo. Ainge should've gotten better for a proven scorer like Walker. But after 127 tries, he made it work.

12. Bruins Trade Joe Thornton to the San Jose Sharks for Marco Sturm, Wayne Primeau and Brad Stuart (2005). "Jumbo Joe" was the team's leading scorer and captain at the time of the trade. Now I admit, he never would've won an MVP as a Bruin. But he had the talent to, and you don't give away guys like that and get little in return. Sturm scored 137 points in 5 seasons with the B's while Thornton had 92 in 58 games for the Sharks the year he was traded!! 'Nuff said.

11. Celtics Trade Chauncey Billups, Dee Brown, John Thomas and Roy Rodgers to the Toronto Raptors for Kenny Anderson, Zan Tabak and Popeye Jones (1998). This is one of the many trades Rick Pitino will never live down. He never gave Billups a chance because the organization didn't see him as a point guard. BUT he loved Kenny Anderson . . . God knows why. I bet as people read this, they'll have forgotten about the other trash included in this deal. Billups went on to win a world championship and become an NBA Finals MVP and five-time All-Star.

10. Patriots Trade Second-Round and Fourth-Round Picks to Move Up Five Spots to Draft WR Bethel Johnson (2003) and 9. Patriots Trade Third-Round and Fifth-Round Picks to the Arizona Cardinals for CB Duane Starks (2005) and 8. Patriots Trade Second-Round and Third-Round Picks to the Green Bay Packers to Move Up 16 Spots to Draft WR Chad Jackson (2006). Where do I begin? Three moves where the Pats clearly outsmarted themselves. Bethel Johnson was a good kick returner and could run fast, but only in a straight line. He was moved to New Orleans and hasn't been heard from again. Duane Starks redefined the meaning of toast. And Chad Jackson never was able to grasp the Patriots offense. The guy Green Bay drafted with the Pats' second-round pick was Greg Jennings. Jackson in his career had 14 receptions for 171 yards and three TDs. Jennings blew past those totals by Week 5 of his rookie season.

7. Red Sox Trade Fred Lynn and Steve Renko to the California Angels for Frank Tanana, Jim Dorsey and Joe Rudi (1980). Lynn won the 1975 Rookie of the Year and MVP. He wanted to play on the West Coast, but the Sox got nothing in return. Tanana went 4-10 in one season in Boston, Dorsey appeared in four whole games and Rudi was 34 and hit below .200 in his one season in town. Lynn rebounded after a bad first year with Cali to make a few more All-Star appearances and is considered by some as a borderline Hall of Famer.

6. Patriots Trade Richard Seymour to the Oakland Raiders for a 2011 First-Round Pick (2009). The trade was widely questioned by Pats fans, as Seymour was part of three Super Bowl winners and got moved . . . for what in return? "Big Sey 93" and Bill Belichick flat-out didn't get along and this is one where BB's ego and arrogance got the best of him. Seymour was needed here in 2009 and 2010. Because despite having the best record in football, New England couldn't stop the run in home playoff losses to Baltimore and the Jets. And to make matters worse, what was considered to be a lock for a top five pick ('cause the Raiders suck), ended up being 17th overall after Oakland's surprise 8-8 season.

5. Bruins Trade Geoff Courtnall and Bill Ranford to the Edmonton Oilers for Andy Moog (1988). I know what you're thinking: the Bruins made the Stanley Cup Finals the year they got Moog. And Edmonton didn't keep Courtnall long. But Courtnall did score over 40 goals for Washington the following season. And in 1990, Ranford won the Conn Smythe Trophy as the NHL Playoffs MVP and a Stanley Cup as Edmonton beat the Bruins. Moog was a very good Bruin, but this deal bit Boston GM Harry Sinden in the butt.

4. Celtics Owner John Brown Trades for Bob McAdoo (1978). This was Brown's way of showing Celtics legend Red Auerbach that he was boss after Auerbach flirted with the Knicks following the 1977-78 season. Red didn't want McAdoo and McAdoo didn't want to be here. With the fans' support, Red won this struggle. McAdoo only lasted 20 games in Boston and when Larry Bird walked through that door the next season, a legend was born.

3. Patriots Trade LB Nick Buoniconti to the Miami Dolphins for LB John Bramlett, QB Kim Hammond and Fifth-Round Pick (1969). Buoniconti became a Pro Football Hall of Famer and a leader of Miami's Super Bowl-winning "No Name Defense." And if there's one Patriots fan under the age of 60 who can tell me what Bramlett and Hammond did for the Pats, I'll streak naked across the field at the 2012 season opener.

2. The Red Sox Trade Pitcher Sparky Lyle to the New York Yankees for JOAT Danny Cater and Infielder Mario Guerrero (1972). Guerrero hit .241 in two seasons with the Sox, while Cater batted .262 with 14 homers and 83 RBI during three years in Boston. Lyle finished third in the 1972 MVP voting and won the 1977 Cy Young Award with the Yankees. A relief specialist, Lyle went 57-40 with 141 saves while averaging 100 innings during seven seasons in New York. And he was a three-time All-Star. This is one reason why the Sox never, ever trade with the Yankees anymore.

1. Red Sox Trade Jeff Bagwell to the Houston Astros for Larry Andersen (1990). The 37-year-old Andersen did his job nicely, helping the Sox to the American League Championship Series by allowing just 18 hits in 21 innings of relief work. But Bagwell went on to win Rookie of the Year in 1991 and the NL MVP in 1994 and play in four All-Star Games representing the Astros. He hit 449 home runs and established a 162-game average of .297/34 HR/115 RBI during a career that nearly took him to the Hall of Fame. Imagine the numbers that the right-handed power hitter would have put up in Fenway? We'll never know.

Our attachment to local sports figures extends beyond the athletic stage. We root for them as people as much as we root for them as players and coaches. When one of them gets hurt or killed, it hurts us. Below is a list of sports tragedies that hurt area fans the most, listed by date of occurrence.

Honorable Mentions. Marquise Hill dies in a jet-ski accident; Jay McGillis of Boston College football is stricken by leukemia and passes away after a courageous battle, with Boston College later naming its spring game in his honor; Jockey Rudy Baez gets injured in a fall; Bruin Ted Green suffers brain damage in a stick fight.

12. Chick Stahl (Died on March 28, 1907). During spring training in 1907, the Red Sox player-manager ended his life by drinking carbolic acid.

11. Cocoanut Grove Fire (November 28, 1942). Following the Boston College-Holy Cross rivalry football game, many supporters traveled to Boston's Cocoanut Grove nightclub. At 10:15 p.m., a raging fire spread through the nightclub, killing 492 people. The fact that top-ranked Boston College was upset that day proved a blessing, as many BC players and fans lives were spared due to the cancellation of their scheduled postgame party at the club.

10. Harry Agganis (Died on June 27, 1955). Known as "The Golden Greek," Agganis was a New England hero. A two-sport star from Lynn and Boston University, Agganis chose to play baseball for the Red Sox despite being drafted in the first round by the Cleveland Browns. In his second year as a Red Sox first baseman, the 26-year-old fell ill and eventually died from a pulmonary embolism. All of New England was devastated.

9. Tony Conigliaro (Injured on August 18, 1967). Angels pitcher Jack Hamilton hadn't hit a batter all season until his errant fastball crashed into the face of "Tony C." The Red Sox player was never the same. He appeared on the cover of *Sports Illustrated* with his eye swollen shut. This image brought to light the severity of the injury that would haunt him the rest of his days.

8. Rocky Marciano (Died on August 31, 1969). The undefeated heavyweight champ from Brockton, Massachusetts retired at age 33. He died the night before his 46th birthday in a plane crash in Iowa that robbed the sports world and New England of an institution.

7. Darryl Stingley (Injured on August 12, 1978). On the precipice of a break-out year, Stingley entered the 1978 season as half of the NFL's most fearsome receiving duo, along with fellow New England wide receiver Stanley Morgan. In preparation for the season, the Patriots were playing the Raiders in Oakland. During the game, Stingley ran a crossing pattern and was leveled by a cheap shot by the "The Assassin" Jack Tatum. Stingley was paralyzed on the play and remained so for the rest of his life. Tatum never apologized. Stingley died 29 years later in 2007 from complications due to the injury.

6. Normand Leveille (Injured on October 23, 1982). The 19-year-old left wing was a rising star in his second season with the Bruins when he was checked into the boards in Vancouver. Later in the game, Leveille fell unconscious, suffering a massive aneurysm that put him in a coma for three months and ended his career. His skate, with teammate Ray Bourque's assistance, on the closing night of the Boston Garden was gallant.

5. Len Bias (Died on June 19, 1986). What could have been? After drafting the University of Maryland star with the second overall pick in the NBA Draft, the Celtics seemed on the verge of solidifying a dynasty reminiscent of their 1960s juggernaut. Following the draft, Bias and friends partook in a late-night dorm party involving significant quantities of cocaine. Autopsy reports would indicate that drug use led to the death of the 23-year-old.

4. Jeff Gray (Suffered Stroke on July 30, 1991). Gray was a vital cog in the Red Sox bullpen. Prior to a game in late July, Gray suffered a stroke and was never the same pitcher.

3. Reggie Lewis (Died on July 27, 1993). The Northeastern All-American and Boston Celtics All-Star had the world in front of him when he collapsed on the court in a playoff game against Charlotte during a cardiac event. He was taken to a local hospital for tests and observations. This was followed by rumors of drug use and midnight hospital transfers. A few months later, the 27-year-old collapsed again on a basketball court and could not be revived, with his tragic death followed by lawsuits, *Wall Street Journal* articles and sad accusations.

2. Travis Roy (Injured on October 20, 1995). The Boston University winger was skating the first shift of his college career when he collided with the boards in the offensive corner. We all stood with his parents as they offered support. Travis was paralyzed by the injury. He has since transitioned from hockey player into a vital member of our Boston community who fights every day to get better and improve other people's lives.

1. Paul Pierce (Stabbed on September 25, 2000). The Celtics forward was playing pool at a Boston night spot called The Buzz Club when he was stabbed 11 times in the back, face and neck, with one of the wounds extending seven inches beneath his skin. Teammate Tony Battie rushed Pierce to the hospital, where he underwent surgery on his lung and later recovered.

Best Red Sox of My Lifetime
:: AG (Born on October 26, 1974)

Pretty self-explanatory, isn't it?

10. Carl Yastrzemski (1961–83). I know his best years were behind him by the time I was hatched. But I can't deny a guy who won a Triple Crown and is No. 1 all-time with the Red Sox in hits (3,419), doubles (646), RBI (1,844), games (3,308), at-bats (11,988) and runs (1,816). Had nice year in 1976 and again in '77. Was a DH towards the end of his career, but I wouldn't feel right not including him. And he's a crusty old goat—I like that.

9. Jonathan Papelbon (2005–). He'd be on the list of the Red Sox All-Time Worst Spellers. But he is Boston's career saves leader. And before you start bitching about the category, we value it in modern day baseball and came to love this jig dancin' lug. So shove the category value and remember that he has a ring and for a time was only behind Mariano Rivera in the entire game as a closer.

8. Nomar Garciaparra (1996-2004). He came on like gangbusters from Pawtucket and took Boston by storm. He was the new sensation that reenergized the hopes of Sox fans for beating the Yankees. In the end, he was traded a few months before the Sox "reversed the curse" and beat the NYY in the 2004 ALCS. I told Nomar to his ear the day he retired from baseball when he signed a one-day deal with the Sox that he would be remembered as a loser because the Sox won once he was traded. He probably hates me, but he was a great player for a period of time. Even I recognize that.

7. Jim Rice (1974-89). He's in the HOF because of good fortune. In his last year of eligibility, they needed someone else to be inducted with Rickey Henderson, so he got the call. I wouldn't have made that call. BUT still a great player who struck fear in the hearts of pitchers. He hated the media as a player, then joined it as a Sox television pregame and postgame analyst. To me that makes him a fraud, as I think he did it to show people he wasn't a dick so he'd get into the Hall of Fame. It worked, but I still think he's a dick and dresses like a pimp 20 percent of the time on television.

6. Mo Vaughn (1991-2003). Won an MVP in 1995 and was a clubhouse leader. I loved Mo. He was fat and lumpy but could move better than expected. He ended up making $17 million in his final year after being traded to the Mets and did nothing for them. And no one, and I mean NO ONE, in Red Sox history could wreck a truck with the scent of unwed mother on him like the "Hit Dog."

5. David Ortiz (2003-). Came to the Red Sox in 2003 after doing nothing with the Twins and became the best clutch hitter in Sox history (even John Henry said so). From 2003 to 2008, you didn't wanna see "Big Papi" at the dish in a key spot if you were an opposing pitcher. Was a top five MVP candidate for five years running from 2003 to 2007. He benefited greatly from having the next guy on this list in the lineup with him.

4. Manny Ramirez (2001-08). He came to the Red Sox after signing a HUGE $160 million dollar deal. He was the best hitter I've ever seen, steroids or not. A freak. And a funny bastard. He whizzed inside the Green Monster. Didn't want to go back to Boston after a rehab stint because he liked Pawtucket so much. Faked it more than a Hugh Hefner girlfriend and ultimately wore out his welcome. But he was entertaining as hell and we're better for Manny having been here in his prime.

3. Wade Boggs (1982-92). In 11 years in Boston, he hit .338 and scored over 1,000 runs. He hung on long enough in the majors to get to 3,000 hits with Tampa Bay and the strippers there thank him, I'm sure. He loved fried chicken, vagish and fell out of a moving truck. That's a man right there.

2. Roger Clemens (1984-96). Won a franchise-tying record 192 games in 13 seasons. Dan Duquette gave him the spark when the Sox didn't re-sign him in 1997 and he 'roided up and took his game to the next level. Will be remembered for his postseason antics (I'm probably being kind), but was a great, great, pitcher. Sure, he was a prima donna, but those 20-strikeout games were the kind of dominance you write books about.

1. Pedro Martinez (1998-2004). In seven years with the Red Sox, he went 117-37 with 22 CG in 201 starts and struck out 1,683. Unfortunately for Pedro, he probably could've had 135 wins if the team had scored some runs for the guy or if the bullpen didn't blow so many of the leads he handed them. He was fun, a little petulant, but was the best pitcher I've ever seen. His performance in 1999 out of the bullpen in Cleveland was the balls. I grew up around football, but Pedro made me love the pitching duel. He was unmatched for most of his time in Boston. I don't blame Grady Little for riding him in 2003 in Yankee Stadium. No. 1 with a bullet.

These athletes always answered the call, no matter the circumstances. They played not only hurt and tired, but at a high level. They played with pride for their teammates, themselves and the city on the shirt that they represented.

Honorable Mentions. Ken Green; Steve Nelson; Uta Pippig; Gary Doak; Sam Gash; John Hannah; John Wensink; Stan Jonathan; Trot Nixon; Carlton Fisk; Jason Varitek; Ted Johnson; Lawyer Milloy; Marvelous Marvin Hagler; Tim Fox; Wes Welker; Vincent Brown; Al Nipper; Dustin Pedroia; Shawn Thorton.

11. Cam Neely. The quintessential power forward, Neely could score, check and fight like no right wing ever had. When a punk like Claude Lemieux wouldn't fight him like a man, Neely simply grabbed him and slammed his head into the boards. Sadly, he suffered a severe knee injury in 1991 from a cheap shot from Ulf Samuelsson that limited him to an average of just over 30 games per season for his last five years in the NHL. But Neely refused to be denied and came back to record 50 goals in the 1993-94 season for the Bruins on virtually one leg.

10. Micky Ward. Even when he pushed his body beyond what seemed humanly possible, his heart refused to let him quit or fall. His dramatic win against Arturo Gatti in 2002 will go down as one of the greatest fights of all time and featured what was certainly one of the greatest rounds (Round 9) in boxing history.

9. Joan Benoit Samuelson. Just 17 days after knee surgery, the runner from Maine willed herself onto the starting line of the 1984 U.S. Olympic Trials for the women's marathon and proceeded to run 26 miles to qualification. She traveled to Los Angeles three months later and won the Olympic gold medal.

8. Bill Buckner. Sure, life is unfair and his game-losing error in the 1986 World Series—when he let a Mookie Wilson ground ball roll between his legs—will forever be associated with him. But that play doesn't define Bill Buckner. In 1985 and 1986, Buckner had back-to-back 100 RBI seasons despite the fact that his ankles were decimated. It hurt just to watch him hobble onto the field, but he still did.

7. Larry Bird. He dove into scorer's tables, slammed his face off the floor and was a prisoner to his own bad back. But he still walked onto the parquet floor, wiped the bottom of his sneakers with his hands and gave us everything he had every night.

6. Dick Hoyt and 5. Rick Hoyt. I can't watch highlights of the Hoyts in the Ironman competition in which they personify the core of human will and not cry. From the Boston Marathon to the sea and streets of Hawaii, this father and son team represents all that is good about family and sports.

4. Steve Grogan. With a brace collared around his neck, Steve Grogan played every game as if it was his last. Over his 16-year career with the Patriots, he always took the ball, whether hurt or not. The image of Grogan diving over a pile to take on two linebackers without hesitation is why we loved seeing #14 under center. During his pro career, he rushed for 36 touchdowns and for over 2,100 yards.

3. Terry O'Reilly. An average skater when he arrived in Boston, he remained in the spoked-B sweater through will and guts. He fought, checked and protected his teammates at all costs. In the end, he willed himself into a good hockey player, making two All-Star teams while scoring over 200 goals and registering over 2,000 penalty minutes.

2. Rodney Harrison. Patrolling the Patriots secondary, Harrison made receivers think twice about running a route within his domain and wince if they did. His great moment of valor came in Super Bowl XXXVIII against Carolina when he partially broke his arm in the final minutes of a three-point game but stayed on the field to make a crucial tackle on the next play (completely breaking his arm in the process). In seven postseason games he led his team to seven victories by registering seven interceptions and recording 61 tackles.

1. Dave Cowens. He played hard and with heart and integrity every night. An undersized center, he would man up in the post or under the rim against giants like Kareem, Bill Walton, Artis Gilmore and Bob Lanier. And though they were taller and bigger, he out-worked them, out-ran them and out-played them. In the end, it was his ankles not his heart that would plague him. His diving steal in the 1974 NBA Finals against the Milwaukee Bucks defined the essence of the man—a true Celtic.

Athletes I Would NOT Want Next to Me in a Fox Hole :: MC

Boston is a blue-collar town and we expect our players to throw some tape on any ailment and go out and play. But when the going got tough, these guys were either in the trainer's room or at home. Game after game, coaches had to scratch their names off lineup cards because they couldn't "go."

10. Matt Young. I wouldn't say this erratic Red Sox hurler from the early 1990s was soft, but being in a fox hole with him would scare me. Matt Young pulling a pin on a grenade and throwing it would put every target he *wasn't* aiming at in jeopardy.

9. Randy Moss. Moss rates as maybe one of the top five athletes to ever play in this town, but he was a diva to his core. In the end, his game was nothing more than a fly pattern and his hand was in the air whether he was open or not.

8. Red Sox 1990 Bullpen. Following a playoff loss, the members of the Boston bullpen strapped ice bags on their arms and backs as a protest against Sox Manager Joe Morgan—because they felt he asked them to warm up too much.

7. Terry Glenn. When Coach Bill Parcells was asked about his mercurial wide receiver, he responded, "She is doing fine." Glenn was an amazing talent out of Ohio State, but was drafted in 1996 against Tuna's wishes. When he played, Glenn was great; when he didn't want to play, he was a boil on the roster of the Patriots. He averaged 11 games a year for six years before shooting his way out of town.

6. Pete McNab. Although paid to put the puck in the net, McNab would often glide his 6-3, 210-pound frame into the corner in hopes of avoiding contact. In 954 NHL games from 1973-87, this teddy bear center was responsible for only 179 penalty minutes.

5. J.D. Drew. Blessed with superstar talent, the right fielder spends too much time on the bench. Seemingly detached from emotion, the aloof Drew missed an average of over 30 games a year in his first four seasons with the Red Sox, causing Manager Terry Francona to white out Drew's name from many a lineup card.

4. Tony Eason. When farm-tough John Hannah states, "[Eason] should have wore a skirt," it tells you a lot about what his teammates thought of the Patriots quarterback. Despite an offensive line of Hannah, Brian Holloway, Pete Brock, Ron Wooten and Darryl Haley, Eason was sacked 59 times in 1984, as he often chose to take a knee instead of stepping up in the pocket or releasing a pass.

3. Manny Ramirez. Oh, no, it's the dreaded hamstring again. One of the greatest right-handed hitters in baseball history, Manny often chose to highjack his talents. In his seven full seasons in Boston, he missed an average of 22 games a year. At $130,000 per game, it's not a bad gig, if you can get it.

2. Pervis Ellison. Maybe they called him "Never Nervous" because he was never on the floor. Brought here in 1994 by Rick Pitino (enough said) and made captain, Pervis proceeded to cash checks and man the far end of the bench in street clothes. For his five seasons in Boston, Pervis was paid over $12.5 million while playing in an average of 38.6 games a year. His best injury resulted from "dropping" a coffee table on his foot.

1. Curtis Rowe. The acquisition of the NBA forward for Paul Silas served as the demarcation between the glory days of the Celtics and a dark age at the Boston Garden. Throughout Rowe's tenure in Boston (1977-79), his effort and sobriety were always in question. Following an indifferent loss, the team was firmly addressed by Red Auerbach. At the end of the tongue lashing, Rowe remarked to his teammates, "Don't worry, they don't put Ws and Ls on your paycheck." Rowe would miss a third of all games in his last two years. In September 1979, Rowe was cut by Bill Fitch for tardiness and for being out of shape. His roster spot was filled by Larry Bird.

Greatest Individual Performances in a Single Contest :: MC

The below list presents great performances in a game, bout or other sporting event performed by area athletes who carved a spot on the totem pole of Boston sports with these performances.

Honorable Mentions. Nomar belts two grand slams in one game; Troy O'Leary collects seven RBI and two home runs in Game 5 of the ALCS vs Cleveland; Bill Mueller hits a grand slam from each side of plate in one game; Micky Ward outbattles Arturo Gatti in their first fight; Flutie torches North Carolina for six TDs; UNH's Ricky Santos throws five TD passes vs Rutgers; Marvelous Marvin Hagler batters and outlasts John Mugabi; John Havlicek's last game; Jim Nance rushes for 206 yards.

18. David Patten (October 21, 2001). The Patriots wide receiver ran 29 yards for one touchdown, threw a 60-yard TD pass to Troy Brown and caught two touchdown passes of six and 91 yards in a 38-17 win over the Indianapolis Colts.

17. Drew Bledsoe (November 13, 1994). Trailing the Vikings 20-0, Drew Bledsoe led the Patriots to a 26-20 overtime victory. In the game, he attempted 70 passes, completing 46 for 426 yards with no interceptions and three touchdowns, including the 14-yard game-winner to Kevin Turner.

16. Fred Lynn (June 18, 1975). The rookie center fielder had a night to remember in Detroit, hitting three home runs (a fourth ball went off the top of the fence and came back for a triple). He knocked in 10 runs while raking five hits. Lynn would go on to win the Rookie of the Year and MVP that season and lead the Red Sox back to the World Series.

15. Ty Law (January 20, 2004). In the AFC Championship Game in Foxboro, Ty Law picked off Colts quarterback Peyton Manning three times while leading the "Homeland Defense" and the Patriots to a 24-14 victory and a trip to the Super Bowl.

14. Alberto Salazar and 13. Dick Beardsley (April 19, 1982). During what became known as "The Duel in the Sun," these two runners ran side by side in the Boston Marathon for over half the race, competing against each other, the fans and police on motorcycles. In the end, though near death from the effort, Salazar pulled away and won by one second.

12. Seabiscuit (June 29, 1937). The great horse ran in the third annual MassCap in front of 40,000 at Suffolk Downs. With Red Pollard in the saddle, Seabiscuit took the lead on the last turn and won by a length.

11. Roger Clemens (April 29, 1986). The righthander from Texas had his coming-out party at Fenway Park in front of 13,414 fans against the Seattle Mariners, striking out 20 batters and walking none.

10. Paul Pierce (May 18, 2008). This was the game that granted the forward entrance into the club of Celtics greats. In a classic Game 7 duel, Pierce scored 41 points, grabbed four rebounds and dished five assists, bettering LeBron James while leading Boston to a 92-87 win over the Cleveland Cavaliers.

9. Babe Ruth (October 9, 1916). In Game 2 of the 1916 World Series against the Brooklyn Robins, Ruth pitched a 14-inning complete game. The Red Sox won 2-1, with Ruth collecting the first RBI of the game.

8. Doug Flutie (November 23, 1984). This win over defending national champion Miami was so much more than a Hail Mary pass. On the day, Flutie threw for 472 yards on 34-46 passing in a performance that propelled Boston College to the Cotton Bowl and Flutie to the Heisman Trophy.

7. Rocky Marciano (September 23, 1952). Marciano knocked out champion Jersey Joe Walcott in Round 13 to win the world heavyweight belt. Marciano had been knocked down in the first round, but got off the canvas to win the fight.

6. Jim Lonborg (October 15, 1967). In Game 2 of the World Series against the St. Louis Cardinals, Lonborg pitched a one-hit shutout—the Cards' lone hit coming with two outs in the eighth inning.

5. Pedro Martinez (September 10, 1999). It's difficult to choose between his many masterpieces: the All-Star game at Fenway Park, the gem against Tampa Bay after Gerard Williams charged the mound, the John Wayne performance out of the bullpen against Cleveland in 1999. But for my money, this one-hitter against the Yankees, in which Pedro struck out 17, was the greatest game I have ever seen pitched.

4. Marvelous Marvin Hagler (April 15, 1985). Brockton's own was fighting for the boxing world's respect and to retain his middleweight championship against Thomas "The Hitman" Hearns. The first round will go down as one of the great rounds in boxing history, a three-minute war. In the third round, shortly after referee Richard Steele came close to stopping the fight because of blood on Hagler's face, the Marvelous One ended the fight on his own terms with an overhand right that sent Hearns to the canvas and sent himself into boxing history.

3. Francis Ouimet (September 20, 1913). The Brookline caddy and amateur golfer stunned the sports world when he won the U.S. Open at The Country Club by beating two of the greatest golfers in the world, Harry Vardon and Ted Ray.

2. Larry Bird (June 8, 1984). How do you choose? His "Duel with Dominique," his 60-point effort versus Atlanta, his knockout punch of Houston (29 points, 11 rebounds, 12 assists)—all are worthy. But I'll submit Game 5 of the 1984 NBA Finals against Boston's rival, the Lakers, and Bird's personal rival, Magic Johnson. In 97-degree conditions at the old Boston Garden, Bird shot 15-20 from the field, scoring 37 points while collecting 17 rebounds in a 121-103 victory. The Celtics went on to win the championship in seven games.

1. Tommy Heinsohn (April 13, 1957). In Game 7 of the NBA Finals, the rookie forward scored 37 points and grabbed 23 rebounds in the 125-123 double overtime victory over the St. Louis Hawks for the Celtics' first championship.

My Top 10 Memories from Lake Placid
:: by Mike Eruzione

Note: Mike Eruzione was the captain of the United States men's hockey team that produced "The Miracle on Ice" at the 1980 Winter Olympics in Lake Placid. The Winthrop native's winning goal, in the third period of the semifinal game against the mighty Soviet Union team, will go down as the greatest goal in American hockey history in what may well have been the most significant moment in American sports history. The below list represents the former Boston University star's most lasting memories of his Olympic experience in Lake Placid.

10. The Goal (February 22, 1980). Scoring the winning goal against the Soviets.

9. The Overall Experience. Being at the other events and watching our athletes compete.

8. Lake Placid. Walking in downtown Lake Placid and really capturing the Olympic spirit on the streets.

7. Practices. The practices between games—some were fun, some were intense.

6. The 2-2 Tie Against Sweden (February 12, 1980). Getting the tie with Sweden with 28 seconds remaining kickstarted our run.

5. The Semifinals (February 22, 1980). Beating the Russians.

4. The Finals (February 24, 1980). Winning the gold medal.

3. National Anthem (February 24, 1980). Standing on the podium and hearing your anthem being played and seeing your flag being raised just a little higher than the others.

2. Teammates. Being with my teammates for six months and truly loving them and what we accomplished.

1. Opening Ceremonies (February 14, 1980). Marching in the Opening Ceremonies, because if I never got there, none of the other things would have happened.

Some of history's finest "sports entertainers" have performed in the city of Boston and throughout New England. Okay, pro wrestling is not a sport due to its predetermined outcomes. But it's athletic in nature and a lot of people reading this book admire top pro wrestlers. Here are the ones I think are the best of the best.

Honorable Mentions. Bret Hart; Shawn Michaels; Bob Backland; Verne Gagne; Killer Kowalski; The Bezerker; Chris Jericho; Jerry "The King" Lawler.

10. John Cena. Billed as a resident of West Newbury, Massachusetts, Cena went to Springfield College and was a football player who looked like a body-builder. He's been the man on both WWE brands, Raw and Smackdown, and a multiple-time world champion. He moves merchandise and in many ways has been the top face (good guy) in WWE since Hulk Hogan.

9. Dwayne "The Rock" Johnson. He wasn't a pro wrestler for a long period of time, but there have been few better. A world champion, he may have the best mic skills of all these greats. "The Rock" went on to make a legitimate movie career for himself and broke down doors for other pro wrestlers to get work in Hollywood.

8. Dusty Rhodes. As I'm writing this, I am in the newsroom at Comcast Sportsnet New England. I told the uninformed here to YouTube the Dusty Rhodes "Hard Times" promo. That's why he's on this list.

7. The Undertaker. "The Dead Man" was the first big man who could do things truly utilizing the top rope. He could fly. He also used less emotion and proved it could be more. Meaning, all he had to do was sit up in the ring after being beaten on and the crowd would pop. Still doing it today, he is the conscience of the WWE locker room. Everyone should aspire to have the level of career success he's had.

6. Bruno Sammartino. WWWF champion for a good chunk of the 1960s and 1970s, he ran the Pittsburgh territory and was the king of Madison Square Garden. Vince McMahon, Sr. realized that he didn't need to put the belt on Sammartino for him to get over with the crowd and he remained a draw into the mid-1980s. Fans in Boston also flocked to the Garden to see him every couple months. I remember a Roddy Piper vs. Bruno cage match at the old Garden that was epic by 1980s' standards.

5. "Stone Cold" Steve Austin. Next to Hulk Hogan and Ric Flair, Austin rates as the single greatest pro wrestling draw of all time. In many ways, he helped WWE stay afloat and then pull away from WCW's challenge in the late 1990s. He was what every guy wanted to be: a foul-mouthed, back-talking, no-crap-taking employee. And give WWE owner Vince McMahon, Jr. credit—he realized that he needed to be the bad guy to make his feud with Austin work, and he was more than willing to be that guy to save his company.

4. Triple H. Hunter Hearst Helmsley came to Vince McMahon, Jr.'s promotion from WCW in the 1990s as a mid-carder and worked his way up the ladder to world champion and eventually married Vince's daughter Stephanie McMahon. He's now huge behind the scenes with the company and does it all, including starring in movies and continuing to wrestle at a high level. In his prime with Degeneration X, Evolution and on his own, the guy could main event anywhere. And he's got the best theme music in the business.

3. Andre the Giant. The most impressive physical attraction in the business . . . EVER. His match with Hulk Hogan at Wrestlemania III will go down as the greatest main event in the history of pro wrestling. Find some earlier Andre matches from his first five years in the biz and you'll see an amazing athlete who could move, run, jump—nothing close to the old man who needed to be carted to the ring in the 1980s. And he was the only guy who didn't need to talk to get people in the building.

2. Ric Flair. My personal favorite, Flair carried the now-defunct NWA Jim Crockett Promotions and then Ted Turner's WCW for over 20 years. His promos were legendary and his brash leadership of "The Four Horseman" made that group hated across the country when wrestling hit WTBS in the early 1980s. He made World Championship Wrestling a must-watch for me after Little League or Pee Wee football. Still around today, he needs to walk away from the biz. But everyone can learn from him and his many, many, many mistakes.

1. Hulk Hogan. The best draw in the history of professional wrestling. Screw Lou Thesz and Verne Gagne and the old timers who could really wrestle. Hogan could go and entertain. He ruled the AWA and then in 1984 became pro wrestling's crossover star because of Vince McMahon, Jr. He got rich and made Vince rich with his charisma. He went on to lead the New World Order in WCW as they overtook WWF in the ratings and became an ATM machine for Ted Turner. He's screwed a lot of people in a dirty business. But . . . ask anyone about pro wrestling and most likely the first name they'll say is "HULK HOGAN."

Sports Guys Who Don't Need a Mask on Halloween :: AG and the Fans

How do you rank ugly people? You just can't. So let's just make fun of them. Here, in no particular order, are the guys that are guaranteed to make people soil themselves when they answer the door on Halloween.

John Lackey and Kevin Youkilis. I lump these guys together because they combine all that is beautiful about "Sloth" from the movie *The Goonies*. Look at Kevin Youkilis and don't tell me you don't see a guy who wants a Baby Ruth. And just listen to any John Lackey audio clip on my radio show and tell me you don't hear the great John Matuszak from the mid-1980s.

Dennis Johnson. God rest, first of all. He could play defense, but he also looked like he could just scare opponents on the court. And he had way too many freckles for one human being.

Sam Cassell and Popeye Jones. These two guys looked like they walked off the spaceship with the rest of the aliens. Amateur Olympic wrestlers have better ears than these two guys. Popeye looks like a deer in the headlights ALL THE TIME and like he could fly away when he's at the free throw line. Cassell is E.T. His teeth are so big, if he went down on a woman he could give her a hysterectomy.

Lyndon Byers. LB was a great fighter for the Bruins and San Jose Sharks in the late 1980s and early '90s. If he deserves to be on this list, it's because of the punches he took. I like him, but was told he had to be on this list by many, including the fans. I spent some time with LB at the Super Bowl in Houston in 2004—great guy. Don't beat my ass for putting you on this list.

David Wells. From Frank Travaline on our Facebook page: "He looked like Bluto from the *Popeye* cartoons." Well played, my friend. Well played.

Paul Pierce. His game is ugly and the people think he is as well. Most say he looks like Beetlejuice from *The Howard Stern Show*. Being compared to a mentally challenged dwarf is not good.

Julian Tavarez. Talk to anyone who covered the Red Sox during Taverez's time here and you'd hear stories of how he would basically parade around naked in the locker room. Combine that with a head that looked like it was in the microwave for too long, plus pock marks leftover after Andre the Giant walked on his face in golf shoes, and you have the brutally honest Sox pitcher.

Zdeno Chara. First of all, he's a 6-9 hockey player. That makes him a freak right there. I'm just waiting for Gomez Adams to call for him to grab him a beer from the refrigerator. "YOU RAAAANG?"

Logan Mankins. When he has the moustache working, he looks exactly like Yosemite Sam. Instead of chasing Bugs Bunny or Donald Duck, he was chasing Robert Kraft around Gillette Stadium over his contract.

Robert Parish. He had to puff on the magic dragon because he couldn't stand the sight of himself in the mirror. In fact, I'd like to put the core of the 1980s Celtics on this list. That includes Larry Bird, Kevin McHale and throw in some Greg Kite and that's a whole pot of ugly.

Delonte West. He's a red-headed guy who has sported an afro, has a birthmark near the corner of his mouth and has a minimum of 10 tattoos, including some on his neck. One website called him "Westerado" after he was arrested in Washington D.C. for riding around like the Terminator, wielding handguns and whatever other weapons he could find. He must have been the most picked-on kid in school with those looks.

The plays below have collectively ripped our hearts out. These moments of sports excellence occurred at the expense of our teams and our Boston sports souls.

11-10. NBA Finals Hook Shots (1974 and 1987). In Game 6 of the 1974 Finals, the Boston Garden crowd waited to charge the floor to celebrate another title . . . then Kareem Abdul-Jabbar hit a 15-foot skyhook over Hank Finkel. That winning shot sent the series back to Milwaukee. Fortunately, the Celtics rebounded from the loss and won Game 7. Magic Johnson would hit his own hook shot in 1987 at the Garden to suck the air out of the old barn.

9. Petr Klima (May 15, 1990). For the first five periods, even his coach didn't trust the Czech. Then in the third overtime, Klima climbed over the boards and scored the golden goal for Edmonton vs. the Bruins in Game 1 of the Stanley Cup Finals.

8. Desmond Howard (January 26, 1997). The Patriots had just regained momentum for Super Bowl XXXI on a Curtis Martin touchdown that reduced the Green Bay Packers lead to 27-21. In the ensuing kickoff, Desmond Howard fielded the kick on the one-yard line and took the ball the distance for a "dagger in the heart" touchdown. Howard would have 244 return yards on the game and be named Super Bowl MVP.

7. Enos Slaughter (October 15, 1946). Did he really score the game-winning and World Series-clinching run against the Red Sox from first on a single?

6. Aaron Boone (May 18, 1999). Grady Little's first mistake was leaving Pedro in too long. His second mistake was allowing Tim Wakefield, who has a propensity for giving up the long ball, to pitch in sudden death in Game 7 of the ALCS. In one of the more devastating manifestations of "The Curse," the Yankees ripped Boston's heart out on a walk-off home run by Aaron Boone in the 11th inning.

5. Ben Dreith (December 18, 1976). "Mr. Dreith, there is a man dressed in all white that wants to talk to you."

4. Mookie Wilson (October 25, 1986). "Little roller up along first. . . ."

3. David Tyree (February 3, 2008). With the Patriots leading Super Bowl XLII, 14-10, the Giants had the ball on their own 44-yard line and it was third-and-5. Eli Manning scrambled out of trouble and threw a pass up for grabs. Little-known Giants wide receiver David Tyree leaped and caught the ball with one hand, pinning the ball against his helmet for a 34-yard reception. The incredible reception with 59 seconds left kept the Super Bowl-winning drive alive. Ugggh!

2. Yvon Lambert (May 10, 1979). The Bruins led with just over a minute left in the Montreal Forum in Game 7 of the Stanley Cup Semifinals when they were penalized for too many men on the ice. Yada, yada, yada, the Canadiens tied the game and then won it in overtime on a Yvon Lambert goal that ripped our hearts out.

1. Bucky "Fucking" Dent (October 2, 1978). The light-hitting shortstop had one home run after the All-Star break and was hitting .243 on the year when he stepped to the plate with two outs in the seventh inning of the playoff game to decide the AL East title. The Red Sox were leading 2-0. With two men on, Dent grabbed teammate Micky Rivers' "suspicious" bat and proceeded to hit a pop-up that fell onto the top of the Green Monster and led the Yankees to victory and the postseason.

Equally important as the players to a team's success are the people who acquire the players. It is critical that they do an efficient and successful job "shopping for the groceries." In a crazed sports environment like Boston, their every move is analyzed and evaluated by the press and fans. The people below oversaw the personnel decisions that allowed our teams to thrive.

10. Lou Gorman. At times, he was too loquacious. But give him his due—he built Red Sox teams that competed throughout his tenure (1984-93). He was the GM in 1986 and that team finished . . . sort of close.

9. The Yawkeys. The Red Sox players loved them and they sustained the team for decades. However, a problem with racial imbalance will forever be tied to their days here.

8. Dick O'Connell. His constructing the Impossible Dream team is enough to put him on this list. Though his 12 years as Red Sox GM (1965-77) were also a great overall success. He drafted Carlton Fisk, Dwight Evans, Rick Burleson, Fred Lynn and Jim Rice. He gave Fenway a winner again.

7. Danny Ainge. In the spirit of his old mentor Red Auerbach, Ainge was as bold as a Celtic GM as he was petulant as a player. He's always been a winner and he brought that winner's DNA with him to the front office of the Celtics. In a few short years, he righted the ship, created salary-cap room and constructed a championship team for the city of Boston.

6. Harry Sinden. He had an innate ability to recognize untapped hockey talent. His acquisition of Cam Neely was brilliant, for it recognized greatness in simple potential. Sure, he was stubborn and inflexible, but you can't take away from him that he built a team that sustained success.

5. Theo Epstein. The Brookline wonder kid who grew up within walking distance of Fenway Park came back home and gave the Red Sox Nation something it hadn't experienced in over eight decades—a World Series championship in 2004. And then three years later, he brought us a second one just for the fun of it.

4. Bill Belichick (and Scott Pioli). Though not technically a front office guy, the man in the hooded sweatshirt is as close to Red Auerbach as anyone in Boston sports history. Belichick built a Patriots dynasty through coaching (and by working closely with his longtime player personnel chief, Scott Pioli), creating a culture of respect for the game and piecing together three championship puzzles.

3. Bob Kraft and the Kraft Family. The moving trucks were circling Foxboro and the team was in disarray. Then New England season ticket holders, the Kraft family, stepped in and bought the Patriots and turned it into a team Boston can be proud of. Thank you!

2. Walter Brown. He did more for Boston sports than probably any other individual in our community. He and his family sustained the Celtics, the Boston Garden and the Boston Marathon. These three gems provided the city with a proud sports identity and enhanced the quality of our lives.

1. Red Auerbach. He was the master of the deal. He drafted, traded and signed free agents. He built championships with coaching and wheeling and dealing like the Larry Bird draft, the Bill Russell trade, the DJ trade, signing Ainge away from the Toronto Blue Jays, getting McHale, Parish and M.L. Carr for surly Bob McAdoo, etc. He was the wizard.

Top 10 Moments of My Career :: by Mike Gorman

Note: Mike Gorman has been the voice of the Boston Celtics on Comcast SportsNet New England for 30 years. His accomplishments in broadcasting are endless. He was kind enough to review his long and storied career and pick his top moments, some of which will probably surprise you.

10. New Bedford Country Club Championship on WNBH Radio, New Bedford, Massachusetts. Golf on radio, from a pay phone overlooking the 18th green. Four hours, one guy to get scores, sold out with 12 minutes per hour of live commercial reads with 48 minutes an hour to fill. It taught me how to make stuff up on the fly. An invaluable experience.

9. Boxing from Worcester on WNBH Radio, New Bedford. Had a commercial book that had three, 30-second reads that had to be done between each round. When I pointed out that there was only 60 seconds between rounds, I was told by the sales manager to simply "read fast." He also told me to "make it exciting, even if it isn't." Hmmmmm.

8. High School Basketball and Football Games on WNBH Radio, New Bedford. Learned my trade there. It was undergrad school, grad school and on-the-job training all rolled into one. You basically had to do everything yourself. Everything.

7. URI Basketball on WPRO Radio, Providence, Rhode Island. First taste of college basketball and my timing was very fortunate. Sly Williams, Jim "Jiggy" Williamson and Irv Chatman. I remember doing a game at Maryland vs. Lefty Drisell and another at Wake Forest. Big time atmospheres that were addictive. I also got the chance to work with Salty Brine. A major break for me. I could never put in words how much he taught me.

GRESH NOTE: For 50 years, Salty Brine was the morning drive host on WPRO-AM. A legend who's in the Radio Hall of Fame.

6. Providence College Basketball on WPRI-TV, Providence. First contact with Dave Gavitt. First contact with Tommy Heinsohn. 'Nuff said. Changed my professional life.

GRESH NOTE: Mike and Tommy have done Celtics games for 30 years now.

5. Big East Television Network. Two or three big games a week in big time buildings with big time crowds and with ESPN just emerging, getting your call on Sportscenter was a big deal. The Big East was Pearl Washington and Patrick Ewing and Chris Mullin and "Send It In Jerome" Lane. And Bill Raftery doing color commentary with Ronnie Perry in the mix as well. Just great game after great game.

4. Big Mondays on ESPN. I worked with Bill Raftery, though when it's with Raf, it never really feels like work. What was there not to like? Thanksgivings in Maui, the Big East Tournament in New York City in March. And all the big games in between on Big Monday. It was an incredible time to be involved with the Big East. Bill Raftery is the one voice you want to hear on a big college basketball game. He makes you laugh a half dozen times and he can do Xs and Os with the best of them.

3. NCAA Tournament on CBS. Network Television, a long putt from #10 above. Games that immediately come to mind: Steve Nash and Santa Clara beating Arizona; any game involving a Big East team; Fang Mitchell and the Coppin State Eagles (my personal favorite). They were/are what the tournament is all about.

2. First 15 Years of Celtics Broadcasts on Prism, Sportschannel and Fox SportsNet. Did the home games throughout the 1980s. Larry, Chief, Kevin, DJ, Danny and Bill Walton. They hardly ever lost at home. This was before the NBA sold out the locals to the networks for the playoffs. Tommy and I did games all the way through the Eastern Conference Finals. Garden sold out every night. Great times.

1. Last 15 years as the Television Play-by-Play Voice for All Celtics Games. What I always wanted to be: "The Voice of the Celtics." I went through some lean years, but Banner 17 is my career highlight. Current Celtics ownership is the best in the 30 years I have been associated with the team. Danny Ainge and Doc Rivers may be the best GM/Coach tandem in the league. Paul Pierce, Ray Allen, KG and Rajon Rondo are a foursome to rival the 1980s. Wasn't sure during the '90s I would be around for another championship team. To be broadcasting a contender once again is a thrill I wasn't counting on.

The men wearing suits in the front office can use their power and money to steer their teams towards championships. These suits steered our teams into dead ends.

10. Bobby Grier. He had a plethora of draft picks from the Bill Parcells deal with the New York Jets, but somehow couldn't identify talent. The Patriots era between Parcells and Belichick marked a state of diminishing returns. Not to mention, the culture of the team ran contrary to the Krafts' mission of greatness.

9. Buddy LeRoux. The one-time Red Sox trainer positioned himself to become a part-owner of the team. On the night that recently deceased Tony Conigliaro was being honored at Fenway Park, LeRoux announced a coup on his partners. The matter ended up in court, where he lost. Taking away from Tony Conigliaro Night further confirmed how little class LeRoux had.

8. Paul Gaston. During his time at the watch, the Celtics plunged to the bottom of the standings. He also threatened to file suit against the *Wall Street Journal* for $100 million after they published a negative story on the death of Reggie Lewis, but never did.

7. Upton Bell. Better known for his talk-show gibberish, Bell called the shots for the Patriots in the early 1970s. His player and coach selections were proof that he didn't know what he was doing. The team's record during his tenure was 9-19.

6. M.L. Carr (GM/Coach). We love M.L. and respect that he took one for the team. But it was a painful process just for the chance to draft Tim Duncan.

5. The Yawkeys. The owners of the Red Sox made both the good and bad GM/Owners lists. Their intolerance caused the Red Sox not only shame, but to miss out on some of the greatest players in the world. Jackie Robinson had a tryout with the Red Sox, but wasn't signed. That means either the Yawkeys and their organization were terrible at evaluating talent, or they were racists.

4. Irv Levin. When he had a chance to sustain a championship team by signing rebounder extraordinaire Paul Silas, he refused to make the necessary funds available. He instead backed deals that replaced the classy Silas with the classless Curtis Rowe and Sidney Wicks. During the Havlicek retirement game, the Boston Garden crowd booed Levin with great passion.

3. Harry Frazee. The Red Sox owner (from 1916-23) needed money to finance his Broadway play *No, No Nanette*. So he sold Babe Ruth, the greatest baseball player in the history of the game, to our sworn enemies, the New York Yankees. The rest is history.

2. John Y. Brown. The whiskey-drinking good ol' boy from Kentucky bought the Celtics and treated the team like a toy. He and his wife, Phyllis George, traded three of Red Auerbach's hard-earned first-round picks to the Knicks for Bob McAdoo. Red threatened to quit in disgust. Brown eventually sold the team to run for the Governor of Kentucky, putting the Celtics back on track for championship ball.

1. Rick Pitino. The used car salesman specialized in bringing lemons to Boston. His massive ego led him to believe he knew more than everyone else and ultimately led to his dismissal.

Most Intimidating Celtics :: by Pat Williams

Note: Pat Williams has been involved with the NBA since 1968. He was named one of the 50 most influential people in the history of the league. He served as general manager of the Philadelphia 76ers for a span of 12 years that included the franchise's glory days of the 1980s. He later co-founded the Orlando Magic and currently serves as the club's senior vice president.

12. Johnny Most. He would walk into the building with his rotund, gargoyle-like face, puffing on that ever-present cigarette and ready to attack on all fronts. When he was in front of that microphone, he would defend his Celtics at all costs against players, referees and fans. When he started yelling, you could hear him all over the Philadelphia Spectrum.

11. M.L. Carr. He was sweet and gracious and kind and friendly, but beneath that M.L. Carr was a savage competitor. When he came into the Spectrum, he stirred up more problems than any other visiting player. It didn't matter to him. He would get into it with players and the fans. And he could play. On some nights, he could take over the game. I hated to see him come into our building.

10. Dennis Johnson. We drafted Andrew Toney in the first round of the 1980 draft. He was a Celtics killer. He was called "The Boston Strangler." In the ongoing chess game between the two teams, the Celtics counterpunched by trading for Dennis Johnson to slow down Andrew.

9. Ray Allen and 8. Paul Pierce. Any time Ray Allen and Paul Pierce come into your building, your team has the deadly assignment of trying to curtail the Hall of Fame shooting of this two-headed monster. It's impossible to keep them both under control.

7. Kevin Garnett. It's the face—the focus, the intensity. It's scary. I don't like to see him step onto the floor against our team. When he arrives, it's always with the attitude of, "I'm gonna get you tonight."

6. John Havlicek. He was a sweet-spirited guy who was soft-spoken, but was also a relentless assassin. No game was ever safe when he was on the other team. He could absolutely wear you down. A reporter once said to Bill Russell, "All Havlicek does is hustle." The Celtic center said in response, "hustle is a talent."

5. Kevin McHale and 4. Robert Parish. Kevin McHale and Robert Parish arrived in Boston on the same day, in the same trade. As a counter move to the Sixers twin towers, Darryl Dawkins and Caldwell Jones, the Celtics brought in these two Hall of Famers in one fell swoop, and it was never the same.

3. Red Auerbach. You were afraid to pick up the phone if you knew it was him on the other end. If he started to talk trade, you made sure you kept your hands in your pockets, because you were never sure what he could do to you. Even as a general manager, he could still influence games, players and officials. He was a presence whenever he was in the building.

2. Bill Russell. The Celtics center was the greatest winner of all time—the greatest defender of all time. When he walked onto the floor with his scowl and will to win, you only felt fear.

1. Larry Bird. My most haunting memory occurred in Game 7 of the 1981 playoffs at the Boston Garden. We had been up 3-1 in the series and had Game 5 won. Somehow the Celtics stole the game back and then beat us in Game 6 at the Spectrum, sending the series back to the Garden. The pressure was so great that you could smell it. I couldn't breathe or watch. Larry Bird hit the key shot to beat us like he always did.

With basketball being invented in nearby Springfield and all those Celtics titles, Boston boasts a rich hoops history that's inspired a lot of envy and hatred from rivals. And some of those rivals have inspired us to hate them back. Here are the ones we have hated and booed the most intensely over the years.

11. Eddie F. Rush. This longtime NBA referee is hated in Boston because Tommy Heinsohn kills him on Celtics broadcasts every time he gets the Green. To Tommy, Eddie is the Antichrist. Like the rest of his colleagues, Rush is an inconsistent referee who can make the NBA a very hateful product. And he's done his share of harm to the Celtics over the years. Still, I truly believe that if Tommy didn't rip the guy from pillar to post, we wouldn't notice every time he's in the house.

10. Ralph Sampson. He was the so-called "Big Man" in the NBA during the mid-1980s who was gonna match up against McHale and Parish. His pro career was not as extraordinary as his college career, so that made him over-rated, petulant and hateful to Boston fans—who saw successful big men for the better part of three decades.

9. LeBron James. I know a lot of current Celtics fans will say he should be higher on the list, but let's call it the way it is: the Celts beat his Cleveland Cavaliers in every big situation in the regular season and in the playoffs. Now he's in Miami and running his mouth along with Dwayne Wade and Chris Bosh. He'll always be viewed in Boston as a guy who should win more. In a town of champions, LeBron will never be viewed as one—no matter how many titles (if any) he wins in Miami.

8. Moses Malone. This big man was the target of many a Celtics legend, including Larry Bird, who once said, "Moses does eat shit." He ran mad smack as a Houston Rocket during the 1981 NBA Finals and Bird and his boys showed him by winning the title in six games. And, of course, his subsequent time in Philadelphia with the 76ers made him a natural Boston rival.

7. Kobe Bryant. This stems from the carryover of the Celtics-Lakers rivalry from the 1980s. Kobe is the new Magic Johnson—the best player on most Celtics fans hate list. He has won one and lost one against the new Big Three in the NBA Finals. He may go down as the best player of all time, but his battles with Paul Pierce will go down in Celtics history, just below Bird vs. Magic.

6. Magic Johnson. His individual rivalry with Larry Bird is the best in the history of basketball. It started with the Michigan State-Indiana State NCAA Championship Game in 1979 and carried onto three of four NBA Finals from 1984-87. Race was a huge factor in this duel and was a catalyst for some of the hatred that came Johnson's way. I think the hatred for Magic in Boston has started to subside, as he and Bird are actually friends. But when they battled on the basketball court, it was sports war at its best.

5. Bill Laimbeer and 4. Rick Mahorn. "McDirty and McNasty," as nicknamed by Johnny Most. The legendary Celtics announcer pulled a nutty in Detroit, uttering that he wasn't supposed to say bad things about them in Detroit, but that he didn't care. These two could have caused a riot in Boston if they wanted to. It was always physical and dirty when they matched up against Kevin McHale and Robert Parish.

3. Kurt Rambis. He did the dirty work for the Lakers in the 1980s. And ironically it was Celtic Kevin McHale's flagrant foul against Rambis in Game 4 of the NBA Finals that helped land Rambis on this list. He drove you crazy in a Dennis Rodman kind of way by being a lunchpail, high-effort guy who made you scream at the TV. But the smart C's fans knew his value to Magic and Kareem. And he was hated for it.

2. Isiah Thomas. The Celtics beat the Pistons in the playoffs in 1985 and 1987 and were the roadblock that Detroit couldn't get past. In 1987, Bird stole the ball off Isiah's inbounds pass, snatching an unlikely victory for Boston and humiliating Isiah...at least in the minds of Boston fans. But Isiah continued to agitate us. He was unlikable as a player. And in this city, he is viewed as a slapdick as both a coach and general manager.

1. Kareem Abdul-Jabbar. With the Bucks and the Lakers, he was a thorn in the side of the Celtics during the 1970s and '80s. He was big, shot the sky hook and at times had a bad hairdo. Those all equal a reason to mock and hate at the same time. He was also one of the all-time greats, which was the main reason Celtics fans disliked him so much.

Players I Admire :: by John Tudor

Note: A local product from Peabody High School, John Tudor made his Major League Baseball debut in 1979 with the Red Sox after being drafted by Boston three years earlier. The southpaw starter led the Sox pitching staff in wins in 1983 and then went to the National League the following year. In 1985, he had one of the greatest seasons by a lefthander in baseball history, going 21-8, with 10 shutouts and a 1.93 ERA. During September of that season, he was extraordinary, going 6-0 and notching four shutouts while leading the Cardinals to the NL East title and National League pennant. A 12-4 record and 2.40 ERA gained him the National League Comeback Player of the Year Award in 1990, which turned out to be his final season. Here, Tudor offers us a list of 10 local athletes he grew up admiring or wanting to be like. With the exception of #1 (Bobby Orr) and maybe #2 (Larry Bird), the athletes on his list appear in no particular order.

10. Derek Sanderson. A great player on a fun team to watch. I loved the way he worked on the ice. Maybe the best short-handed player of all time. Pretty darn good fighter, too.

9. Terry O'Reilly. I think there is a hockey theme here somewhere. The toughest player to wear the Bruins uniform. Not given enough credit for his offensive abilities, Terry was the working man's hockey player. What he lacked in God-given talent, he made up for with sheer determination and grit.

8. Bobby Miller. Another hard-working hockey player. My second favorite Bruin when it comes to short-handed situations. Really good guy, but not much of a softball player. LOL.

7. Mosi Tatupu. Breaking the hockey theme with a really good football player. Mosi worked hard for everything he got. This guy was one classy individual. We all miss him.

6. Johnny Pesky. I'm not quite old enough to really remember seeing him play, but you couldn't ask for a better person. A true ambassador for the game of baseball.

5. Steve Grogan. Since the emergence of Mr. Brady, we tend to forget how good and reliable Steve was. The toughest QB to play in New England and possibly the NFL. Another fairly soft-spoken guy if you were to meet him on the street. But my bet is he was just the opposite on the field and in the locker room.

4. Ray Bourque. Great Hall of Fame player. Hard-working professional and always willing to put the team ahead of himself. Ray always seems to put himself in the right situation to do and say the right thing. Excellent role model for us all.

3. Tom Brady. I have more of an adult's perspective on Brady. I admire him in ways that are different from how I admired athletes when I was a kid. Not only is he a great player, but he handles himself with amazing class. In today's fishbowl world, he always seems to say and do the right thing. He just goes out and lets his play on the field do the talking. He acts like he has been there before. He just continues to compete until the whistle blows.

2. Larry Bird. Another working man's player. Nothing pretty or flashy about him or his game, but I don't think there has ever been a more competitive athlete to roam the Garden floor. As a kid growing up in New England, I think he was second only to Bobby Orr in athletes I would pay to watch. Pure money with the game on the line.

1. Bobby Orr. Do I really need to say anything else? I grew up in the Big Bad Bruins era. I always wanted to be like Orr, as did most New England boys at that time. Great player and even better role model.

The endeavor of athletics demands that players physically challenge one another in an effort to force their will upon their opponents. Sometimes the end result is victory. Sometimes the end result is loss and/or injury. The below list represents a compilation of demoralizing injuries inflicted upon some of our favorite players.

Honorable Mentions. Gord Kluzak's knees; Robert Edwards' knee injury on the beach; Dave Cowens' feet; Clayton Weishuhn's knees; Kevin McHale's foot; Rodney Harrison's knee—twice; Jerry Remy's knees; Nomar's wrist; Tom Brady's knee; head injuries of Ted Green and Marc Savard.

12. Wes Welker (January 3, 2010). In a meaningless game against the Texans in Houston, Wes Welker suffered a devastating knee injury with the playoffs a week away. The Patriots never recovered and were dominated by the Baltimore Ravens one week later in Foxboro.

11. Jim Lonborg (Winter of 1968). The reigning Cy Young winner was warned not to ski in the offseason. The pitcher didn't heed the warnings and suffered a broken leg while on the slopes. He was never the same pitcher for the Red Sox, going 27-29 over the next four years before being traded to the Milwaukee Brewers.

10. Ted Williams (July 11, 1950). In the first inning of the 1950 All-Star game, Williams crashed into the scoreboard while catching a Ralph Kiner fly ball. He broke his elbow in the collision. He wouldn't play again for the Red Sox until September 7. The Red Sox finished four games out of first place.

9. Ted Williams (March 1, 1954). On the first day of spring training, Williams crashed into the left-field wall and broke his collar bone. He wouldn't play his first regular-season game until May 15. Williams would go on to hit .345 to lead the league, but too few at-bats would cost him the batting title.

8. Tony Conigliaro (August 18, 1967). In the midst of the Impossible Dream season, the Red Sox slugger with movie star charisma was hit in the face by a Jack Hamilton pitch that ended his season and forever derailed his career and life.

7. Carlton Fisk (June 28, 1974). No catcher blocked the plate like Carlton Fisk. On June 28, 1974, Cleveland Indian Leron Lee decided to go right through Fisk's knee to get to home plate. Doctors said Fisk would never play again. Fisk willed himself back onto the field and started his first game since the injury on June 23, 1975. He hit .331 for the season.

6. Jim Rice (September 21, 1975). With the postseason just weeks away, the rookie sensation was hit by a Vern Ruhle pitch that broke his wrist. The injury caused Rice to be unavailable for the playoffs. Cecil Cooper took his spot and struggled mightily, going 1 for 19 in the World Series against the Cincinnati Reds.

5. Patriots Exhibition Nightmare (September 1, 1989). In the final exhibition game of 1989, the Patriots lost three defensive starters—for the season! Ronnie Lippett (Achilles tendon), Andre Tippett (shoulder) and Garin Veris (knee) all were injured in a game that starters usually sit out. The team was never able to recover from the devastating injuries and finished 5-11 on the season.

4. John Havlicek (April 20, 1973). The Celtics won 68 games in the 1972-73 season and were the favorites to win the championship. However, in Game 3 of the Eastern Conference Finals, John Havlicek was sandwiched by a New York Knick pick and injured his right shoulder. Havlicek would shoot lefty for the rest of the series, but it wasn't enough. The Knicks won the series in seven games and went on to win the NBA title.

3. Cam Neely (May 1991). Multiple cheap shots by Ulf Samuelsson during the 1991 Conference Finals took a toll on the great right wing. The Ulf-induced injury led to a degenerative hip condition for Neely, which ultimately led to the premature end of his career.

2. Larry Bird (July 30, 1989). "Larry Legend" reported to Camp Millbrook with the rookies after recovering from devastating foot injuries. During a scrimmage, he was undercut by rookie Kelvin Upshaw and fell on his back. The rest was history.

1. Bobby Orr (Career). He first injured his knee in his rookie season of 1966-67. Unfortunately, the knee injuries would only get worse for Orr. Over the next eight seasons, he had his knees operated on 12 times. By age 27, his career was virtually over. His injuries robbed sports fans everywhere from witnessing even more of his brilliance.

Five Sports Figures I *Think* Hate Me :: AG

I know that I have offended, disgusted or flat-out pissed off many folks over the years. The following are the ones I have pissed off to the point that I'm pretty sure they will never place me on their Christmas-card lists.

5. Willie McGinest, Former Patriots DE. When his play dipped under Head Coach Pete Carroll, I used to call him "Millie." He played soft sometimes back then and I called it like I saw it. I came to find out he is a very likeable guy.

4. Max Lane, Former Patriots OL. To this day, every time I mention his name I can't help but think of how he got turtled by Reggie White in Super Bowl XXXI. I've said it on the air so often that people who didn't know what "got turtled" meant, do now.

3. Jacoby Ellsbury, Red Sox Outfielder. So I *may* have called him a "pussy" on Twitter (@greshandzo), causing Sox Manager Terry Francona during the 2010 season to publicly question media "tough guys." I've only put him on the think list because he'll be around a while and maybe I can change his mind.

2. Theo Epstein, Red Sox General Manager. In 2006, I asked him a rare radio interview tough question. Apparently I made him a smidge upset and he gave me a terse, "That's fine. But you're wrong." He never appeared on that station I worked for again. I think he's plenty smug, but with a pair of World Series rings, he should be.

1. Charlie Moore, NESN Fisherman. When my on-air partner Scott Zolak told me this clown had a fishing challenge show on ESPN called *Beat Charlie Moore*, my reply was, "With what!?" This guy drives me nutz, and for as much as I've crushed him on the radio, I'm sure he feels the same way about me.

Four Sports Figures (and One Institution) I *Know* Hate Me :: AG

Okay, I am *positive* I'm never getting on any of these guys' Christmas-card lists.

5. Nomar Garciaparra, Former Red Sox SS. On the day he retired, I told him that he'd be remembered as a loser because the Red Sox reversed the curse the year they traded him. He wasn't happy. Neither was the club. Oh, well.

4. Todd Rucci, Former Patriots OL. He used to get run over so often while trying to protect Drew Bledsoe, I nicknamed him "Roller Skates" Rucci. I knew all about that because I wore them while trying to block for Chris Hixson as an OL at URI.

3. Brian Rose, Former Red Sox P. I remember running into this dink while he was pitching for Pawtucket. He walked around with an undeserved sense of entitlement. He was way overhyped and did a whole bunch of nothing while in the bigs. I used to point out how overrated he was every time he pitched. I heard he didn't like that, but I had fun.

2. Brown University. This is the institution that had me do fill-in work as a football radio color analyst. I uttered the phrase "snot blowers"—which the athletic director and other boosters found to be offensive. The AD fired me over the phone, saying, "I don't want your schtick affiliated with my athletic program." (I was a talk-show host on that radio station as well.) And yet, when their married play-by-play guy got busted with a hooker, he got a second chance. And I'm the one who messed up?

1. Doug Flutie, Former Boston College QB. While doing a talk show with the hooker guy, I was challenged by him off air to say to Doug Flutie's face at an interview at the AAA All-Star Game in Pawtucket everything I've said about him on the radio (I think he's way overrated). I did. Flutie got up and walked away after our radio equipment came unplugged right after the question. He was pissed. My then-partner was aghast. I was beaming with pride.

These people brought out the best in one another while competing as partners. Side by side, they helped our teams win or graced us with the pleasure of witnessing (or listening to) their united work.

Honorable Mentions. Tom Brady and Wes Welker; Drew Bledsoe and Ben Coates; Dave Cowens and Paul Silas; Andre Tippett and Donald Blackmon; Manny Ramirez and David Ortiz; Fred Cusick and Johnny Peirson.

15. Dick Hoyt and Rick Hoyt. The marathon team of Hoyt and Hoyt represent all that is good about sports. They show that it is possible to fulfill one's potential by persevering and challenging the limits of one's abilities.

14. Gil Santos and Gino Cappelletti. It wouldn't be an autumn Sunday without Gil and Gino on the radio and the volume on the TV turned off.

13. Jim Plunkett and Randy Vataha. In 1971, this QB-WR pairing came to New England from Stanford and immediately connected. The sight of Vataha running under a Plunkett long bomb was a thing of beauty. In their rookie seasons, the two connected for nine touchdowns—the longest going for 88 yards. In all, the two former Cardinals would join forces for 16 touchdowns as Patriots.

12. Sean McDonough and Jerry Remy. McDonough was the greatest talent to broadcast a sporting event in Boston sports history. A Friday night baseball game with McDonough and Remy bantering back and forth was a special presentation.

11. Tom Brady and Randy Moss. Their undefeated 2007 regular season proved that the quarterback and wide receiver formed one of the greatest tag teams in sports history. Brady threw for 50 touchdowns and 4,806 yards that season, with Moss catching 23 of those touchdown passes and accumulating 1,493 receiving yards.

10. Will Cloney and Jock Semple. The two administrators of the Boston Marathon sustained the world's greatest race for over four decades. Cloney was the steady captain, while the fiery Scotsman Semple breathed life into each year's race.

9. Gino Cappelletti and Babe Parilli. The two Patriots played together in Boston from 1961 to 1967. Parilli threw passes to Cappelletti and held for his kicks. They racked up eight Pro Bowl selections between them during this period.

8. Cam Neely and Craig Janney (1988-92) or Adam Oates (1992-97). In 1992, Janney and Oates were actually traded for each other. However, with their amazing playmaking skills, both played a pivotal role in helping Cam Neely become the greatest right wing of all time. All three averaged more than a point a game for the B's during their tenures in Boston.

7. Doug Flutie and Gerard Phelan. The two Boston College Eagles were room-mates off the field and a deadly quarterback-wide receiver combination on the field. Flutie won the Heisman and produced over 10,000 yards of offense for BC. Phelan had 1,714 receiving yards and 107 catches and was on the receiving end of Flutie's famous Hail Mary TD pass against Miami.

6. Larry Bird and Dennis Johnson. The two Celtics seemed to always be on the same page. Nothing was sweeter than a backdoor pass from DJ at the top of the key to a cutting Bird. However, their greatest connection was when Bird fed DJ for a game-winning layup after Bird's great steal against Detroit in the 1987 playoffs.

5. Jim Rice and Fred Lynn. They arrived in Boston in 1975 as rookies and helped the team to the World Series by combining for 43 home runs, 207 RBI and a .320 batting average. Rice would go on to the Hall of Fame and Lynn would have made it, too, if he had stayed at Fenway Park.

4. John Hannah and Leon Gray. The two offensive linemen came into the league together in 1973. They guarded the left side of the Patriots line for six years. In 1978, they cleared the way for the NFL's top running attack with 3,165 yards and 30 touchdowns. That offseason, Gray was traded to Houston, and New England's ground game suffered, falling to 15th in the NFL the following season. The Patriots quarterbacks suffered, too, getting sacked 49 times compared to just 16 times the previous season.

3. Phil Esposito and Bobby Orr. Two of the greatest players in NHL history, they skated for the Big Bad Bruins. The pair fed off each other, making the B's an offensive juggernaut and two-time Stanley Cup champions. The Art Ross Trophy is awarded to the National Hockey League player who leads the league in scoring at the end of the regular season. In the seven seasons between 1968-75, the winner was either Orr (two times) or Esposito (five times). In 1,256 games, the two combined for 1,900 points.

2. Tom Brady and Bill Belichick. The two geniuses form the greatest quarterback-coach combination in the history of the NFL. Together, they have won at a pace (a .776 winning percentage and three Super Bowls in four years) never seen before in the sport. And their level of success will probably never be witnessed again in the NFL.

1. Red Auerbach and Walter Brown. The two men teamed up to create the greatest dynasty in sports history. As the team owner, Brown sustained the Celtics through the tough times until Auerbach could steer the team towards dominance.

My Favorite Bruins :: by Rick Hoyt

Note: Rick Hoyt is one half of the father-son marathon/triathlon team of Dick and Rick Hoyt. Rick is the spark that makes the team go. He inspired his dad to start their running in 1977 by suggesting that his father push him in his wheelchair, and they haven't stopped since. Rick, who is stricken with cerebral palsy, loves to compete and loves sports. He never forgets to remind his dad that he beats him in every race. A graduate of Boston University, Rick's greatest loves outside his family are hockey and the Bruins.

5. Zdeno Chara. The current Bruins captain and defenseman let my family use his luxury box in 2007 and we got to meet him after the game. Zdeno wanted my father to be his personal trainer, as he was thinking of trying to do a few triathlons over the summer months.

4. Lyndon Byers. A former Bruins player and a radio host, he usually interviews dad and me at the starting line of the Boston Marathon.

3. Cam Neely. Played right wing for the Bruins in the Eighties. I have a picture of Cam Neely, Dave Cowens, my dad and me at a fundraiser for the New England Museum of Sports.

2. Gerry Cheevers. Was the top Bruins goalie in the Seventies. He was in the net when Bobby Orr won the Stanley Cup. I was a goalie on a street hockey team as a kid.

1. Bobby Orr. In Game 4 of the 1970 Stanley Cup Finals, Bobby Orr went flying over the ice after scoring the winning goal. That was the same year I used my voice-activated computer to say my first words: "GO BRUINS."

My Favorite Marathon Memories :: by Dick Hoyt

Note: Dick Hoyt is one-half of the father-son marathon/triathlon team of Dick and Rick Hoyt. Dick, the father, has pushed, pedaled and/or swam the team in over 1,000 races, including three decades worth of Boston Marathons and the Ironman competition in Hawaii. Beloved from Hopkinton to the Back Bay and around the world, Dick Hoyt is the shining personification of parental love.

5. Milestone. If it comes down to one race a year, Rick and I would like it to be the Boston Marathon.

4. Boston Marathon Count. We have completed in 28 Boston Marathons so far, with our best time being 2:48:51 in 1986. It will be our 30th Boston Marathon in 2012 when Rick will be 50 years old (and I will be 71). That is our goal right now

3. Running for Easter Seals in 2006. For Team Hoyt's 25th Boston Marathon, Rick and I decided to raise money for Easter Seals of Massachusetts. We were able to raise over $360,000 and it all went to Easter Seals of MA. The Boston Athletic Association (B.A.A.) also presented Rick and me with the prestigious Patriot's Award that year.

2. The 100th Running in 1996. For the 100th running of the Boston Marathon, Rick and I were honored as Centennial Heroes by the B.A.A. and their sponsor John Hancock.

1. First Boston Marathon in 1981. For Team Hoyt's first Boston Marathon, the B.A.A. rejected our application, as we were different than all the other runners. They never saw a runner pushing someone in a chair before. They said we could line up behind the wheelchair athletes (they propel their own running chairs) and run without a number. Our time was 3 hours and 18 minutes.

Red Sox Pitchers I Would Give the Ball to for Game 7 :: MC

If I had my choice of any Red Sox pitcher to start a do-or-die Game 7, these are the ones I would hand the ball to before that fraud from Texas! What would be the use? He'd look for Terry Cooney to get tossed, cry if he saw Dave Stewart or sit in the dugout while someone else tried to close out his game.

12. Jon Lester. When this topic was posed to Red Sox GM Theo Epstein, he strongly suggested that I add Jon Lester to the list. Lester may have only won two postseason games, but he does have a 2.57 ERA in six starts and a 3-to-1 strikeout-to-walk ratio (39-13). Theo, you were right!

11. Sonny Siebert. The right-handed pitcher had the innate ability to rise to the occasion. Siebert's duels against Oakland's Cy Young winner Vida Blue in 1971 were electric, playoff-like events in which Siebert pitched like an ace in both games, going 1-0 with a no decision.

10. Dennis Eckersley. "The Eck" was one of the most feared starters in baseball before being transformed into a closer. Down the stretch in 1978 when every game was an elimination game, Eckersley was 4-0 with a 0.81 ERA.

9. Mel Parnell. One of the top southpaws ever to pitch for the Red Sox, Parnell was not afraid to take the ball when called upon. He pitched on one day of rest 12 times in his career, going 9-2 with 11 complete games. In August and September, he was 55-25 during a career that spanned from 1947-56.

8. Derek Lowe. The lanky righty proved again and again, that the hotter the spotlight, the better he pitched. In the 2004 postseason, he won three games—each one clinching its respective series.

7. Josh Beckett. The hard-throwing righty has a 7-3 career postseason record and two World Series rings. Beckett has proven that he can beat the Yankees—in New York in October. That is enough evidence for me.

6. Bruce Hurst. In the 1986 postseason, the lefty was the Red Sox ace, going 3-0 with a 2.13 ERA.

5. Babe Ruth. "The Bambino" was a true ace when he was a pitcher for the Red Sox. Ruth thrived in the postseason, compiling a 3-0 record with a 0.87 ERA.

4. Pedro Martinez. Exhibit A: Pedro's six-inning, no-hit relief appearance against Cleveland in Game 5 in 1999. Exhibit B: For his career, Martinez was 6-2 in the postseason.

3. Jim Lonborg. In 1967, the Red Sox ace took the mound 42 times, never saying "No" when asked. Lonborg pitched on three days of rest 19 times. During a nine-day span in October of 1967, he pitched three complete-game wins, beating the Twins in the pennant clincher and the Cardinals twice in the World Series. After just two days of rest, he took the ball again in Game 7, but finally ran out of gas during his fourth start in 12 days.

2. Curt Schilling. One of the greatest postseason pitchers in baseball history, Schilling posted a 2.23 ERA and 11-2 playoff record, including a win in "The Bloody Sock Game."

1. Luis Tiant. If a big game needed to be pitched, Tiant would get my nod. In the postseason, he was 3-0. Tiant was not afraid to pitch a complete game (unlike a certain pitcher in the 1986 World Series). In Game 5 of the 1975 World Series, Tiant pitched a complete game while throwing 158 pitches.

This list is a compilation of amazing sports stats that defy sports logic. The athletes responsible for them range from Boston's greatest team player to a local goalie that set an NCAA record. The great thing about sports statistics is that they are tangible and finite, even when they are as unbelievable as these stats.

22. Rudy Baez Goes on a Roll. Jockey Rudy Baez rode seven winners at Rockingham Park on the same day (September 27, 1991) on his way to compiling a record 413 wins at the same track in a single year.

21. Rick Miller in a Pinch. During the 1983 season, the Red Sox outfielder went 16-35 (.457) as a pinch hitter.

20. Todd Day's Day. The backup guard averaged 12 points per game for the Celtics in the 1995-96 season. However, on December 22, 1995, the streaky shooter poured in 41 points, including a team-record 24 points in one quarter.

19. The Bruins 20-11 Club. In the 1977-78 season, the Bruins had 11 players score at least 20 goals: Peter McNab (41 goals); Terry O'Reilly (29); Bobby Schmautz (27); Stan Jonathan (27); John Ratelle (25); Rick Middleton (25); Wayne Cashman (24); Greg Sheppard (23); Brad Park (22); Don Marcotte (20); and Bobby Miller (20).

18. Ted Cox Starts With Six. As a Red Sox rookie in 1977, Ted Cox started his career with six hits in his first six at-bats.

17. Wade Boggs on Base. Over a five-year period from 1985 to 1989, Boggs averaged 321 walks and hits per season.

16. Nick Buoniconti Interceptions. In Buoniconti's 91 games with the Patriots, the future Dolphin grabbed 24 interceptions—from the linebacker position.

15. Luis Tiant's Pitch Count. In the 1975 World Series, "El Tiante" threw 368 pitches in 11 days, including 158 in Game 5.

14. Ted Williams on Base. In 1949 at the age of 30, Ted Williams got on base 358 times through 194 hits, 162 walks and twice getting hit by a pitch.

13. Dick Greenlaw Saves. On December 14, 1955, RPI goalie and Melrose High School graduate Dick Greenlaw saved an NCAA record 78 of Boston University's 87 shots at the Boston Arena. Sports anchor Don Gillis would later say, "Greenlaw saw more rubber than the Mass Turnpike." Led by forward Jackie Parker, BU would take 128 shots in all on way to a 9-0 victory.

12. Nomar Before and After the *Sports Illustrated* Cover. Before showing off his shirtless, ripped body on the March 5, 2001 *SI* cover, the Red Sox short-stop played in 142 games per season with a .333 batting average. After the cover, Nomar appeared in just 93 games per season with a .297 average.

11. Steve Grogan "Running Back." In 1976, the Patriots quarterback ran for 12 touchdowns in the last 13 games of the season.

10. Phil Esposito Shots. During the 1970-71 season, Espo took 550 shots in 78 games, averaging 7.05 shots per contest for the Bruins.

9. Robbie Ftorek Scoring. In Ftorek's senior season at Needham High School, the hockey great scored 54 goals and added 64 assists in a 23-game season.

8. Tom Jackson Reports. "They (the Patriots) hate their coach (Bill Belichick)." The ESPN commentator made the aforementioned remark after New England's opening game in 2003. Since Jackson's report, the Pats have com-piled a 101-26 regular-season record (.795) and won two more Super Bowls under their "hated" head coach.

7. Ted Williams' Triples. "The Splendid Splinter" had more career triples than did speedster Rickey Henderson (71 to 66), despite playing in almost 800 less games.

6. "Quarterback" Andy Johnson. In 1981, Patriots running back Andy Johnson threw the ball nine times for seven completions and four touch-downs, compiling a quarterback rating of 118.7.

5. The Monster vs. The Mick. In Mickey Mantle's prolific career, he stuck out 12 times in 16 at-bats against Red Sox reliever Dick Radatz.

4. Bobby Orr Plus. In the 1970-71 season, Bobby Orr recorded a plus/minus of +124.

3. Jim Rice and Triples. In 1978, Jim Rice had 13 triples before the All-Star break for the Red Sox.

2. Tight End Mike Vrabel. While with the Patriots, the linebacker and part-time tight end caught 10 passes, all for touchdowns.

1. Bill Russell's Rebounding. On February 5, 1960, Bill Russell grabbed 51 rebounds against the Syracuse Nationals. In his career, he collected 40 or more rebounds in a game 11 times.

These were the best of times and the worst of times. Over the years, there have been many examples of great play confirmed by the statistics. There have also been plenty of examples of incompetence and bottom-line bad play that have been validated by numbers. The below list is representative of play that was unsatisfactory.

13. Anemic at Fenway (2001). Utility infielder Craig Grebeck might have looked like Kelly Leak from *The Bad News Bears*, but he didn't hit like him. In 43 plate appearances for the Red Sox, Grebeck had just TWO hits for a .049 average.

12. Not Worth the Ride. In 1,026 at-bats as a Red Sox catcher, Doug Mirabelli had zero triples and cost the Red Sox the money needed to have a State Trooper escort him to Fenway.

11. Name in Record Book. Tim Wakefield has done a lot of good things in Boston, but he is also the Red Sox leader in home runs allowed (376), walks allowed (1,048), hits allowed (2,768), earned runs allowed (1,392), wild pitches (110), hit batters (168) and losses (160).

10. Sam "Bam" Puts Pats in a Jam. From 1973 to 1977, New England running back Sam "Bam" Cunningham fumbled 39 times in 62 games.

9. Bone Chips or Not, Still Bad (1978). Butch Hobson played for Bear Bryant at Alabama and was tough. However, stats are stats. Even allowing for his elbow woes in the 1978 season, Hobson committed 43 errors in 133 games (.899 fielding percentage).

8. Just a Little Bit Outside (1997-2006). Bruins defenseman Hal Gill had a 2.6 shooting percentage for Boston, scoring 20 goals on 780 shots during his eight seasons with Boston.

7. The Wiggle and The Truth Turning it Over (2000-01). In just one season, Antoine Walker and Paul Pierce combined for 563 turnovers, or an average of 6.92 per game.

6. A Swing and a Miss (2004-05). In just over a season, Red Sox second baseman Mark Bellhorn struck out 286 times in 806 at-bats, or once every 2.8 at-bats.

5. O-fer for Aparicio (May 19 to June 1, 1971). Red Sox shortstop Luis Aparicio set a major league record as a positional player by going hitless in 44 straight at-bats in 1971. During the stretch, Aparicio's batting average dropped from .206 to .154.

4. O-fer America (1985-2011). U.S. runners have not won a Boston Marathon in over a quarter-century. Zero. American athletes have gravitated to more "appealing" sports while African runners have come to Boston motivated and have left with a wreath and money.

3. No Golden Glove for Matt Young (1992). In the 1992 season, you needed an "E" ticket for the Matt Young roller coaster. Every time the Sox pitcher touched a batted ball, it was an adventure. On the year, Young had eight assists and six errors for a .625 fielding percentage.

2. Joe Kapp Off-Target (1970). The Super Bowl quarterback came over to the Patriots from the Minnesota Vikings and was anything but super. In 10 starts, the Pats registered a 1-9 record while Kapp's touchdown-to-interception ratio was 0.17 (4 TDs/17 INTs).

1. 6-4-3 for Jim Ed Rice (1982-85). In a four-year span, the Red Sox power hitter came to the plate in a force-out situation 925 times and hit into 131 double plays (14.1 percent). He hit into more double plays than anyone else in the league all four years. He also holds the distinction of hitting into the most and second-most double plays in a season (36 and 35) in baseball history.

Eccentrics, hot heads and maniacs? The Boston sports world has been littered with them. Whether acting out on the field, in the locker room, in their homes or at some nightclub, these combustible competitors provided us with plenty to talk about.

Honorable Mentions. Terry Glenn; Ricky Davis; Duane Thomas; John Burkett; Rasheed Wallace; Monty Beisel; Blaine Lacher; Jimmy Piersall; Marty McSorley; Keith "Burger King" Foulke.

11. Terry O'Reilly. Nicknamed "The Taz" after the Tasmanian Devil, O'Reilly played hockey with such emotion that sometimes the line between fury and playing physical got blurred. With the Bruins on the verge of being eliminated by the Quebec Nordiques in April of 1982, referee Andy Van Hellemond was breaking up an altercation when O'Reilly reacted by slapping the official across the face. The rugged right winger would be suspended at the beginning of the following season for 10 games for his hot-tempered conduct.

10. Sidney Wicks and 9. Curtis Rowe. The two talented forwards came to the Boston Celtics in 1976 at a low point in the franchise's history and added to the me-first culture that was suffocating the shamrock on the front of the Celtics shirt. Ultimately, the two UCLA products would be sent on their way, but not before establishing a legacy of selfish play and boorish behavior.

8. Corey Dillon. Despite a rap sheet as long as a first-down chain, the running back was fairly tame in New England as long as you didn't go over to his locker.

7. Wil Cordero. In June of 1997, the Red Sox infielder was charged with hitting his wife with a phone, trying to choke her and threatening her life. The fans at Fenway let him know he was no longer welcome in our community. Following the 1997 season, he was released.

6. Manny Ramirez. Whether he was urinating inside the Green Monster, throwing traveling secretaries to the ground, mourning the loss of yet another grandmother or testing positive for a banned substance, the brilliant hitter was unpredictable, unreliable and undependable. In other words, he was "Manny being Manny."

5. Byung-Hyun Kim. Known for giving up leads late in games (see Scott Brosius and Derek Jeter in 2001), BK also could stir it up with the fans. This ability manifested itself when the side-winding righty didn't take kindly to the Fenway crowd's disdain during the 2003 playoffs and showed them his displeasure by flipping Red Sox Nation the bird. The next time he was introduced to the Red Sox crowd, he wore socks on his hands to prevent another demonstration.

4. Marvin Barnes. The gifted power forward brought his ABA ways to the Celtics in the late 1970s. Everybody liked Marvin and all agreed that his talent was limitless. Unfortunately, when you get a guy with the nickname "Bad News," you know there is going to be baggage. Marvin loved basketball, but not as much as partying, which he did at an All-Star level in hotels, bars airports and even on the Celtics bench.

3. Carl Everett. You know you're a ticking time bomb when you get thrown out of Red Sox Family Day in consecutive seasons. Head-butting umpires, yelling at reporters with curly hair and displaying your basic psycho behavior is enough to make this list.

2. Wade Boggs. He could hit and get on base and will himself invisible and serve as a speed bump for his wife and woo Margo on the road and drink beers at prolific levels. Now I know why he ate all of that chicken.

1. Irving Fryar. The Patriots got the wide receiver from Nebraska with the first overall pick in the 1984 draft. In the ensuing years, he caught passes, returned punts and found mischief. Some of his trouble was harmless, while some of it caused serious problems. At halftime of a home game, he sped off in his car and crashed into a tree. While gallivanting with fellow Patriots wide receiver Hart Lee Dykes in Providence, he got into a fight with other bar patrons—a dispute that involved guns, jail and blood. However, no event demonstrated how Fryar's game suffered due to his misbehavior more than the 1986 Super Bowl, in which Fryar played with a severed tendon in his finger reportedly caused by the wrath of his knife-wielding wife.

The 11 Things I'll Never Understand About Boston Sports :: AG

I'd like to think that I get sports—period. I've worked in Providence, New York and for two national radio outlets—ESPN and Sirius/XM. Yet there are some things about our lovely New England and, more importantly, the city of Boston and its fans, I'll never understand. The following things perplex me the most.

11. Fans Hating on Grady Little. Yes, he left Pedro Martinez on the mound with a 5-2 lead in the eighth inning of Game 7 of the 2003 ALCS—when many fans said Pedro was shot. Yes, Pedro and the Sox promptly lost the lead and the game—and Grady got fired over it. But to me, the manager did the right thing—you ride your stud. Sox fans will ALWAYS disagree.

10. Use of the Phrase "Old-Time Hockey" by Bruins Fans. This is the smartest hockey fanbase in the country, yet there is this obsession here with doing things the way Espo, Orr and Middleton did, and that just doesn't work in today's NHL. The game's rule changes effectively retired "old-time hockey." The players of 2011 are bigger, stronger, faster and less physical. You may still see an element of OTH here or there, but its heyday is long gone. So let's stop calling sports radio shows wishing it would come back.

9. Thinking That Someone Is a "Good Guy" Just Because He Plays Hard. One name—Nomar Garciaparra. He played hard, played well and was considered by the fans to be a "good guy." The media knew differently. Nomar was an a-hole to 90 percent of the media and wasn't "Mr. Popular" in the clubhouse. But when he was traded, fans called sports radio shows to say, "You don't do this to a good guy." In the end, fans learned that he was an emperor with no clothes.

8. When There's a Coaching or Managing Opening, Fans Lobby for Former Star Players or Broadcasters with No Coaching Experience. When the Red Sox needed a manager in 2004, I got a ton of calls about how NESN analyst Jerry Remy should get the job. No experience, not a coach, just give him the job cause he says good things on the air. Or if the Pats need a QB coach, it's "Cawlll Grogan. Stevie Grogan would be great." UGH . . . drives me nuts. Just because they could play it or describe it, doesn't mean they'd make the com-mitment to coach it.

7. Pink Hat Fans. These are people who go to the games because it's cool to do so. The people who bum tickets from a friend so they can be seen at the game and be "kind of" interested in who wins. These are the people who just want a cool Facebook status for three days. And this isn't exclusive to just ladies.

6. Pink Hats Who Don't Think They're Pink Hats. Sorry, my sweetheart of a wife, but you qualify (and thank God she has now accepted this because of me). It doesn't mean that she loves sports any less . . . BUT when you ask questions like, "Who's the guy who coached for Green Bay and he has a funny last name. He coached with that guy who you're friends with. C'mon you know who he is?" Or refers to the down-and-distance marker in football as the "upside-down exclamation point" and wants to know how she can get that job . . . she is a Pink Hat. Somewhere in this, there's a new line of jokes for Jeff Foxworthy.

5. Fans Kicking Superstar Players in the Nads on Their Way Out of Town. Very few, and I mean very few, athletes leave Boston with dignity. You come in with all the fanfare and hope, and after giving it your all, you get crapped on when it's time to go. Sit down and think how many times you've cursed someone you once cheered and ask, "Was it justified?"

4. When Guys Leave the Red Sox, There Always Seems to be a Smear Campaign. I think this is where some fans learned the behavior described above. It can't just be that a player wants to go elsewhere because of money or because the Sox don't want to re-sign him. There has to be some dastardly motive to everything, along with his declining skills or warts. I believe this all stems from people not wanting to be the bad guy, and in the end, the player and the organization come out looking bad. The ugly divorce rate in sports here is almost 100 percent.

3. Big Free Agents Are Saviors. And that leads to unfair expectations. Take John Lackey, for example. In 2010 for the Red Sox, he had, for the most part, a Lackey-type year. But he was THE free-agent signing in the offseason for the Sox and we all saw $18 million next to his name. So a 14-11 record with a 4.40 ERA didn't cut it. He was himself, as in what he's always been. But because he was showered with money and praise, he was crushed in the off-season and labeled a disappointment. Players don't magically get better just because they get paid more money.

2. The Celebrity Fans Who Crawl Out From Under Rocks for Big Games. Donnie Wahlberg aside, I don't think I've run into one "celebrity fan" who knows what they're talking about. But dammit, when they can pull rank and sit courtside to mug for the cameras, those Brady and KG jerseys look good on them. Spike Lee may be a douche, but the guy shows up for Knicks vs. Clippers games just like he does for Lakers games.

1. "Sweet Caroline." The song, that song, that @#$%ing song. I swear people don't even know all the words to this Neil Diamond hit. But for some reason, it gets the royal treatment during every major sporting event. Is singing "SOO GOOD, SOO GOOD, SOO GOOD" that fun? Throw in "Tessie" by the Dropkick Murphys and "Dirty Water" by the Standells and you have the makings of a cocktail that would cause me to jump off the Tobin Bridge. Instead of waterboarding, if the military made people listen to these songs on a loop, we would have found Bin Laden much sooner.

These seven athletes and one coach were billed as franchise changers, but fell way, way, way short of those expectations.

8. Jim Plunkett. The Patriots made the Heisman Trophy winner the first overall pick in the 1971 NFL draft, but got very little in return for their investment besides interceptions and losses. From 1971-75, Plunkett threw 62 TDs and 87 INTs as the Pats went 24-46 during his tenure. He ended up winning two Super Bowls with the Oakland Raiders.

7. Joe Thornton. Maybe some will feel I'm being too tough on "Jumbo Joe," as he did have a few good postseasons and became an MVP after being traded to San Jose in 2005. But he never became the leader Bruins fans wanted after the club made him the top overall pick in the 1997 NHL Draft. The biggest problem with Thornton is that former GM Mike O'Connell got a bunch of slapdicks in return for the guy. But O'Connell was never positioned as a savior, so I couldn't put him on this list.

6. Len Bias. Picked by the Celtics second overall in the 1986 NBA Draft, Bias never even played in the NBA because he died of a cocaine overdose two days after the draft. He and Larry Bird were supposed to win us more NBA titles, but the brilliant efforts of Red Auerbach to gain the high pick went for nothing. Pot is okay by me, coke isn't.

5. Adalius Thomas. Signed by the Patriots out of free agency in 2007, Thomas did help the Pats to a perfect regular season. But his play slipped after that and he and Bill Belichick couldn't get along, so he was released before the 2010 season. I will always remember in 2009 how he and three others were late for meetings because of a snowstorm. For all the money the Pats ponied up to sign Thomas, he should've gotten himself a driver. And when the Pats finally hired one for him, they told him to drive Thomas right out of town.

4. Kenneth Sims. The first overall pick in the 1982 NFL Draft only played one full 16-game season in his career with the Pats. Known as "Game Day" because he didn't like to practice, the defensive end also didn't like sacking quarterbacks and earning his money. He was released after the 1989 season and was busted for coke. Not the kind you drink . . . and that tub of goo drank a lot of it.

3. Gord Kluzak. The first name called in a 1982 NHL Draft that featured Phil Housley, Scott Stevens and Dave Andreychuk, ol' Gord comes up a bit short, playing the fewest games of any top overall draft pick in NHL history.

2. Jose Offerman. Signed by the Red Sox in 1999, Offerman was viewed as GM Dan Duquette's solution for losing Mo Vaughn to Anaheim. We all knew it wouldn't work and it didn't. Offerman was an All-Star in 1999, but proved better at hitting people than baseballs after that. He hit a guy with a bat in a 2007 independent league game and beat the crap out of an umpire in a 2009 Dominican league game he was managing. If he'd played with that fire in Boston, maybe Duquette would've been right.

1. Rick Pitino. He walked through that door in 1997 and was out by the middle of 2001 after amassing a sterling 102-146 record with the Celtics. He will be remembered for his great rant about "how all the negativity in this town sucks." We wouldn't have been negative if you had just ONE, ONE winning season, Rick. And to boot, he had Red Auerbach removed as team president . . . ego runneth over.

The Top Five Reasons Why Soccer Doesn't Suck :: by Taylor Twellman

Note: The second overall pick in the 2002 Major League Soccer draft, Taylor Twellman scored over 100 goals for the New England Revolution and made 29 appearances for the U.S. national team. After concussions forced him to retire following the 2010 season, Taylor made a quick transition into TV broadcasting. Here he lists the most compelling reasons for you to start watching more soccer.

5. The Games Are 90 Minutes of Nonstop Action with No Commercials. As a fan, you can drink with no shutoff, unlike a seventh-inning cutoff in baseball or the middle of the second period at a hockey game. And with nonstop action, the kids will not get bored.

4. The World Championships Are Held Every Four Years. Every national team in the world has a chance to qualify, which is why the world loves soccer—it's not exclusionary. Think of it as a worldwide NCAA March Madness Tournament.

3. Hottest Athletes in the World. And we play with uniforms that show off our bodies. Short shorts. Tight shirts. And no jocks!!

2. It's Affordable. MLS teams now have their own soccer-friendly facilities and you can take a family of four to a game with all the niceties for under $200, if not less. And teams that don't play in soccer-only buildings play in NFL-type stadiums. Not bad.

1. The Rest of the World Plays It. Can that many people be wrong? It's a sport that we Americans don't dominate, so for some in the U.S., it doesn't matter. But that "should" make it more appealing.

Top Five Reasons Why Soccer Sucks :: AG

Taylor decided to tell us why soccer's cool. So I will tell him why he's wrong.

5. The Games Are Soooooooooooo Boooooorring. I'd rather sit through a class on 18th-century existential imperialism. Not enough action other than a bunch of dudes running around who may or may not speak English.

4. My Wife Thinks Soccer Players Are Hot. I already have enough to contend with in this world; I don't need her ogling and fantasizing about men she can't have. And on this issue, I think I speak for the entire male species.

3. What the Hell is a Red Card and a Yellow Card? I don't know what this means. When do they give a red or yellow? And what's the difference? What are fouls and what aren't? They should explain this during games so us normal sports fans can understand. Like FOX *tried* to do when they broadcast the NHL.

2. America Doesn't Care, So Why Should I? We have the NFL, NBA, NHL, MLB, PGA, NASCAR and others. Why would I watch something that is way less exciting than those sports? And I don't give a damn if some kid in Angola plays it on some piece of land over there. I'm never going there and just don't care.

1. The World Cup. Very simply, if the sport was so popular, they'd hold the World Cup every year. But FIFA is smart enough to not water down the product so people don't lose interest, 'cause even they know, it's not that interesting.

Top 10 Reasons Why NASCAR Doesn't Suck (That Bad) :: AG

My wife Betsey and her oldest, Connor, are huge NASCAR fans. You wouldn't think NASCAR was a big New England thing 'till the circuit comes to Loudon, New Hampshire and the joint is jammed. When we met in 2009, I didn't understand why they liked it the way they did. Then I went to two NASCAR races in 2010 and the Daytona 500 in 2011 and learned a lot about the sport that could endear it to those who open their minds—like I was forced to do because of a hot blonde.

10. Booze, Booze and Boos. You get to bring alcohol to the races. As in, you can bring in a cooler of hooch, beer, moonshine or whatever you fashion in tying one on. And, as I've found out, the races are so long, you need all you can gather. I also didn't know that there are a lot of NASCAR fans who hate some of the more successful drivers. The fans are as passionate and loyal as any fans I've seen. They boo during driver introductions, just like fans at any other pro event.

9. Joe Gibbs Owns Multiple Teams. He coached the Redskins in the NFL, so the team concept is right in his wheelhouse. I was shocked to learn that the "team" is important and it's paramount to winning a race. And Kyle Busch is a Gibbs driver. He'd be a great pro wrestling villain.

8. Lots of "Different" People. If you're a people watcher, then this sport is for you. Check out 80-year-old ladies screaming obscenities at the top of their lungs, hillbillies with vulgar tattoos, the prototypical fat guy sweating while drinking his moose juice then taking off his shirt to expose the "3" shaved into his hairy back. I was at a race where a guy was throwing jello shots to people in the stands. He then got into a fight and was pummeled by some young whipper snapper. Teriffic! Better people watching than the airport or local mall.

7. A Surprising Amount of HOT Chicks. You'd be shocked. Thank God one of the selling points to get me to go was my wife telling me that there'd be a lot of eye candy. And of course, I didn't believe her. But I saw bikinis, tank tops, Daisy Duke shorts and lots of fake boobs. It's a Gresh guarantee that wherever you sit at a NASCAR race, you will be ogling some hottie nearby. Just like my wife does.

6. The Venues. I've come to learn that every racetrack is different and cool. Like going to different NFL or college stadiums. The speedway in New Hampshire is different from Dover, which is different from Daytona. The racers may be driving an oval, but the ambiance and feel is each unto its own.

5. Food. And don't roll your eyes because I'm larger than the average bear. We're talking BBQ, sausages, beer, funnel cakes, gin, whiskey, steaks. You name it, they'll probably have it. And by major sports standards, it's fairly priced.

4. The Technology. We all want to know what's going on behind the scenes at any sporting event. If we could listen to NFL coaches on their headsets, we all would. Well, in NASCAR, you can listen to the crew chiefs interact with their drivers. And it's uncensored! You rent these TV/Walkie Talkie units and listen in. Which is why you see fans wearing headsets in the stands. Best 50 bucks you'll ever spend.

3. Driver Rivalries. There are always guys who have scores to settle with someone out on the track. From people just hating on the success of Jimmie Johnson, to Brad Keselowski and Kyle Busch almost killing each other last year, someone is always pissed at someone else. And when they race side by side at 180-200 miles per hour, you're just waiting for the inevitable.

2. Cheating Death. Maybe some will actually find this too cerebral, but wrecking doesn't do it for me. It's seeing if the guy inside can walk away. Lots of folks like wrecks . . . few take the time to notice that the drivers usually hit a wall at 125 mph and get out of the car and cuss someone out. I like the wrecks, just for a different reason.

1. Driver Accessibility. From the merchandise trucks, to walking around pit road right before a race, to signing a million autographs, NASCAR drivers do what all pro athletes should do. They realize that the fans pay their salaries and so they treat them with respect. And NASCAR itself almost requires them to do it. Now I do realize that if the driver is popular and is cool, he'll move more merchandise. But most of these drivers are pretty down to earth and way cool. Major League Baseball could learn something from these cats.

When compiling this list, I had to make sure that I included some guys who weren't Yankees. That was hard. I had to workshop this list with some colleagues because the Red Sox-Yankees rivalry makes you forget that there are other hated players in MLB.

10. Dave "Smoke" Stewart. This Oakland A's and Toronto Blue Jays pitcher just owned the Red Sox. His intensity made him very unlikeable, and so did his success. He was 3-0 against the Sox in the postseason with an ERA under 1.40. And against Roger Clemens, it was a smoke show. The guy lived up to his nickname.

9. Billy Martin. First off, he's a Yankee, so he's automatically got two strikes against him. But there's so much more. In 1952, he and Red Sox outfielder Jimmy Piersall got into a fist fight before a game and you can take it from there. He was manager of the Yanks for much of the late 1970s and early 1980s when they were battling the Sox for AL East supremacy. The only good thing about Billy was that he was such a hothead, when he pulled Reggie Jackson out of a game in June of 1977, he and Reggie almost came to blows in the dugout.

8. Darryl Strawberry. He was a part of the 1986 Mets team that won the World Series against the Red Sox, but some forget that he was also a member of the Yankees in 1996 and during his injury-plagued seasons of 1997, '98 and '99. In 1999, he hit a big home run in Fenway to help the Yankees beat the Red Sox in the ALCS on their way to a world championship. Everyone loved chanting "DARRYLLL, DARRYLL." But when he wasn't coked up, the guy had Hall of Fame talent.

7. Reggie Jackson. "Mr. October" was also "Mr. Red Sox Killer" pretty much every month of the season. In the 1975 ALCS (which the Sox won, by the way), he hit .417 for Oakland. But it was the big plays and consistent performances vs. the Sox that also made you want him on your team. Like his homer off Reggie Cleveland in the bottom of the ninth inning in September of 1977 that ultimately set the Yanks apart from the Sox and the Baltimore Orioles to win the division. The Yanks won the World Series that year and he's been quoted as saying that was the most memorable home run of his career. And, of course, he was right in the middle of the "Boston Massacre" in 1978.

6. Albert Belle. The Cleveland Indians, Chicago White Sox and Baltimore Orioles slugger always found a way to get big hits against the Red Sox. In

1995, Sox first baseman Mo Vaughn won the MVP award because the media didn't like Belle. But in Game 1 of that season's ALDS, Belle hit a big home run that prompted then-Sox Manager Kevin Kennedy to ask the umps to check his bat for cork. Belle then flexed his bicep at Kennedy from the dugout while mouthing, "There's your fucking cork." Albert was a first-class asshole, and that's probably disrespectful to first-class assholes.

5. George Bell. The Toronto Blue Jays big bopper drew Boston's ire, in part, because in his heyday he was one of the best hitters in the game. Some will remember his 1993 brawl with Aaron Sele in which Mo Vaughn knocked him on his rear end. In his day, Bell was one of the most feared hitters in baseball. And he was guaranteed to get booed at Fenway every game.

4. Roger Clemens. I could probably do just a list on him alone. There's his spring training walkout in 1987 over his contract. His 1990 playoff failure. The way he left in free agency, telling everyone he wanted to get closer to his Texas home—then signed with Toronto. And he eventually ended up as a Yankee and pitched well in the postseason to eliminate the goat tag. He's a Hall of Famer, but also a clown and a parody of himself.

3. Aaron Boone. This unlikely Yankee hero sent the Red Sox home in 2003 when the Sox were one run away from the World Series. His 11th-inning homer off Tim Wakefield in Game 7 of the ALCS made a whole region question their sanity and faith in humanity. He did very little overall as a Yankee, but his place in Red Sox history was secured that night. He'll never be forgotten. If not for World Series wins in 2004 and 2007, we'd still be hearing about the "Curse of the Boonebino."

2. Alex Rodriguez. He was almost a member of the Red Sox in 2003, but the deal was shot down by the players association because A-Rod was going to reduce his salary and that would have set a bad precedent. He then became a Yankee and went from beloved figure to most hated overnight. Then came the fight in Fenway Park on July 24, 2004, when he brawled with Sox catcher Jason Varitek. Later that year in the ALCS, A-Rod swiped at Bronson Arroyo while the Sox pitcher was trying to tag him at first base. The play was ruled interference and he was crucified in Boston and will be as long as he's a Yankee.

1. Bucky Dent. The home run he hit in the 1978 American League Eastern Division playoff game at Fenway gave the Yanks a 3-2 lead in a game that they'd go on to win, 5-4. The guy hit only 40 home runs in the big leagues, but one of them ripped out the hearts of Red Sox fans, earning Bucky Dent the nickname of the mother-of-all swear words. That makes him No. 1 automatically.

Over the history of Boston sports, our players have been the authors of many great moments. However, there have been times when opposing players also produced great performances. The below list recognizes the best of them.

Honorable Mentions. Michael Vick torches Boston College; Wilt Chamberlain grabs 55 rebounds in a game against the Celtics; LeBron scores 47 points in Game 7 vs. Boston in 2008.

16. Mark McGwire vs. Red Sox (June 10-11, 1995). In a two-game stretch at Fenway Park, Oakland Athletic Mark McGwire hit five home runs. His Red Sox victims: Erik Hanson, Stan Belinda, Zane Smith, Zane Smith and Zane Smith.

15. Acie Earl vs. Celtics (April 12, 1996). A 1993 first-round pick by Boston, Acie Earl managed only a career high of 15 points in his two seasons with the Celtics. In 1995, the Toronto Raptors picked him up in the expansion draft. As a Raptor, he returned to Boston and put a Raptor single-game record of 40 points on the Celtics.

14. Sammy Baugh and Dan Sandifer vs. Boston Yanks (October 31, 1948). Redskin quarterback Sammy Baugh threw for 446 yards and four touchdowns on 17 of 24 passing in Washington's 59-21 victory. In the same game, Skins defensive back Dan Sandifer had four interceptions, two of which he ran back for touchdowns.

13. O.J. Simpson vs. Patriots (1973). In two games against New England in 1973, O.J. had two standout performances, running for a combined 469 yards and three touchdowns.

12. Mark McGwire in the Fenway Park Home Run Derby (July 12, 1999). Even if the balls were juiced and/or he was juiced, McGwire put on an awesome power display in the All-Star Home Run Derby. His 13 home runs in the first round lit up the Boston sky and sent thousands of fans scavenging on Lansdowne Street for a souvenir.

11. Bernie Parent vs. Bruins (1974 NHL Finals). The Bruins had the best record and were the No. 1 team in the NHL in scoring until they met goalie Bernie Parent and the Flyers. His Stanley Cup-clinching 1-0 shutout still frustrates the Gallery Gods.

10. Joe Washington vs. Patriots (September 18, 1978). In a rain-soaked Monday night game in Foxboro, Colts running back Joe Washington ran for 53 yards, caught two balls for 41 yards and a touchdown, threw a 54-yard touchdown pass and then ran for 112 yards on kickoff returns, including the game-winning return with just over a minute left.

9. Ron Tugnutt vs. Bruins (March 21, 1991). The Quebec Nordiques goalie was virtually impenetrable. In the 3-3 overtime game, Tugnutt saved 70 of the 73 Bruin shots. On the night, Boston outshot the Nordiques almost three-to-one. With eight seconds left in overtime, Tugnutt stoned a Ray Bourque 20-foot slap shot with an amazing glove save. Bruins announcer Fred Cusick yelled, "He saved the best for last!" At the end of the game, the Boston Garden crowd stood in admiration and Cam Neely prodded the opposing goalie to take a bow.

8. Darryl Sittler vs. Bruins (February 7, 1976). Up in Toronto, the Maple Leaf center had six goals and four assists in a single game against Boston. Bruins rookie goalie Dave Reece was victimized for all 10 points.

7. Elgin Baylor vs. Celtics (April 14, 1962). The Los Angeles Laker scored 61 points in Game 5 of the NBA Finals. Despite Baylor's unstoppable performance, the Celtics would go on to win the series in seven games.

6. Joe DiMaggio vs. Red Sox (June 28-30, 1949). When "Joltin' Joe" came to Fenway Park in late June of 1949, he was still suffering from bone spurs that had prevented him from playing in a game that season. Unfortunately for the Red Sox, DiMaggio played in this series. He led the Yankees to a three-game sweep of the Red Sox with four home runs and nine RBI. The Fenway crowd gave him a standing ovation.

5. Dominique Wilkins vs. Celtics (May 22, 1988). In the greatest duel in Boston Garden history, Dominique and Larry Bird staged a prolific shootout in Game 7 of the Hawks-Celtics playoff series. Dominique scored 47 points. However, the Celtics would win the game, 118-116, on Larry Bird's 34 points—20 of them coming in the fourth quarter.

4. Jerry West vs. Celtics (1969 NBA Finals). In the 1969 Finals, Jerry West averaged 37.9 points against Boston. This included an NBA classic performance of 42 points, 13 rebounds and 12 assists in a losing effort in Game 7. At the conclusion of the series, West was named NBA Finals MVP, the only time that a member of a losing team was so recognized.

3. Nolan Ryan vs. Red Sox (1974). In three games against the Red Sox in 1974, Nolan Ryan struck out 53 batters (15/19/19). In the second of the three games, played on June 14, Ryan pitched 13 innings and threw 235 pitches (Boston pitcher Luis Tiant was the losing pitcher after throwing 14.1 innings).

2. Ken Dryden vs. Bruins (1971 NHL Playoffs). The Bruins had the best record in the NHL at 57-14-7, while scoring 108 more goals than any other team. But in the quarterfinals of the playoffs, rookie goalie Ken Dryden shut down the Big Bad Bruins in seven games. The upstart Canadiens went on to win the Stanley Cup and Dryden was named the MVP of the playoffs.

1. Michael Jordan vs. Celtics (April 20, 1986). In a Boston Garden classic, the second-year Chicago Bull scored 63 points against the Celtics in Game 2 of the 1986 NBA Divisional Playoffs. Jordan shot 22 for 41 from the field and 19 for 21 from the foul line. The Celtics won the game in overtime, 135-131, on the way to the championship. But Jordan was the story on this night.

Best Quotes in Boston Sports History
:: by Dan Shaughnessy

Note: Dan Shaughnessy has written about area sports for over 20 years for the *Boston Globe*. The Groton, Massachusetts native graduated from Holy Cross before launching a sports writing career that's seen his work featured in national publications like *ESPN The Magazine*. He appears on regional and national radio and TV shows, such as *Pardon the Interruption* and *Rome Is Burning*. Shaughnessy has contributed to and authored a number of books, including *The Curse of the Bambino* and *Reversing the Curse*. During all his years as a sports journalist, he's heard a lot of great quotes from players, coaches, broadcasters, fans and front office people. Here are his favorites, in no particular order.

9. Red Sox Pitcher Pedro Martinez: "The Yankees are my daddy." This came after a loss to the Yankees in 2004 when they hit him around pretty hard. Everytime Pedro pitched in Ruth's house, regardless of uniform, Yankee fans reminded him of those comments by chanting, "Who's your daddy." He plays it off well, but I think he wishes he never uttered those words.

8. Red Sox Pitcher Curt Schilling: "I guess I hate the Yankees now." Schill uttered this prior to the 2004 season when he was traded to the Red Sox from the Arizona Diamondbacks.

7. Patriots Head Coach Bill Parcells: "If they're gonna let you cook the dinner, they oughta let you shop for some of the groceries." This was the classic line from Parcells in his farewell press conference after having many backroom disagreements with Patriots owner Robert Kraft. Bill was a total control guy and he didn't have it in New England. So he left. But he left the organization in a better place. As he always does. I think if Kraft had it to do over again, things may have ended up differently.

6. Celtics Head Coach Rick Pitino: "Larry Bird's not walking through that door." After a March 1, 2000 loss to Toronto, Pitino laid into the media, which had been on him for not winning enough. This is the full quote and is the definition by which the Pitino era is remembered:

> "Larry Bird is not walking through that door, fans. Kevin McHale is not walking through that door, and Robert Parish is

not walking through that door. And if you expect them to walk through that door, they're going to be gray and old. What we are is young, exciting, hardworking and we're going to improve. People don't realize that, and as soon as they realize those three guys are not coming through that door, the better this town will be for all of us because there are young guys in that [locker] room playing their asses off. I wish we had $90 million under the salary cap. I wish we could buy the world. We can't; the only thing we can do is work hard, and all the negativity that's in this town sucks. I've been around when Jim Rice was booed. I've been around when Yastrzemski was booed. And it stinks. It makes the greatest town, greatest city in the world, lousy. The only thing that will turn this around is being upbeat and positive like we are in that locker room...and if you think I'm going to succumb to negativity, you're wrong. You've got the wrong guy leading this team."

5. Red Sox General Manager Lou Gorman: "The sun will rise. The sun will set. And tomorrow I'll eat lunch." A great line from Lou Gorman when in 1987 Roger Clemens walked out of camp in a contract dispute. Clemens was a prima donna but he could deliver the goods. Few dealt with Clemens' antics with the humor that Gorman did.

4. Celtics Forward Larry Bird: "Moses does eat shit." During the 1981 NBA Finals, Houston center Moses Malone said he pooped on the Celts in the press. And that he could go back to his hometown of Petersburg, Virginia and get four guys and beat Bird's crew. He couldn't do it with professionals. The Celts, behind Bird, won Games 5 and 6 to wrap up the series. When a fan held a sign during the 1981 championship rally that said "Moses does eat shit" Bird laughed and acknowledged that fan in the crowd.

3. Celtics Broadcaster Johnny Most: "Havlicek stole the ball!" This famous call was made by the legendary Celtics play-by-play man at the end of Game 7 of the Eastern Division Finals. Johnny Most had a lot of great calls in his time, but this was his best.

2. Celtics General Manager Red Auerbach: "Am I supposed to win here, or take care of local yokels?" Red's response when asked why he passed on Bob Cousy in the draft. Instead of Coos, he took 6-11 Charlie Share. Cousy became a Celtic when his Chicago Stags team folded and he was acquired in a dispersal draft. He didn't hold the "local yokel" line against Red and the rest is history.

1. Red Sox Pitcher Roger Clemens: "We have to carry our own luggage." When asked about how it felt losing Bruce Hurst to San Diego to free agency in 1988, he complained about team management and uttered this line to defend how bad things were in Boston. It's like the broke woman complaining how she's not getting as much money from the federal government and that she can't buy cigarettes.

Best Quotes Not Picked by Shaughnessy :: AG

My friend Dan Shaughnessy missed some of my favorite Boston sports quotes in his list above. Here are a few more of the most memorable mutterings from our town's sports scene, listed in no particular order.

Red Sox OF Carl Everett about Dan Shaughnessy: "You and your curly haired boyfriend." When Everett said that dinosaur fossils were manmade fakes, Shaughnessy dubbed him "Jurassic Carl." So Carl fired back to then *Boston Globe* beat writer Gordon Edes, in a tirade in the Red Sox clubhouse, the line in question. He then said, "Bye, bye, bye. All you *Globe* motherfuckers get out of here." Good times with Carl and friends. This is one of the many reasons I love Dan.

Pats coach Bill Parcells to an unnamed QB (overheard by my radio partner Scott Zolak): "You couldn't hit a bull in the ass with a fist full of rice." Don't know exactly who Tuna uttered this to or where the colorful phrase came from, but it's pretty self explanatory.

University of Rhode Island offensive line coach Jack Peavey to a young OL named Gresh: "Go hit the fucking guy. Stop creeping up to the linebacker like the Hamburgler does to a hamburger." Okay, so I'm taking some creative license here by including a quote that won't matter to pretty much anyone but me—but I think it's funny as hell. There were 10 players in the room at the time—all linemen—and we were watching game film. I wasn't aggressive enough on a draw play that we ran against Boston University, and that line came out. I still laugh when I think of that line, not to mention get hungry.

Bill Belichick to Tom Brady: "Do your job." Tom Terrific told me this was his favorite quote. We're just all glad he did as he was told.

Curt Schilling, replying to a question about the Yankees' mystique and aura: "Those are dancers in a nightclub." One of the rare times Curt made everyone in America laugh.

Everyone has their bucket list, especially when it comes to sports. I've been to five Super Bowls, an NBA Finals, a World Series and the early rounds of an NCAA Tournament. But there's a lot left that I want to do.

11. See Big Fight in Vegas. Just a big fight, regardless of weight class, at a Vegas strip casino. My only problem with it? I'm afraid of getting shot! A few drinks, and people all amped up is a recipe for disaster. I'd have to roll with my brother Steve and my boys Nelson and Charod—three guys who are 6-3 or taller and weigh at least 300 lbs. We'd just have to keep little defensive back Rod's mouth shut.

10. Play Golf at Pebble Beach. I will never forget when Tiger Woods absolutely obliterated the field there in the U.S. Open and that's when I said, "I need to play this course to completely understand the scope of this feat." One of my friends played this course and shot 79. I know I won't do that, but I wanna try.

9. Go to the Pro Bowl in Hawaii. I know no one gives a damn about the game. But c'mon, it's in Hawaii for God's sake. I'm just curious to see how, if at all, it resembles the Super Bowl. And it gives me an excuse to pay $10,000 for a vacation.

8. See a Football Game in Every SEC Stadium. It is the king conference in college football and I've been to a few stadiums in the SEC, plus their title game in Atlanta and it was AWESOME. So I need to see them all.

7. Play Golf at St. Andrews in Scotland. You see it every once in a while on TV for the British Open and hear about its rich history and lineage. I've gotta go play links golf.

6. Go to Tokyo for a Sumo Tournament. I've always wanted to go to Japan and be the biggest person there in my mind. But I'd love to go to the Tokyo Dome and see fat guys push each other around. And if I can also catch a big pro wrestling show there, where they take it way too seriously, it would be perfect.

5. Go to the Final Four. Yes, I've never been. Watching Butler in the 2010 National Championship Game reminded me why the country gets hooked on the NCAA tourney. And I wanna see all three games. Not just the national championship. I'd eat this up.

4. Watch the Super Bowl. IN LAS VEGAS! This is next on my list because it's the most realistic. I love the Super Bowl and I love Las Vegas, so why not combine the two. The prop bets, just the general handicapping and the buzz of it all. Vegas is always happening and I'd love to see how ridiculous it is for the Big Game!!

3. Go to the BCS National Championship Game, But Only at the Rose Bowl. I'm a huge college football fan and have always wanted to see the Rose Bowl, so for me it's a way of combining the two. I've been to all the other BCS sites and for me the Rose Bowl is special. Hopefully for me, Boise State will be in the game I go to so all the asshole purists have their panties in a bunch.

2. Saturday and Sunday at the Masters. For a golf fan like me, there's nothing like it. And surprisingly for me, the snobbery at Augusta National helped create the legend of The Masters. Tournament organizers only allow two commercials an hour during TV coverage, helping make it the biggest event on the PGA Tour.

1. The Kentucky Derby. I can't even count how many people I've lied to over the years in telling them I've been to Churchill Downs. In the old days, winning this or the Indianapolis 500 meant you were a superstar. That's not the case any more with the Indy 500, but the Derby still matters. The thrill, the pageantry, the hats, the booze. That's my Kentucky Derby and I want to soak it all in.

Top 10 Events I've Covered :: by Tony Massarotti

Note: Tony Massarotti has been covering sports in the city of Boston for over 20 years. He did it first for the *Boston Herald,* where he was the Red Sox beat writer, and now does it for the *Boston Globe,* where he is a columnist. He also is co-host of the afternoon drive show on 98.5 The Sports Hub. Tony has covered a lot of sporting events in his time and he was kind enough to rank and share his favorites.

10. Larry Bird's Retirement. For someone who grew up in the 1980s, Bird was an iconic figure. When the call came on the morning of August 18, 1992 that Bird was retiring, time seemed to stop. Bird's best years were well behind him, but the end seemed to have such finality for a young sportswriter who thought he might never cover anything bigger.

9. The 2006 U.S. Open. The first major golf championship I ever covered. Phil Mickelson was on the verge of becoming the No. 1 player in the world when he hit the 18th tee and went *poof*. Geoff Ogilvy goes down in history as the winner, but Mickelson lost it. What a collapse.

8. The 2008 U.S. Open. Playing on one knee, Tiger Woods defeated Rocco Mediate in a playoff. Still, it's here for selfish reasons. One year, I covered the Open in San Diego during the day, then drove to Los Angeles for Games 3, 4 and 5 of the Celtics-Lakers at night. What a week.

7. The 2007-08 Celtics Season. A year after winning a mere 24 games, the Celtics acquired Kevin Garnett and Ray Allen. They went 66-16 during the regular season, then grinded their way through the playoffs before defeating the Lakers in the finals. The crowning achievement for the Golden Age of Boston Sports.

6. Super Bowl XLII. The home teams don't *always* have to win, do they? The Patriots were 18-0. The Giants were huge underdogs. Aside from being one of the most heartbreaking defeats in Boston sports history, it was perhaps the greatest Super Bowl ever played.

5. Roger Clemens' Second 20-Strikeout Game, September 17, 1996. In his final win as a member of the Red Sox, Clemens tied the club record for wins (192) and shutouts (100) while recording his 100th career complete game. At this point, no one else ever had recorded 20 strikeouts in a nine-inning game. Clemens had done it twice.

4. Roger Clemens' Departure From the Red Sox. An event that changed Red Sox history. Before Clemens departed, Red Sox superstars were lifelong members of the organization. Once he left, no one was safe anymore. Part of the Red Sox legacy died when he departed. But the club became better for it.

3. Pedro Martinez Strikes Out 17 at Yankee Stadium, September 10, 1999. The greatest game I've ever seen pitched. Against the dynastic Yankees, Martinez threw two pitches from the stretch. He retired the final 21 batters, 15 by strikeout. Twelve of the final 15 Yankee batters whiffed.

2. The 2003 ALCS. In my mind, you can't have one without the other. They are forever intertwined. Aaron Boone begot Curt Schilling, Keith Foulke and Alex Rodriguez among others. Over the course of the 2003 and 2004 seasons, the Red Sox and Yankees played 52 games: Boston won 27; New York won 25. Each won an ALCS.

1. The 2004 ALCS. More than the World Series victory over the St. Louis Cardinals, it was the defining moment in modern Red Sox history. What a comeback for the Red Sox. What a collapse for the Yankees. What an unimaginable story.

The Nutmeg State is bipolar. Half its residents are crazy New York fans; the rest are loyal, cerebral, charming Boston fans. Somewhere around New Haven, the light side of the moon becomes the dark side of the moon and Yankees hats start popping up. Here are the 13 best things about Connecticut, in no particular order.

13. Best Pizza at Frank Pepe's in New Haven. White Clam Pizza.

12. Two Best Olympians from Connecticut. Bruce Jenner and Dorothy Hamill.

11. Boston College Basketball Guards from Connecticut. Ernie Cobb, John Bagley and Michael Adams all starred for the Eagles at the Heights.

10. Julius Boros. The Fairfield golfer beat Jack Nicklaus and Arnold Palmer at the U.S. Open played at The Country Club in Brookline, Massachusetts in 1963. He won three majors in all.

9. Most Points Scored by a Player in a Game for UConn. Men: Bill Corley poured in 51 points against the University of New Hampshire (January 10, 1968). Women: Nykeshia Sales scored 46 points against Stanford (December, 21, 1997).

8. Connecticut Natives Who Played for the Red Sox. Mo Vaughn (Norwalk), Jimmy Piersall (Waterbury), Kevin Morton (Norwalk), Jeff Bagwell (oh wait a second, he never made it up . . . ugggh), Rico Brogna (Watertown), Walt Dropo (Moosup), Darren Bragg (Waterbury).

7. Best Hartford Whalers. Ron Francis, Sylvain Turgeon, Mike Liut, Kevin Dineen, Pat Verbeek, Geoff Sanderson, Blaine Stoughton.

6. Captain George Bush. Future President George H.W. Bush led Yale to the 1947 College World Series.

5. The Yale Bowl. The football stadium for the Yale Bulldogs was the model for the Big House in Michigan and the Rose Bowl in Pasadena.

4. "Boston Billy" Was From Newington. The greatest marathoner ever, Bill Rodgers, lived in Connecticut and starred for the Wesleyan University track team.

3. National Championships in Basketball. UConn's men's hoops team won the national title in 1999, 2004, and 2011. The women won it in 1995, 2000, 2002, 2003, 2004, 2008, 2009 and 2010.

2. Top Five High School Players from Connecticut (According to Bijan Bayne). Calvin Murphy (Norwalk), Walter Luckett (Kolbe Cathedral), Johnny Egan (Hartford-Weaver), John Williamson (New Haven-Wilbur Cross), Lloyd Hinchey (Norwich Free Academy).

1. Talk About a Winner—Chris Drury. The Trumbull star was the winning pitcher in the 1989 Little League World Series. He won the 1995 NCAA men's ice hockey championship with Boston University and the 1998 Hobey Baker Award as the top NCAA men's ice hockey player. Moving on to the NHL, Drury won the Calder Memorial Trophy as the league's top rookie for the 1998-99 season, then won the Stanley Cup two seasons later with the Colorado Avalanche. On top of all that, Drury has won a pair of silver medals while playing with the U.S. men's hockey team at the 2002 and 2010 Winter Olympics.

Top 10 Boston Bands and Musicians
:: by Rich Shertenlieb

Note: Rich Shertenlieb co-hosts *The Toucher and Rich Show,* the wildly popular morning drive show on 98.5 The Sports Hub. At their core, the hosts are music guys. So Rich knows his bands and musicians and was nice enough to do something for this book that we were completely unequipped to do—write this list.

10. Neil Diamond. He's not from Boston, he's never lived in Boston, he's a Dodgers fan. Then why the hell is "Sweet Caroline" played at every Red Sox game? Thanks to Neil Diamond, the Pink Hats have a theme song. If you take a girl to a Red Sox game, and she tells you that her favorite part of the game is singing "Sweet Caroline" . . . show her something shiny to distract her, ditch her, and go date a Bruins fan.

If it weren't for Neil Diamond, there'd be . . . peace on Earth.

9. Dropkick Murphys. It's one thing to hear the DKM anthem "Shipping up to Boston" playing at the end of a tight Celtics-Lakers game. But now the song is so popular that it has been inexplicably used during random Atlanta Falcons/Carolina Panthers games. Just another example of how the rest of the country just wants to be us.

If it weren't for the Dropkick Murphys, there'd be . . . no music played at any Boston sporting event.

8. Extreme. Extreme was the side project of the most loved singer of Van Halen.

If it weren't for Extreme, there'd be . . . no Van Halen.

7. James Taylor. Sure he's a legend blah blah blah . . . but when James Taylor sings the national anthem before a Boston sporting event, it's like having your monster truck show start with a mandatory showing of *Beaches*.

If it weren't for James Taylor, there'd be . . . no one to steal the crown of "Dentist Office Music King" from Phil Collins.

6. The Cars. The Cars were proof that there will always be a place for catchy pop songs and that butt-ugly lead singers will always get laid. When Ric Ocasek stood next to supermodel Paulina Porizkova, it looked as if the

Victoria's Secret Fashion Show had been infiltrated by Emperor Palpatine.

If it weren't for The Cars, there'd be . . . no Weezer, soundtrack to the greatest scene from Fast Times at Ridgemont High—make that soundtrack to the greatest scene of any movie ever.

5. New Kids on the Block. Dreamboats. My first seven minutes in heaven was in a sixth-grade closet lined with NKOTB posters. She imagined I was Jordan, I imagined I hadn't lined my closet with NKOTB posters. But you'll never hear me talk trash about any band with Donnie Wahlberg. My man has been a Celtic faithful, attending almost every game, even during the Wally Szczerbiak era.

If it weren't for NKOTB, there'd be . . . no N'SYNC, Backstreet Boys, Ron Pearlman dream-fodder.

4. Pixies. Stop reading this now and buy anything with their name on it. As I'm making this list, I'm realizing that the front men of Boston bands are not the most attractive people, unless you're talking about. . . .

3. The J. Geils Band. Last summer, lead singer Peter Wolf was a guest inside the NESN broadcast booth during a Red Sox game and I thought the Ghost of Christmas Past had come to visit Don Orsillo.

If it weren't for the J. Geils Band, there'd be . . . no one to open for the Spin Doctors at the Chili Cook-Off.

2. Boston. I'm still waiting for Nirvana to pay royalties to Boston for ripping off the main riff of "More Than a Feeling," then repackaging it and naming it "Smells Like Teen Spirit."

If it weren't for Boston, there'd be . . . no music ever played on WZLK-FM (classic rock in Boston).

1. Aerosmith. The only band in the world who could end a song like "Rag Doll" with the following: "Dah deebie yaba doobie, daw daw det . . . daba, det, dooba-dat doodoo-dat-dooba-dat doodoo-dat doodoo-dat doodoo-dat dooba-dah . . . yah boobity boobity boobity boobity boobity baw! Baw buh buh baba baba babuh bow ah, bah wana buh nana nana bow, wah . . . (fade out)" and manage to make it sound badass.

If it weren't for Aerosmith, there'd be . . . no Guns N' Roses, Motley Crue, rock and roll frontmen who look like Carly Simon.

The Allure of the Green Monster :: MC

Like a temptress, Fenway's left-field wall has enticed many a Red Sox GM to bring big-swinging, right-handed hitters to Boston to pepper the wall or the screen or the Monster seats. Sadly, more times than not, these big swingers have swung and missed. I know everyone loves the big ball, but. . . .

Honorable Mentions. Don Baylor; Dick Gernert; Andre Dawson; Tony Armas; Tom Brunansky.

13. Rudy Pemberton, 6-1, 185 lbs. Another right-handed hitter who was projected to hit better at Fenway than he had at the more spacious parks he had previously called home. But after hitting just three home runs in two seasons (1996-97) at Fenway, he was out of Boston and the majors.

12. Tony Perez, 6-2, 175 lbs. Perfect symmetry—he hit 40 home runs and hit into 40 double plays from 1980-82 for Boston.

11. Dante Bichette, 6-3, 215 lbs. He had been a Triple Crown contender in Colorado, but who isn't in that park? He came to Fenway and wasn't a Triple crown contender, striking out 98 times and hitting into 16 double plays in 137 games during the 2000 and 2001 seasons.

10. Rob Deer, 6-3, 210 lbs. Deer came over from Detroit in a mid-season deal in 1993 to provide some pop. In his first game at Fenway, he hit a home run and was 3-4, an effort the Fenway crowd cheered wildly. For the rest of the year, he hit .179.

9. Butch Huskey, 6-3, 244 lbs. What a name for a big hitter—BUTCH HUSKEY! But his name and size turned out to be a lot scarier than his production in Boston. He only contributed seven home runs and 28 RBI to the Red Sox cause for the 1999 season before leaving for Minnesota.

8. Walter Dropo, 6-5, 220 lbs. He was so big that his nickname was "Moose." Between 1949-52, he hit 51 home runs and knocked in 229 RBI for the Sox.

7. Bob Bailey, 6-1, 180 lbs. "Beetle" Bailey was brought to Boston in 1977 to provide some punch from the bench, but only managed four home runs and nine RBI in two seasons. In the 1978 playoff game against the Yankees, Goose Gossage was quoted as saying, "Thank you" when he saw the righty standing in the batter's box. Gossage threw three pitches by the pinch hitter and Bailey walked back to the dugout.

6. Jack Clark, 6-2, 175 lbs. Signed as a big-money free agent, the four-time All-Star brought to Fenway the potential of not only the big ball, but the big ball in big moments. In the end, "Jack the Ripper" bought too many Mercedes Benzs and struck out too much, hitting just .236 with 33 home runs in 1991 and 1992, then retiring.

5. Danny Cater, 6-0, 170 lbs. I know you need some pop from the right-hand side. But trading Sparky Lyle for an average-at-best hitter? In 211 games between 1972-74 in Boston, Cater hit 14 home runs and struck out 406 times. Sparky Lyle saved 35 games for the Yankees in 1972 and later won a Cy Young Award with New York.

4. Jose Canseco, 6-3, 195 lbs. No one swung a bigger right-handed bat than Jose. He came to Boston in 1995 with a big reputation for the long ball and off-the-field antics. In the end, he was just another past-his-prime hitter who carried a big stick.

3. Orlando Cepeda, 6-3, 210 lbs. A great hitter for the San Francisco Giants, Cepeda came to Boston in 1973 to fill the new role of designated hitter. Cepeda had a bad leg, which made it painful to watch him run. He could still swing the bat though, once hitting four doubles in a game at Kansas City.

2. Wily Mo Pena, 6-3, 270 lbs. In theory, the Red Sox did have a lot of starting pitchers going into the 2006 season, giving the impression that Bronson Arroyo was expendable. However, history proves that you can never have enough arms. The Red Sox moved the slinger to the Cincinnati Reds for this big bopper, who only hit 16 bops in 157 games in Boston before getting shipped out in the midst of the 2007 season.

1. Dick Stuart, 6-4, 215 lbs. You know you're big when you attend Sequoia High School in Redwood California. The big first baseman could hit the big ball, hitting 75 home runs during the 1963 and 1964 seasons in Boston. But during those two years, he also had 53 errors at first base and was so deficient defensively that he earned the nickname "Dr. Strangeglove."

Top New Hampshire Golf Courses :: Jane Blalock

Note: Jane Blalock was named LPGA Rookie of the Year in 1969 and won 27 tournaments during a career that gained her induction into the New England Sports Hall of Fame. She still holds the LPGA Tour record of making an amazing 299 straight cuts. Here, the Portsmouth, New Hampshire native offers us a list of the top courses in her beloved Granite State.

10. Breakfast Hill Golf Club. A new course enjoyed by all and in excellent shape.

9. Abenaqui Country Club. A classic hidden gem next to the crashing waves of the Atlantic Ocean.

8. Lake Winnipesaukee Golf Club. A new addition to the NH scene with a fantastic design and gorgeous scenery.

7. Hanover Country Club. One must be in good condition to walk the hills of Hanover, but it's a beautiful (and tricky) course.

6. Concord Country Club. An extremely well-manicured course and interesting layout.

5. The Balsams. Worth the long journey north, it's a real classic with breathtaking views.

4. Manchester Country Club. A real gem with a great Donald Ross design, it has been the home to many national and state championships.

3. Wentworth by the Sea Country Club. It presents spectacular views of the water and a real challenge in the wind and serves as home of The Handa Cup.

2. Lake Sunapee Country Club. Scenic, interesting and classic Donald Ross.

1. Portsmouth Country Club. I grew up on this course, so I am partial—a true championship test on Great Bay.

These are the athletes, officials, and organizations hated most by Patriots Nation. Before reading this list, remember that the Pats have only been consistently good for a short period of time. And if you aren't winning, you aren't creating rivalries. And with no rivals, there's not much hatred. So if you followed the Patriots in the 1960s and you hated a team or individual player, you probably won't find him here.

10. Former Patriots Owner Victor Kiam. He sold the team to James Orthwein, who almost took the Pats to St. Louis. In fact, my radio partner Scott Zolak has a St. Louis Patriots hat from that whole fiasco. Thank God Robert Kraft owned Foxboro Stadium because of Billy Sullivan's incompetence. If not for that, the club's proposed move away from New England probably would have happened. I couldn't imagine Boston and New England not represented in the NFL.

9. Former Denver Broncos Tight End Shannon Sharpe. He made the NFL films highlight reel forever when he uttered into a phone on the sidelines of the old Foxboro Stadium on November 17, 1996, "Mr. President, call in the National Guard! We need as many men as you can spare! Because we are killing the Patriots! We'll call the dogs off! Send the National Guard please!" The guy's a Pro Football Hall of Famer, so he can run smack. I don't mind it, but a lot of fans around here will never forgive him.

8. Former Miami Dolphins Head Coach Don Shula. At a game in Foxboro Stadium on December 12, 1982, a work-release parolee used a small snowplow to clear a path for kicker John Smith to kick a field goal that led to a Pats 3-0 win over the Dolphins. Shula went nuts on the sidelines, calling it "the most unfair act" in the history of the league. Shula griped about this for years and years and years. The Dolphins didn't play in Foxboro in December for at least the next three seasons, and the Pats played games in the heat of Miami in September of 1983 and 1984. Coincidence? Or was it payback because of Shula's stroke with the NFL?

7. The NY Sack Exchange. This was the Jets defensive line of the early 1980s—Marc Gastineau, Joe Klecko, Marty Lyons and Abdul Salaam. In 1982, this group recorded 66 sacks and Gastineau was an ass that everyone could hate. Plus, they were Jets. So that created something automatic right there in the minds of Pats fans.

6. Former San Diego Chargers Running Back LaDainian Tomlinson. After eliminating the Chargers from the playoffs in 2006 in San Diego, some of the Pats players did the "Lights Out" dance at midfield, mimicking San Diego DE Shawne Merriman, who did the dance after every sack. An indignant LT responded, "When you go to the middle of our field, when you start doing the dance that Shawne Merriman is known for, that's disrespectful to me. And I can't sit there and watch that. And so, yeah, I was very upset. And just the fact that they showed no class at all. Absolutely no class. And maybe that comes from their head coach. So you know, there you have it." Combine that with the fact that the Pats shut his ass down in nearly every playoff game (except in 2010 when he was with the Jets) and you have a recipe for hatred.

5. Former NFL Referee Ben Dreith. He made the third-down roughing the passer call in Oakland against Pats DT "Sugar Bear" Hamilton in the 1976 playoffs with about a minute to go that cost the Pats a win. I think for Dreith's safety, he never refereed a Pats game again. Some feel the "tuck rule" no-fumble call in New England's 2001 playoff win over the Raiders made up for this disaster. But plenty of others still hate Dreith.

4. Eric Mangini. This former Pats defensive coordinator and Jets and Browns head coach is fingered in one of the ugliest scandals in Patriots history. He was the head coach of the New York Jets in 2007 who ratted out the Patriots for illegally videotaping other teams signals on the sidelines and creating the "Spygate" scandal. Mangini then led the Jets to the playoffs and really cemented himself as a permanent member of the hated list. Mangini was actually a bit player in all of this, as Jets GM Mike Tannenbaum was the real rat. But Mangini was the point man and direct connection to the Pats, so he gets the blame.

3. Rex Ryan and the Rest of the Current New York Jets Organization. Right on up to owner Woody Johnson. Mike Tannenbaum, Rex Ryan, Mark Sanchez— all of 'em. The Jets beat the Pats in the divisional round of the playoffs in 2010 at our place! Ryan talks like the Jets are the kings and the Pats are their loyal subjects. And it makes Rex hated in these parts. When the Jets are on the schedule, it means big ratings, big money, big hype and big hate.

2. Former Oakland Raiders Safety Jack Tatum. His name is synonymous with dirty play. His hit in a 1978 preseason game permanently paralyzed Pats WR Darryl Stingley from the chest down. Tatum wrote in his book (which he entitled, *They Call Me Assassin*) that he tried to contact Stingley in the hospital, but the Stingley family disputes that. Either way, Tatum capitalized on paralyzing someone and never showed remorse.

1. Colts Quarterback Peyton Manning. The reason he's No. 1 is because he's the biggest threat to the mantle of "quarterback god" bestowed upon Tom Brady. In the early 2000s, Manning and the Colts just couldn't beat the Pats. Then came 2006, when the Colts finally got a win in the playoffs vs. Brady and the Pats in the AFC Championship Game. The rivalry and the hatred was on. But for Patriots Nation, beating Peyton means everyone gets to see "Manning Face" and that's the best face you can ever see.

All of us Boston sports fans are like Rain Man. Consciously or subconsciously, sports are always on our minds. At the strangest moments, visions of Davie Tyree traverse the lobes of our brains, seeking to escape, but to no avail. We remember where we were when special sporting events happened. However, we can't remember to pick up milk.

Here are a couple dozen random streams of Boston sports consciousness.

24. Celtics Aren't the Celtics. In 1978, Celtics owner Irv Levin moved the team to California and the Celtics became the San Diego Clippers. John Y. Brown then purchased the Buffalo Braves and renamed them the Boston Celtics. He completed the transaction by serendipitously maintaining the rights for Larry Bird (Levin wanted Freeman Williams) and trading for Dave Cowens, bringing the Celtic great back to Boston.

23. Tony Conigliaro Croons. Tony C. was so big in the 1960s that he signed a record contract. He released songs called "Playing the Field" and "Play Our Song."

22. Thank You, St. Louis. Boston teams beat all four St. Louis squads in championship showdown. The Celtics won NBA Finals over the St. Louis Hawks in 1957, 1960 and 1961. The Red Sox swept the St. Louis Cardinals in the 2004 World Series. The Bruins beat the St. Louis Blues in the 1970 Stanley Cup. The Patriots beat the St. Louis Rams in the 2002 Super Bowl.

21. Boston Sports Props. Red Auerbach's cigar and rolled up program; Gerry Cheevers' scarred mask; Bill Belichick's hoodie; Bob Montgomery's plastic helmet; Marvelous Marvin Hagler's burgundy robe; Don Cherry's dog Blue; the Brown Family pistol that has signaled the start of the Boston Marathon for over 100 years; Dee Brown's pump-up sneakers at the NBA dunk competition; Ace Bailey's (rest in peace) turtleneck; Bill Rodgers' gloves.

20. John Lennon Dead. It was during a Patriots-Dolphins *Monday Night Football* game on December 8, 1980 that Howard Cosell announced that John Lennon had been shot and killed.

19. The Impossible Dream Album. Every New England home had a copy of *The Impossible Dream: The Story of the 1967 Boston Red Sox* album narrated by Ken Coleman.

18. Boston Sports Bars for Before the Game. Ironhorse (down below at the old Garden); Fours (voted best sports bar in America by *Sports Illustrated*); Scotch and Sirloin; Sullivan's Tap; Red Wing on Route 1; any car with its trunk open in the parking lot at a Patriots game; Baseball Tavern (rooftop); Cask 'n Flagon; Eliot Lounge (was the legendary watering hole for runners after the Marathon).

17. High School Sports Dynasties. Reading High School Track didn't lose for three decades under legendary coach Hal Croft; Catholic Memorial hockey won 12 Super 8 titles; Everett High School has won eight Super Bowls since 1997; in 1914, Everett won the national championship, going 13-0 and outscoring opponents 600-0.

16. Old Teams. New England Tea Men (NASL soccer), Boston Breakers (USFL football), Boston Lobsters (WTT pro tennis team), Boston Braves (baseball, football, hockey and rugby).

15. Agent Wars. Bob Wolfe battled Red Auerbach over Larry Bird; Jerome Stanley used Brian Shaw to make his point; Jerry Kapstein with Fred Lynn; Howard Slusher with John Hannah and Leon Gray; Scott Boras played unfair with Mark Teixeira; Alan Eagleson was a bad guy who represented Bobby Orr; Marshall Medoff tried to steal the Boston Marathon.

14. Physical Specimens. Vincent "The Undertaker" Brown; Ben Watson; Ted Johnson; Zdeno Chara; Chuck Connors; Sam Gash; Charles Bradley; Xavier McDaniel; Rich Garces.

13. Dubious Distinction. Red Sox pitcher Tracy Stallard gave up Roger Maris' landmark 61st home run in 1961.

12. Unique to Us. Charles Regatta; Boston Marathon; high school football on Thanksgiving Day; *Candlepin Bowling* (Don Gillis' show on Saturday ranked as the highest-rated sports show for years); Cape Cod Baseball League.

11. Eddie Popowski. I loved when foul balls came to him in the third-base coach's box. When he threw the ball back to the pitcher, he wrapped the ball behind his back and it came out over his shoulder (somehow).

10. *Sports Illustrated* Cover Appearances. Larry Bird (16); Tom Brady (15); Ted Williams (11); Marvelous Marvin Hagler (9); Bill Russell (9); Bobby Orr (5); John Havlicek (5).

9. Batting Practice Pitcher. Ted Olson pitched for the Red Sox in 1938 and 1939. Over 57.2 innings, he recorded an ERA of 7.18.

8. Historical Regular Seasons That Didn't Lead to Championships. The Red Sox won 99 games in 1978, but lost to the Yankees in a divisional playoff game; the Patriots won 16 games during 2007 regular season, then lost in the Super Bowl; the Celtics won 68 games during the 1972-73 regular season, but lost in the Eastern Conference Finals; the Bruins won 57 games in 1971-72, but didn't make it out of the quarterfinals in the NHL playoffs.

7. "Ain't No Stopping Us Now." The McFadden and Whitehead song became the mid-1980s Celtics anthem. Ahh, the good ol' days of disco and championship Celtics teams.

6. Jobs Wendell Kim and Rene Lachemann Couldn't Do. Traffic cop; air traffic controller; maitre d'; crossing guard; harbor master; and, oh, yeah, third base coach.

5. Foxboro Traffic. There is a reason to stay in the parking lot tailgating after the game—Route 1 traffic.

4. Sunset of His Career. Dan Duquette was right about Roger Clemens—his career was on the decline and he wasn't worth the money. But amazingly he "found" his fastball.

3. Dwight Evans' Throw. It was a thing of beauty to watch Evans wind up and throw a strike to peg an overambitious runner trying to score or go from first to third.

2. Bruins Song. Remember when the Bruins were on TV 38 and the broadcast started with a speeded-up version of "The Minute Waltz?" That was awesome.

1. Hagler vs. Mugabi. The fight was an all-out war and Hagler's greatest fight. Mugabi was a warrior, but Hagler was the greatest middleweight of all time.

Top 12 People From Rhode Island :: AG

I moved to the state of Rhode Island in 1989 when I was a sophomore in high school. We lived in Westerly, where I didn't fit in right away because I wasn't Italian. I am now in the Westerly High School Athletic Hall of Fame. That qualifies me to do this list.

Honorable Mentions. Rocco Baldelli; Bill Almon; Billy Andrade; Will Blackmon; Brian Boucher; Keith Carney; Mike Cloud; Brad Faxon; Dave Gavitt; Joe Hassett; Chris Ianetta; Dan Wheeler; Chris Terreri; Mark van Eeghen; Richard Hatch; Elizabeth Hasselbeck; Shanna Moakler; Meredith Vieira.

12. Boxer Vinny Paz and 11. Boxer Peter Manfredo. Paz was a five-time world boxing champion and was one helluva tough guy, a world-class fighter. Now he's just a world class ass. He waltzes around the state like he's still in his prime and deserves to have his butt kissed. In his day, he could go, but he never developed anything to do after boxing. Peter Manfredo was on the show *The Contender*, making it to the finals and earning his way to a big fight against Jeff Lacy, who outclassed him. He's now the NABF middleweight champion. Good enough to beat fringe guys, but not good enough to beat top fighters.

10. Vincent "Buddy" Cianci. Only in the state of Rhode Island could the mayor of the state's biggest city get driven from office because of an assault against a man who was banging his wife at the time. Buddy then became a talk show host, ran for office again, won, but got sent to prison because the Feds got him on one of 34 counts of a federal indictment. He rebuilt the city of Providence into what it is today. He got things done. He's now a highly rated talk show host again in Providence. He can win any election he wants if he runs. He's that good.

9. Jeffrey Osborne. Have a mediocre event where you need someone safe to sing the national anthem? He's your guy. He's well-known enough, so people don't boo, but they don't remember that he sang the anthem. I guess that's what "On the Wings of Love" does for someone. He beats out John Cafferty and the Beaver Brown Band.

8. Mena Suvari. I didn't know that she was from Rhode Island until I looked it up. She's not on this list for her Rice-A-Roni commercial. She's here for showing her tits to Kevin Spacey in *American Beauty*. Cinematic genius, right there.

7. Ruth Buzzi. The Westerly, Rhode Island native was a regular on *Rowan and Martin's Laugh-In* during the late 1960s and early '70s, so how could I not mention her? If you're a fan of early Nick-At-Nite reruns, you saw her as the grumpy old lady on the park bench who hit Artie Johnson with her purse.

6. Peter Farrelly and 5. Bobby Farrelly. Funny film directors who have created a franchise based on their names. If you see their names in a movie's opening credits, you know what to expect. My personal favorite is *Kingpin*. Ishmael was a great character.

4. Lou Lamoriello. The grand poobah of the New Jersey Devils has won three Stanley Cups and made some of the shrewdest moves in hockey history—like firing Claude Julien when the Devils had the best record in franchise history. His teams have made the playoffs all but two years during his 20-plus year tenure. He was also the Providence athletic director who hired Rick Pitino in 1985, which led to the Friars reaching the Final Four two years later.

3. Ernie DiGregorio. Led Providence College to the Final Four, then he was selected third overall by the Buffalo Braves in the 1973 NBA Draft. He won NBA Rookie of the Year after averaging 15-plus points a game. He was traded to the Lakers in the late '70s and ultimately fizzled out of the league because of bad knees. He's now a celebrity host at Foxwoods Resort Casino. The best athlete ever from the state of Rhode Island.

2. James Woods. He's been nominated for two Emmys and two Oscars and was awesome in such movies as *Casino*, *Once Upon a Time in America* and *Ghosts of Mississippi*. He's also poked fun at himself on the Fox TV show *Family Guy*, appearing as himself. Which leads us to....

1. Seth MacFarlane. The creator of *Family Guy*, he owes a lot of his success to Comedy Central, which aired reruns of the show after Fox cancelled it. After the CC reruns made the show a hit, Fox restarted production on new episodes and it became one of the most successful comedies in television history. McFarlane now also oversees production of *The Cleveland Show* and *American Dad*. He boasts a net worth of about $250 million and has sex with lots of hot chicks in Hollywood. We should rename the state MacFarlane Land.

My Top 10 Moments in Broadcasting
:: by Dave Goucher

Note: Dave Goucher has been the radio voice of the Boston Bruins for over a decade. The Boston University grad has also called hockey games on radio for his alma mater, for the Wheeling Thunderbirds and for the Providence Bruins, as well as for NHL Radio's Game of the Week on Westwood One. Named New England's top play-by-play announcer by the Associated Press in 2003, 2006 and 2007, the Pawtucket native also serves as WBZ's play-by-play announcer for the Boston Marathon. Dave is a fine man and was nice enough to share his thoughts on the highlights of his career. (See Dave's Top 5 moments in 2011 on page 260.)

10. 1993 Beanpot, BU vs. Harvard. Not all of my most memorable moments as a hockey play-by-play announcer have been with the Bruins. Many of them occurred long before, either in college or in the minor leagues. I consider all of it one big body of work. My senior year in college, I called the Beanpot title game between BU and Harvard. My Terriers lost, but there was great up-and-down action in the second period and I used it to make my first resume tape (yes, it was still a cassette tape in those days). I called games in college with my best friend at BU, Rich Keshian. He passed away suddenly in 1999 and one of my most prized possessions is a framed black-and-white picture he gave me of us calling the Beanpot from the radio booth at the old Boston Garden. It hangs in my home office to this day.

9. BU vs. Maine in 1993. The Black Bears had a powerhouse team that season, with Paul Kariya, Jim Montgomery and the Ferraro twins among the guys on their roster. Into February, they had not lost a game all season until the Terriers staged a rally from a 6-2 deficit in Orono to win 7-6 in overtime. Mike Pomichter set up Mike Prendergast for the game-winner and I can still see my partner Rich standing on top of a folding chair in our little broadcast area with his arms raised over his head yelling, "Yes, yes, yes!" We put the call of the winning goal as the outgoing message on our answering machine for months. Maine still went on to win the NCAA title. That game was their only loss of the season.

8. Providence Bruins Championship Parade in 1999. Not all the moments I remember most fondly happened in the broadcast booth. In 1999, I was calling Providence Bruins games in the AHL when they won the Calder Cup. The year before, the P-Bruins had finished dead last in the league. The next year, they were having a parade through the streets of downtown Providence. I'll never forget riding around in a convertible with the sidewalks jammed and tickertape raining down from office windows or emceeing the rally in front of 10,000 people at City Hall. Broadcasters can be in this business at all different levels for decades and never have the opportunity to call their team winning a championship. I feel fortunate that I had the chance to do it.

7. P-Bruins vs. Rochester, Game 5 of the 1999 Calder Cup Finals. After rolling through the regular season and the first three rounds of the playoffs, the P-Bruins stood on the brink of a championship, leading Rochester 3-1 in the series. They had not lost a home playoff game all year and were not about to start, easily wrapping up the title with a 5-1 victory before a sold-out home crowd of 11,909. As the final few minutes ticked away, I began to think about what I was going to say at the end, reminding myself, "Don't screw this up, you're going to have to live with this." What came to mind was they had just "completed" an incredible season. They had been the best team in the league all year, putting up the best record in AHL history—a combined 71-24-4 through the playoffs—and winning the Cup was an appropriate and fitting ending. So as the clock hit zero, I yelled: "This incredible season is complete!" I still have my line charts and scoresheet from the game, along with a championship ring.

6. Bruins vs. Flyers, Game 7 of the 2010 NHL Eastern Conference Semifinals. I know you're wondering why this would be in my Top 10. Here's why: to me this list is about the games I'll remember most, good and bad, when I'm retired and sitting on a beach somewhere. As a broadcaster, you become emotionally attached to the success or failure of your team. Never was this more evident to me than while calling this game. The backstory is that I had called four previous Game 7s for "my team"—either in the minors or in Boston—and my team had lost them all. So I decided before the game to just try and enjoy the moment and not get too caught up in the score. But when it got to 3-0 Bruins in the first period, it was impossible not to think of a Bruins-Canadiens Conference Finals matchup. Then when the Flyers scored late in the first period, I had a sinking feeling. And when they scored a power-play goal in the third to take the lead, I knew it was over. The year before, the Bruins had lost Game 7 in overtime to Carolina and I didn't think it would be possible to feel more disappointed at the end of a season. A year to the day later, I found out I had been wrong.

5. Bruins vs. Sabres, NHL Exhibition Game in 2000. A preseason game? No doubt about it. It was the first Bruins game I'd ever called and I was scared to death. I'd spent seven years riding the buses in the minors, working in Wheeling, West Virginia and Providence before finally making it to the NHL and getting the job I'd always wanted. I don't remember a time when the Bruins were not a part of my life and now I was their radio announcer. In the preseason, the team usually flies into a city the day of the game, as opposed to arriving the day before during the regular season. We flew into Buffalo mid-afternoon and on the bus ride from the airport to the arena, I held out my hand in front of me and it was shaking. I was nervous about doing my first game and even more nervous about interviewing then-Head Coach Pat Burns for the first time. Pat could be an intimidating man and I was the new guy. But he made it easy. The game couldn't start fast enough, and once it did I was fine. I was calling a hockey game, just as I'd done for years. I still have the ticket from my first regular-season game against Ottawa. But by then, I'd called three exhibition games and most of my nerves vanished just after the puck dropped in Buffalo.

4. Bruins vs. Flyers, Game 1 of the 2010 NHL Eastern Conference Semifinals. Playoff weather feels different. It's the springtime and it's usually warm. The atmosphere in the rink feels different too. It's a feeling of anticipation and drama that doesn't exist during the regular season. And it would be hard to top the drama on this first day of May. Marc Savard returned from a seven-week absence due to a concussion and scored in overtime to take the opener of the series against the Flyers. The Bruins seemed to be in control of the game, with three two-goal leads, only to find themselves in OT. They stormed the Flyers early on and finally broke through on Savard's goal, a bullet that sailed just under the crossbar. His reaction was priceless, pumping his fists as he crossed the ice and tossing his stick into the stands. He had taken a vicious cheap shot from Matt Cooke of the Pittsburgh Penguins and been through some very dark days after the concussion, unable to go outside, but there he was back on center stage, writing the perfect final line of a storybook return.

3. Bruins vs. Sabres, Game 4 of the 2010 NHL Eastern Conference Quarterfinals. Truth be told, it was the first-round matchup the Bruins wanted. They had fared well against the division-champion Sabres during the regular season and were now looking to take a commanding 3-1 lead in the series. It wasn't looking good though, trailing 2-0 after the second period. But the Bruins scored twice in the third and set the stage for not one but two overtimes. Broadcasting overtime playoff games is exhilarating and nerve-wracking at the same time. Every time the puck goes in the offensive zone, you think the game might end. I am usually on the edge of my seat, literally. The Bruins have experienced the pain of "too many men on the ice" penalties in the playoffs. But this time, they were on the other side of it when the Sabres were caught with six skaters. And the Bruins looked to a player who was out of work halfway through the season to be the overtime hero. Miroslav Satan, who had his best seasons in Buffalo, put home a backhander to win it for Boston. In overtime, I always hope it's a clean goal, whoever scores it, and this one was.

2. Bruins vs. Canadiens, Game 6 of the 2008 NHL Eastern Conference Quarterfinals. Easily the most enjoyable and exciting game I've called at the TD Garden. The Bruins were down 3-2 in the series and had been a bit of a Cinderella story just to make the playoffs. They didn't clinch a spot until the next-to-last day of the season and were huge underdogs against top-seeded Montreal. The B's won Game 5 in Montreal to stay alive and now they needed to win again. They overcame three deficits, but when they finally took the lead with just over four minutes left, it only lasted 11 seconds. The teams scored six goals in the third and the swings in momentum were enormous. But Marco Sturm's late game-winner, after he barreled over Roman Hamrlik twice and leaped over Carey Price to put home a rebound, sent the Bruins back to Montreal. The noise level at the Garden was ear-splitting. I'd never heard the place so loud and I haven't since. And after a few years of being on the fringes of the Boston sports scene, this game put the Bruins back on the map.

1. 2010 Winter Classic at Fenway Park, Bruins vs. Flyers. It was more than just the game. It was the days leading up to it, including skating at Fenway and standing rinkside as the snow fell during Bruins practice on New Year's Eve. I grew up a Bruins fan and a Red Sox fan and those two passions merged in one place. I made the walk the Bruins were going to make, from the clubhouse, down the tunnel to the Red Sox dugout. I couldn't help but think of all the legends who had made that same walk. I remember counting the number of stairs from the dugout up to the field/rink (there are nine). I got to Fenway early on January 1. I wanted to be there when it was empty, the calm before the storm. It was perfect weather for an outdoor game (34 degrees and cloudy) and we had the window of the broadcast booth open to feel the elements. When Marco Sturm scored in overtime, it set off a roar from the crowd that I'd never heard at a hockey game. And long after it was over, I found myself not wanting to leave the booth. I made my way down to the grandstand and looked around. Over 38,000 fans had headed out into the night to celebrate. Fenway was empty again.

The two greatest arenas in Massachusetts are sports and politics. Depending on the day, one can be more treacherous than the other. Sometimes these two worlds intersect. The below list is representative of these clashing worlds.

10. Governor Ed King at Bobby Orr's Retirement. Did he really think that the fans weren't going to boo him?

9. Auditor Joe DeNucci. The Newton resident was never afraid to mix it up with anyone—in politics or in the ring. DeNucci fought more times at the Boston Garden than any other boxer. He had a career record of 54-15-4 and served a quarter of a century as State Auditor.

8. Senator Edward Kennedy. The good Senator represented the Commonwealth for almost five decades. He also caught a touchdown pass for the Crimson in the annual Harvard-Yale game.

7. Town of Foxboro. Fed up by the behavior of unruly Patriots fans, the town of Foxboro banned night games at the stadium. The final straw was a *Monday Night Football* game in which the fans' behavior got as far out of line as their blood alcohol levels. One fan was arrested when he urinated on a man who was administering CPR to another fan who had suffered a heart attack.

6. Mayor Menino Apologizes. After several egregious umpiring calls against the Red Sox in the 1999 ALCS, some Red Sox fans voiced their displeasure and threw plastic bottles onto the field. The following day, Mayor Menino felt compelled to apologize to the world.

5. Pie Pours Beer. At the 1970 Stanley Cup celebration at City Hall, Bruin Johnny "Pie" McKenzie shared his libation with Mayor Kevin White by pouring it over White's head.

4. Governor Endicott Peabody. The future governor was an All-American lineman at Harvard who was voted into the College Football Hall of Fame.

3. Governor John Volpe. In Red Auerbach's final game as head coach on April 28, 1966, the Celtics led the Lakers in Game 7 of the NBA Finals by 10 points with 35 seconds remaining. Governor Volpe had convinced the Boston coach to allow him to light his last victory cigar. The ambitious politician approached the bench and lit the stogie. Instantly, the Lakers were ignited and rallied. Los Angeles closed to within two points before the Celtics finally secured their championship.

2. President John F. Kennedy. An avid sportsman who was once on the cover of *Sports Illustrated*, JFK loved all sports—including the famous touch football games played at the Kennedy compound in Hyannis. Kennedy skippered Harvard's sailing team, with a crew that included his brother Joseph, to an NCAA national championship.

1. Mayor Raymond Flynn. The South Boston resident was a multi-sport standout at South Boston High School. He matriculated to Providence College where he was an All-East Basketball player, MVP of the NIT and had his number retired. He served three terms as Boston's mayor and served as U.S. Ambassador to the Holy See (the Vatican).

Top 99 Massachusetts High School Athletes
:: by Mayor Raymond Flynn

Note: Raymond Flynn served as Boston's mayor from 1984 to 1993. Shortly after he left office, Flynn was appointed U.S. Ambassador to the Holy See (the Vatican). Prior to his career in politics, Flynn established himself as one of the best all-around athletes to ever come out of Boston. His basketball prowess made him a star for Providence College and landed him a tryout with the Celtics. Mayor Flynn's athletic feats in multiple sports at Southie High would have earned him a spot high on this list if the humble mayor hadn't compiled the list himself.

But Mayor Flynn wanted to highlight the area's other great high school athletes. In his words: "Over the years, the Boston area and state of Massachusetts have produced some of the finest high school athletes in the country. While following high school sports has been of great interest to many, including me, it's very difficult to compile a list without unintentionally omitting some obvious other great ones. Most of my choices are athletes and games that I actually saw or followed closely in the news.

"I'm hoping that in paying tribute to these outstanding high school athletes, we can shed some attention and recognition on these and other deserving athletes in the future. This is not a complete list of great high school athletes from the state but just the beginning of the discussion."

99. Averrill Roberts. Boston Latin Academy.

98. Bob Bigelow. Winchester High School, Penn, Kansas City Kings.

97. Lee Brothers. Lexington High School.

96. Bill Smithers. Somerville High School, Holy Cross.

95. Dukie Walsh. Matingnon.

94. Bob Nicholas. South Boston High School, Boston Patriots.

93. Sully Nector. Chelsea High School.

92. Fred O'Hearn. Boston Tech High School, Bowdoin, NHL.

91. Lenny Dempsey. Medford High School.

90. Doug Arangio. East Boston High School.

89. Bobby Leo. Everett High School, Harvard University.

88. Dana Barros. Xaverian High School, Boston College, Boston Celtics.

87. Leo Osgood. Jamaica Plain High School, Northeastern University, Milwaukee Bucks.

86. Bill Hanson. Catholic Memorial High School.

85. Dick Jauron. Swampscott High School, Yale, NFL.

84. Mark Charos and George Williams. Archbishop Williams High School.

83. Andrea Higgins. Fontbonne Academy, Boston University.

82. Will McDonough. English High School.

81. Eddie Pellagrini. Roxbury Memorial High School, Boston College, Boston Red Sox.

80. Ed Burns. Arlington High School hockey coach.

79. Jerry Remy. Somerset High School, Boston Red Sox.

78. Russ Halloran. Newton North High School, MLB.

77. Jack "The Shot" Foley. Assumption High School, Holy Cross, Celtics.

76. Rich Dubee. Bridgewater Raynham, MLB.

75. Roscoe Baker. Roxbury Memorial.

74. Jackie Hughes. Malden Catholic, Harvard University.

73. Mike Fidler. Malden Catholic, Minnesota North Stars.

72. Leo Smith. Boston College High School, Boston College.

71. Bill Donlan. Boston College High School, Boston College.

70. Dan Sullivan. Boston Technical High School, Boston College, Baltimore Colts.

69. Tommy Bilodeau. Boston Latin School.

68. Dick Lucas. South Boston High School, Boston College, Philadelphia Eagles.

67. Marty Pierce. Matignon High School hockey coach.

66. Makalia Long. University of New Hampshire.

65. Michael Prendergast. Catholic Memorial, Boston University.

64. George Burke. North Quincy High School, University of Massachusetts.

63. Don Trembley. Lawrence Central Catholic School.

62. Chris Herren. Durfee High School, Boston College.

61. Ralph De Leo. Boston Tech High School.

60. The Sullivan Family. South Boston High School, Boston College/Boston University.

59. Kevin Coughlin. South Boston High School, University of Michigan.

58. Pete Varney. North Quincy High School, Chicago White Sox.

57. Sarah Behn. Foxboro High School, Boston College.

56. Dave Silk. Thayer Academy, Boston University, Olympics.

55. Bill and Bob Cleary. Belmont High School, Harvard, Olympics.

54. Jim Craig. Oliver Ames High School, Boston University, Olympics, NHL.

53. Mike Eruzione. Winthrop High School, Boston University, Olympics.

52. Bob MacGillivray. English High School, North Carolina State.

51. Steve Flynn. South Boston High School.

50. Charlie Bunker. Dorchester High School.

49. Ralph Colsen. East Boston High School.

48. Don Gentile. South Boston High School, University of Mississippi.

47. John Varone. East Boston High School, University of Miami.

46. Butch Wade. Boston Tech High School, University of Michigan.

45. Frank Casey. Boston Latin High School.

44. John "Boots" Connelly. Boston Latin High School, Boston College.

43. Glen Tufts. Bridgewater Raynham High School.

42. Rumeal Robinson. Cambridge Rindge and Latin, University of Michigan.

41. Greg McMurtry. Brockton High School, University of Michigan, New England Patriots.

40. Billy O'Dwyer. Don Bosco High School, Boston College.

39. Tom Gastall. New Bedford High School, Boston University, MLB.

38. Russ Gibson. Durfee High School, Boston Red Sox.

37. Don Allard. Somerville High School, Boston College, Boston Patriots.

36. Paul Carey. Boston College High School, Stanford University, Baltimore Orioles.

35. Tenley Albright. The Winsor School, USA Figure Skater.

34. Joe Ciulla. Woburn High School, Columbia University.

33. Gerry O'Leary. Boston English High School, Holy Cross.

32. Dick "Turk" Farrell. St. Mary's of Brookline, Philadelphia Phillies.

31. Steve DeOssie. Don Bosco High School, Boston College, Dallas Cowboys.

30. Steve Sarantopoulos. Brockton High School, Providence High School.

29. Mike Pagliarulo. Medford High School, New York Yankees.

28. Karl Hobbs. Cambridge Rindge and Latin, University of Connecticut.

27. Manny Delcarmen. West Roxbury High School, Boston Red Sox.

26. Terry Driscoll. Boston College High School, Boston College.

25. Billy Hewitt. Cambridge Rindge and Latin, University of Southern California, NBA.

24. Jerry August. Matignon High School, Boston University.

23. Richie Hebner. Norwood High School, Pittsburgh Pirates.

22. Nancy Kerrigan. Stoneham High School, Olympics.

21. Rod Langway. Randolph High School, UNH, Washington Capitals.

20. Wilbur Wood. Belmont High School, Chicago White Sox.

19. Danny Murphy. St John's Prep, Chicago Cubs.

18. Mark Bavaro. Danvers High School, Syracuse, New York Giants.

17. Jack Concannon. Matignon High School, Boston College, Chicago Bears.

16. Fran Duggan. South Boston High School, Boston College.

15. Ronnie Perry, Jr. and Ronnie Perry, Sr. Catholic Memorial, Somerville High School, Holy Cross.

14. Jack O'Callahan. Boston Latin School, Boston University, Olympics, Chicago Blackhawks.

13. Bobby Carpenter. St. John's Prep, Washington Capitals.

12. Tony Conigliaro. St. Mary's High School, Boston Red Sox.

11. Howie Long. Milford High School, Villanova, Oakland Raiders.

10. Bill Monbouquette. Medford High School, Boston Red Sox.

9. Joe Bellino. Winchester High School, Naval Academy, Boston Patriots.

8. John Cuniff. Don Bosco High School, Boston College, New Jersey Devils.

7. Doug and Darren Flutie. Natick High School, Boston College, CFL, NFL.

6. Ted Donato. Catholic Memorial High School, Harvard, Bruins, Olympics.

5. John Thomas. Cambridge Rindge and Latin, Boston University, Olympics.

4. Jimmy Walker. Boston Trade, Providence College, Detroit Pistons.

3. Robbie Ftorek. Needham High School, NHL.

2. Patrick Ewing. Cambridge Rindge and Latin, Georgetown, New York Knicks.

1. Harry Agganis. Lynn Classical, Boston University, Boston Red Sox.

I think hockey hatred runs the deepest and burns the longest. My friend Howie Sylvester, who produces the Bruins on 98.5 The Sports Hub, named five of these guys off the top of his head. These are the guys that Bruins fans have railed on most over the years.

10. Art Skov. Infamous referee who made the call against Bobby Orr with inside three minutes to go in Game 6 of the 1974 Stanley Cup Finals, with the Bruins down just a goal. That penalty all but handed the Cup to the Philadelphia Flyers. Skov also sent Orr to the box in Game 6 of the 1972 Stanley Cup Finals for 10 minutes, but that time the B's were able to close it out with Orr scoring the game-winner. The Flyers once had a 12-game-winning streak with Skov as the referee and he used to call penalties on Orr—a double whammy in Boston.

9. Keith Magnuson. The Chicago defenseman was hated in these parts from 1969-79 as a major fighter who would run guys like Derek Sanderson from behind and into the boards. He got into numerous fights with Bobby Orr. He appeared on the cover of *Sports Illustrated* at the peak of the Bruins-Blackhawks rivalry.

8. Brad Park. The longtime New York Ranger was always second fiddle to Bobby Orr when folks talked about the best defenseman of the 1970s. Just like the Rangers were seemingly second fiddle to the Bruins. Park once described the Bruins as "bloodthirsty animals who have turned present-day hockey into a brutal sport." Then he was traded here and all was forgiven!

7. Gilles Lupien. A 6-6 defenseman who really was a borderline NHL player, but his size and willingness to fight kept him in the league for a few years. He'd fight everybody and couldn't skate very well. Good enough reasons to hate the guy . . . AND he played for the Montreal Canadiens. That sealed the deal for those in Boston.

6. Pat Quinn. In 1969, the Toronto Maple Leafs defenseman and Bobby Orr got into a heated exchange after the whistle that led to a dogpile fight. But then a few weeks later in the playoffs with the B's, up 6-0 in the second period, Quinn knocked Orr out near the blue line. That led to a major shit show for Quinn every time he came to Boston. The B's won the series against

Toronto, but Quinn put himself on the most wanted list forever with that one.

5. Chris Nilan. Despite being born in Boston, this heavily penalized defenseman wasn't regarded as a hero native son. He played for nearly a decade for the Montreal Canadiens and then briefly for the New York Rangers. At the end of his career, he realized his boyhood dream and played for the locals for two seasons starting in 1990. He led the world in penalty minutes and once got 42 in a single game against the Hartford Whalers. We hated him until he came here, and we hated him hard.

4. Ken Dryden. He was drafted by the Boston Bruins, but never played for them. Instead, he became a Hall of Fame goalie for the Montreal Canadiens. A six-time Stanley Cup champion, Dryden won four consecutive titles from 1976-79. People always remember he was a Bruin for a day and that he killed Boston in the postseason. He was one of the two biggest reasons why the Canadiens dominated the 1970s.

3. Matt Cooke. This Pittsburgh Penguins goon delivered a possible career-ending hit on the B's Marc Savard in 2010. The play became even more infamous when none of Savard's teammates took issue and beat the shit out of Cooke. The next meeting between the two teams resulted in a mega-fight between the B's Shawn Thornton and Cooke where he got rolled. Every time the B's play the Pens, Cooke is a marked man.

2. Claude Lemieux. The guy was a skilled scorer and would instigate a fight as quick as he could score goals. He and Cam Neely had their battles whether he was in a Canadiens or New Jersey Devils uniform. If you don't remember this clown, go to YouTube and type in "Claude Lemieux vs. Steve Leach line-brawl 1995." You'll understand after that.

1. Ulf Samuelsson. He played in 1,080 games, scored 332 points and accumulated 2,453 penalty minutes. That's about all you need to know about "Ulfie." His hit on Cam Neely during Game 3 of the 1991 Wales Conference Finals is the one that most say shortened Neely's career. Neely is now the President of the B's and is beloved in Boston. As long as Neely remains in good standing, Ulf will be at the top on this list.

My 10 Favorite Boston Bruins Fights
:: by Ken Casey of Dropkick Murphys

Note: Ken Casey is the bass guitarist and vocalist of the red hot Irish-American rock band Dropkick Murphys. Their song "Shipping Off to Boston" now serves as an anthem for our great city. Formed in Quincy in the mid-1990s, the band has released seven albums to date.

10. Derek Sanderson vs. Montreal Canadiens. This was before my time, but amazing nonetheless. Bruins/Canadiens benches clear; Cashman and Sanderson go on a rampage. Police and fans get involved. Sanderson throws a Canadiens jersey into the stands in the Garden on his way to the penalty box.

9. Terry O'Reilly vs. Clark Gillies. An O'Reilly nemesis. They had some epic battles.

8. John Wensink Challenges the Minnesota North Stars. After battering Minnesota right wing Alex Pirus, Boston's John Wensink challenged the entire Minnesota bench, capping an epic 1977 brawl that generated so much bad blood that it set the stage for an even bigger brawl in a 1981 Bruins-North Stars game at the Garden that featured a record-breaking 406 penalty minutes.

7. Lyndon Byers vs. Craig Berube. The Byers uppercut was scary business, just ask Philly's Berube. Side note: one night in the late 1980s, I heckled Byers around 2 a.m. outside of Sean's in Faneuil Hall and he chased me halfway up State Street. Who knew the bastard could run so fast? He almost got me.

6. Cam Neely vs. Scot Kleinendorst I & II. Former Adams Division foes the Hartford Whalers come into the Garden in 1987 and Kleinendorst drops Neely with a punch right on the button. The crowd is shocked. But have no fear— next period Cam settles the score with a savage beating, shattering Kleinendorst's nose and skating off to some classic commentary by old friend Derek Sanderson.

5. Terry O'Reilly's 1987-88 Bruins. Lead by Neely, Miller, Byers and Head Coach Terry O'Reilly, the Bruins pound their way through the Sabres, Canadiens and Devils on their way to the Stanley Cup Finals.

4. Terry O'Reilly vs. Dave Schultz, Any and All. O'Reilly epitomized everything we love about the Bruins—tough, hardworking, ton of heart.

3. P.J. Stock vs. Steven Peat—or Anyone Else, for That Matter! The little bastard had a lot of heart. The Bruins hadn't seen a little guy that tough since Stan Jonathan. Between the wave and the P.J. Stock Crew t-shirts that put Sully's Tees on the map (courtesy of Ian Larabee), the fans ate it up!

2. Bruins Go Into the Stands at Madison Square Garden. Could it ever get any better than this 1979 battle? Don't mess with the Big Bad Bruins or they will come into the stands and beat you to a pulp with your own shoe!

1. Stan Jonathan vs. Pierre Bouchard. Jonathan switches hands in this 1978 fight and drops Bouchard, breaking his cheekbone. Blood everywhere. Ref covered in blood. The brutality of old time hockey in its rawest form.

The 10 Most Wonderful Things About Vermont's Three-Year Run in the NCAA Men's Basketball Tournament :: by Tom Brennan

Note: Tom Brennan served as head coach for the University of Vermont men's basketball team from 1986–2005. He guided the Catamounts to three straight NCAA tournaments. In 2005, his team achieved their program's first March Madness victory and became the tournament darlings with an upset over Syracuse, which had won the tournament two years before. The all-time leader in games coached and wins at Vermont, Tom retired after that season and now calls college games on national radio and does shows on satellite radio from the comfort of his home in Vermont. A wonderful guy with an amazing zeal for life, Tom was kind enough to share with us the highlights of his March Madness experiences.

10. Being That Guy. I was lucky enough to be the coach of those teams. This is actually reason nine through one as well; but I'll try and be a bit more versatile.

9. Doing the Unthinkable. That starting in 2003, we went three years in a row to the NCAAs. Vermont had never been in postseason play in the 100 previous years.

8. Patience. We accomplished a goal that took 16 years to attain. I'm still kind of shocked that they kept me around after my sizzling 14-68 start in my first three years at Vermont.

7. Belief! Having been to the tourney in 2003 and 2004 and having much of the team back, we really believed that we could compete with the "Cuse" in 2005. At Vermont, how cool is that!

6. Containing Myself. The sheer joy I felt when the horn went off vs. Syracuse was overwhelming. I actually thought I might burst and they would find me in pieces throughout the arena.

5. See No. 10!

4. Achieving the Goals I Set for Us. That all the hard work and dedication of all the players, coaches and staff in the previous 15 years was totally rewarded. Patience IS a virtue.

3. Perspective. We were all part of something so meaningful. It was so much greater than all of us combined.

2. Thank You Four-letter Network. That the whole year of 2004-05 was chronicled in a series on ESPN called *The Season*. I can't wait to show my grandchildren and it NEVER goes away.

1. School and Personal Pride. More important than anything, how proud we were able to make our university, alumni, community and state. Thanks again, boys—I'll never forget you.

Note: Gary Tanguay is from Rumford, Maine. He's the host of the New England Patriots Radio Network pregame, halftime and postgame shows, as well as the face of Comcast Sportsnet New England.

10. Chester Greenwood. Inventor of the ear muff, which was the precursor to the headsets that NFL coaches and NASCAR pit crews wear today. Don't visit Farmington, Maine on Chester Greenwood Day. You will not get through town because of the parade.

9. Bitsy Ionta. Pine Tree Baseball League. Why is Bitsy on this list? Because, I hit the only home run of my short-lived baseball career off of him, that's why. I was playing for the Mexico team (no, not the country . . . ha) and he was pitching for the Dixfield Dixies in the Pine Tree League, which is one of the oldest baseball—not softball people, but baseball—leagues in the country. Bitsy was a crafty vet, who played into his sixties and got hitters out not with speed, but by making the ball dance. One of his pitches came my way and didn't dance. It was beautifully flat and I crushed it . . . oh, a good 150 feet down the right-field line. Okay, it was a short porch, but was that my fault?

8. Stan Thomas. Mexico, Maine's only major leaguer, he graduated from my high school about 14 years ahead of me and played for Texas and the Yankees. We were the only kids excited when a Stan Thomas baseball card showed up in a newly bought pack.

7. L.L. Bean. Leon Leonwood Bean was the great outdoorsman whose name remains on that big store in Freeport where drunken college kids go at three in the morning. He invented the Bean boot as a young man and legend has it that his first batch all fell apart. He replaced every pair free of charge and that approach to customer service went on to make his store famous.

6. Cindy Blodgett. The best basketball player to ever come out of Maine. No, not the best woman basketball player, the best basketball player—period. While at the University of Maine, she led the country in scoring twice. I knew she was big when I saw her meet with Larry Bird at the Fleet Center before a Pacers-Celtics game. Larry didn't meet with just anybody.

5. Ricky Craven. NASCAR driver from Newburgh, Maine. This guy was the real deal. I loved my guys at Oxford Plains Speedway like Tiger White, Stan Horne and Al Hammonds, but Craven made it to the big time in the 32 TIDE Car. He had two NASCAR wins and 41 top 10s before moving to a broadcasting career. A great guy who I had the pleasure of interviewing at the Las Vegas Motor Speedway while covering a Ruiz-Holyfield title fight. How did I end up at a racetrack while covering a fight? What happens in Vegas stays in Vegas.

4. Mike Emrick. One of the two greatest hockey announcers to come out of Maine. He is not a native, but he performed play by play for the AHL Maine Mariners in Portland. After three seasons, he moved up to the Philadelphia Flyers. I can't believe it took him that long.

3. Gary Thorne. The other great hockey announcer to come out of Maine. I knew Gary before he was famous when he was the cool guy that taught business law at the University of Maine at Orono. He also was the hockey team's play-by-play announcer. For a summer, he announced for the minor league Maine Guides and a season later he was in the big leagues with the Mets. And as they say, the rest is history.

2. Jud Strunk. The anchor of "The Farmington Maine Sports Report" on *Laugh In* during the early 1970s, he was also known for his folk hit "Daisy a Day." Heck, the guy was even on *The Tonight Show*.

1. Billy Swift. "Swifty" was THE MAN in college. After a brilliant career with the Black Bears, he was a first-round draft pick by Seattle. But his best season was with the Giants when he went 21-8 in 1993. I moved out of a house at school and Swifty moved in after me. All I can recall is there was a blow-out party and I lost my $200 security deposit. Damn.

These are the people whose work area fans love to read, watch and listen to. Their opinions have mattered and helped us shape our own views about the local sports scene.

12. Ron Borges. A *Boston Herald* columnist who doesn't mince words and one of the most insightful boxing analysts on the planet. I love the guy. Many other people hate him, but that means people are reading and listening to him.

11. Dan Shaughnessy. Stands out because of his curly hair and incredibly biting columns. No one in Boston can take out the carving knife and turn someone into a gutted fish like him. Another favorite of mine.

10. Sports Radio. Yes, I said it. With the creation of 98.5 The Sports Hub to challenge WEEI, local fans have more choices than ever to get their sports information and hear opinions. With up to 20 percent of the Boston radio audience listening to sports radio, it's the most listened-to format in the city. And with online streaming, there are now people all across the country listening to the best sports opinions in America.

9. Don Gillis. The former Channel 5 sportscaster is regarded as the pioneer of the 11:23 p.m. sportscast. He hosted Red Sox pregame and postgame shows and hosted a weekly radio show called *The Voice of Sports*. Imagine the nightly news with no sportscast...oh, sorry—Fox 25, you've already done that. Gillis shouldn't be forgotten in Boston sports history.

8. Glenn Ordway. The longtime sports radio host on WEEI created a show that allowed him to get big ratings, yet insulate himself from criticism. He had rotating guests that did most of the boastful talking, while he sat back as a traffic cop and basked in the shouting and ratings success. He worked with Johnny Most for Celtics broadcasts and did some Bruins as well, so he definitely has his play-by-play stripes. He has his place as a "voice" but few will remember anything he said that was controversial because he never did. You can decide if that makes him a genius or poser.

7. Jackie MacMullan. She's in the Basketball Hall of Fame for a reason. She's one of the best ever to cover the NBA. She began writing for the *Boston Globe* in 1982 and quickly won the respect of everyone from Red Auerbach to Larry Bird to the editors of *Sports Illustrated*. She's since moved on to ESPN, making a smooth transition to television and radio. She's written numerous books and left her job at the *Globe* to spend more time with her kids. And she's still the best, most recognized female sports voice in America.

6. Ray Fitzgerald. He worked for the *Boston Globe* from 1965 until his death in 1982. He was the Massachusetts Sportswriter of the Year 11 times and was one of Boston's first huge sports voices. His columns were funny, glib and always had a point. Not many people my age in this city have any idea just how influential Ray was.

5. Bob Lobel. The longtime Channel 4 sports director became a legend because of the late night show *Sports Final*. His use of the panic button and the classic phrase, "why can't we get players like that?" after a player was traded away from Boston, is still a part of the Boston sports lexicon. We need to remember what he was and not what he is now. And he was an icon.

4. Eddie Andelman. He is regarded as the creator of sports radio. He is also a successful businessman making tons of dough in the real estate world and the creator of the Hot Dog Safari, an event that benefits the Joey Fund. His distinct Boston accent makes him stand out everywhere he goes. I say "Hi, how ahhh yeahhhh" like him all the time on the air because I do respect the hell out of the guy.

3. Peter Gammons. The longtime *Boston Globe* baseball writer was one of the two reasons I ran to get my Sunday *Globe* in the early 1990s. His Notes column was the most comprehensive baseball column in the country. He was hired by ESPN as their baseball insider and he became a national icon. Some joke that Red Sox GM Theo Epstein is a part of "Gammons Youth" because of Gammons' intense TV exposure and how much he influenced a generation of baseball fans. His schedule is now scaled back to just working NESN and the MLB Network. But to me, he is the only baseball insider I remember.

2. Will McDonough. The other reason I ran to get my Sunday *Globe*. He was THE sports columnist at the *Boston Globe*. His NFL Notes were right on, every time. He's a throwback to the old AFL and had connections at every NFL team once the leagues merged. He nearly always nailed the top 10 picks in his NFL draft preview. In 1979, he punched New England DB Raymond Clayborn after he poked Will in the eye. He was on the *NFL Today* on CBS and the *NFL on NBC* and his sudden death in January 2003 shocked everyone. One of the greatest ever and one of a kind.

1. Bob Ryan. He started at the *Globe* in the early 1970s with Peter Gammons and is universally regarded as one of the preeminent sports voices in our country. He was a Celtics beat writer and had coaches yelling at him that a player was called for a foul because of something he wrote. He's clashed with a few, but that's because he speaks his mind. He's on TV and radio and is still writing today. He's got an opinion on everything and is respected by EVERY-ONE in the media business. Tony Kornheiser has it right: Bob Ryan is "the quintessential American sportswriter."

Boston Red Sox Mount Rushmore :: AG

We know what Mount Rushmore stands for and why those four faces are on the national monument. But deciding on JUST four faces for this franchise was so tough. I know everyone won't be happy with this list, but it will spark more debate than any of the Mount Rushmores to follow in this book.

Honorable Mentions. Pedro Martinez, the only modern-day player who, in my opinion, could've cracked this list; Jimmie Foxx, a perennial MVP candidate while in Boston and even won one in 1938 (take out his last season in Boston and he averaged 40 HR and 125 RBI here); Roger Clemens, who had 192 wins for the Sox, just like Cy Young did, but the shadow of steroids still hangs over him and once he left and became a Yankee. . . .

4. Carl Yastrzemski. All-time team leader in hits, RBI, runs, at-bats, doubles and he won a Triple Crown. So he's not "Mr. Happy" all the time. I think he's mellowed as he's gotten older, but his numbers tell the story for younger generations of Sox fans who haven't connected with him. When your stats rival what Ted Williams did, you're damn good. There are four generations of Red Sox fans who have an attachment to Yaz and I wish he was around more and would embrace Sox fans now. He's an icon, but he could be so much more if we'd get to know the guy. Regardless, he deserves this honor.

3. Cy Young. His 192 wins as a pitcher are still a Red Sox team record, tied with Roger Clemens for the most in club history. This spot probably could've gone to Pedro or Clemens, but some of the numbers set Cy apart. Young started 297 games and threw 275 complete games in a Red Sox uniform. And his Sox ERA was 2.00—ridiculous in any era. And he jumped to the American League when he came to Boston in 1901, so there was an adjustment period for him. The best pitcher in each league gets an award named after this guy, so how can he not be etched into the side of our baseball mountain? And let's not forget, he also had nine saves...hey, they all count towards a legacy.

2. Babe Ruth. Let's see: he only played from 1914-19 with Boston, but his curse lived until 2004. The Sox sold him for what would amount to $2.5 million dollars today, because to get the player-for-player equivalent for him just couldn't be done. He pitched, he hit, he was a larger-than-life presence. He MADE . . . MADE . . . the New York Yankees what they are today. Even though Ruth was only here for six seasons, he's linked as much to the Red Sox as he is to the Yankees. It just happens to be in a negative way. My eight-year-old stepson even knows the Sox blew this one. This link between the Bostons and New Yorks will never die because of "The Babe."

1. Ted Williams. I will forever regard "Teddy Ballgame" as the greatest hitter who ever lived. The only guy who can challenge him right now is Albert Pujols, and he still has a loooonnngggg way to go. His career ended in 1960, and yet we still compare today's hitters to Ted. If nothing speaks to his greatness, that should, in a nutshell. His on-base percentage one year was .551—.551! That would cause Theo Epstein and Bill James to have sportsgasms if they could find anyone like that today. It's a shame what has happened to his remains as he was manipulated by his scumbag son until his death in 2002. His head is frozen in some facility in Arizona. Just disgraceful. But his face would shine on this monument.

Top 11 Role Players in Boston Sports History
:: AG and the Fans

We asked our fans at the book's Facebook page via my radio show at 98.5 The Sports Hub, to list their best role players. These were predominately guys who played on winning teams because we're now more aware of the phrase "role player." Thanks for the great contributions from Jason Whitford, Mark Lenehan, Ed Finch, Frank Travaline, Rob McMahan, Kris Waterman, Jimmy Olsen, Hank "The Crank" Johnson, Cori Marie, Andrew Cardente, Kevin Kelly and Abbie Smith.

11. Mosi Tatupu and 10. Larry Izzo. Two guys who did the same thing, just in different eras. Izzo was a key signing from the Miami Dolphins when Bill Belichick sunk his teeth into his first real free agent class in 2001. BB identified that he needed a special teams ace and he got one for seven years with Izzo. Mosi, who was with the Pats from 1978-90, played some at running back, but was a standout special teamer covering kicks. Both excelled at doing the garbage work needed to help teams win at the highest level.

9. Shawn Thornton. In four years with the Bruins, he's become a fan favorite as the enforcer. He skates hard, is good with the media and rarely loses a fight. He won a Stanley Cup in 2007 with Anaheim, and another with the Buins in 2011.

8. Kendrick Perkins. Drafted by the Memphis Grizzlies in the first round of the 2003 NBA Draft and traded to the Celtics, he grew from a raw high schooler to one of the pieces of the Celtics 2007-08 championship team. He would draw charges, grab rebounds and be the legitimate tough guy that Kevin Garnett portrays himself as. He was traded in 2011 to Oklahoma City, just when fans were really starting to appreciate what he did for the C's.

7. Doug Mirabelli. He played with the Red Sox from 2001-07, with a short stint as a San Diego Padre at the beginning of the 2006 season. The Padres traded Mirabelli back to the Red Sox when the Sox couldn't find a suitable replacement for him as Tim Wakefield's personal catcher. Mirabelli arrived at the airport where a police escort was waiting to get him to Fenway for a game that night against the New York Yankees. He arrived at Fenway at 7 p.m. and was behind the plate at 7:13 p.m. Now that's a role player right there.

6. Dave Roberts. Brought in by GM Theo Epstein in 2004 to be a defensive specialist and add speed off the bench, he stole the most famous base in Red Sox history. Sox down 4-3 in the bottom of the ninth, facing elimination against the Yankees in Game 4 of the ALCS, Roberts stole second as a pinch runner after a Kevin Millar walk. Bill Mueller then singled, Roberts scored and the greatest comeback in baseball history was on.

5. James Posey. Signed in the 2007 offseason by the Celtics to be a shooter from deep and a defensive guy who could do multiple things off the bench, Posey turned out to be a steal for Danny Ainge. Often the forgotten man, he'd knock down the occasional big shot and was allowed to flow at times offensively because he'd see man-to-man defense with everyone worrying about Ray Allen or Paul Pierce. He played so well, he opted out of his remaining contract with Boston and signed a $25 million deal with New Orleans in 2008. But for one year and a ring, he did yeoman's work here.

4. Troy Brown. What didn't Troy Brown do? He returned punts, kicks, played defense, caught passes, ran reverses. He was "Mr. Everything" for the Pats from 1993-2007. He'll be a Patriots Hall of Famer someday, and he earned his way onto this list. He did what was asked of him and did it to the best of his abilities. He was a fire extinguisher; you broke the glass in case of emergency and Troy fixed everything. His signature play for me was in the playoff game in San Diego in 2007 when Tom Brady threw what should've been the game-ending interception to Marlon McCree. Troy stripped McCree of the ball and the Pats went on to score a touchdown and win the game on a last-second field goal. That play was Troy in a nutshell.

3. Tim Wakefield. The knuckleballer would let you know he wasn't happy about his role unless he was starting, but this Red Sox pitcher has done it all. Starter, short relief man, long relief man, closer—you name it and he's done it. And at the end of the day, he may end up as the winningest pitcher in Red Sox history. A real asset to the organization for 15 years now, even if he's not always happy with his role.

2. Dennis Johnson. He was brought to the Celtics from Phoenix in a 1983 trade to match up against bigger guards like Andrew Toney of the Philadelphia 76ers. And play defense, he did. He was named to the NBA All-Defensive team three times as a Celtic and knew when to facilitate to Bird, McHale and Parish. But he could also score and do his own thing when needed. He didn't need to be a star here with the Big Three around and he fit in perfectly.

1. Kevin Faulk. I absolutely love this guy. He's the best third-down back in the NFL for about five years running. He can pick up the blitz, return kicks and play special teams if needed. He has the respect of everyone in the organization, Bill Belichick included. Kevin Faulk is every bit as important as Troy Brown was.

Within the confines of the arena, the athletes have the opportunity to determine who is superior. However, sometimes the world that surrounds the sports stage has an impact on the event or even overshadows the proceedings. In the following list, fans, weather and other outside forces shifted the focus from the athletic happening to the hostile elements surrounding it.

14. Red Sox vs. Indians in Fog (May 27, 1986). In front of 6,661 fans at Municipal Stadium in Cleveland, the Red Sox beat the Indians 2-0 in a fog-shortened, six-inning game. After the game, Sox pitcher Dennis "Oil Can" Boyd uttered the famous quote about the stadium situated on Lake Erie, "That's what happens when you build a ballpark by the ocean."

13. Patriots Exhibition on Fire (August 16, 1970). Prior to New England's first exhibition game of the 1970 season at Alumni Field on the Boston College campus, a fire broke out under the bleachers. Fans were forced to evacuate to the field. After the fire was brought under control, the game was played and the Patriots lost 45-21.

12. Wembley Stadium Storm (October 6, 1980). Following Marvelous Marvin Hagler's dominating victory over Englishman Alan Minter in London, the angry crowd showered the new middleweight champion with bottles. Hagler and his team had to run under the cover of the English Bobbies while those around the ring used their chairs as shields to protect themselves from the unruly Wembley Stadium crowd.

11. Killer Plane at Shea Stadium (December 9, 1979). At the conclusion of the second quarter of a Patriots-Jets game, the halftime show was provided by remote-controlled airplanes. Unfortunately, during the event, one of the "pilots" lost control of his machine. The plane subsequently dove into the crowd, killing a New England fan.

10. Route 1 Electrocution (December 22, 1983). Following the Patriots playoff-clinching victory over the Cincinnati Bengals, New England fans rushed the field and tore down the goal posts. Some of the rambunctious revelers decided to march the goal post up Route 1, where it came in contact with electrical wires, resulting in the electrocution of five fans.

9. Fire Outside Fenway Park (June 17, 1972). In the first game of a double-header against the Chicago White Sox, a four-alarm fire broke out over the right-field wall at the Vendome Hotel. Throughout the afternoon, smoke rose over Kenmore Square and cast an eerie pale over the matinee event. While the Red Sox split the doubleheader, tragedy enveloped downtown Boston, as nine fireman perished in the blaze.

8. Suffolk Downs Riot (August 11, 1945). In the 11th running of the Mass Cap, favorite Johnny Jr. was the first horse to cross the wire. However, race stewards disqualified the favorite and gave the championship to the previous year's winner, First Fiddle. When the disqualification was announced, fans rioted and attacked the steward's stand. Police with tear gas and shotguns were called in to quell the equine-inspired uprising.

7. Boston College vs. Alabama at Sullivan Stadium (November 23, 1983). On the day after Thanksgiving, a brutal rain/ice storm consumed Foxboro in the midst of the Boston College-Alabama football game. At halftime, with the Crimson Tide leading 13-6, the power went out. Moments before the game was to be cancelled, electricity returned. A scrappy BC team, led by linebacker Steve DeOssie, turned the tide on the Tide and rallied to beat the national power 20-13.

6. MIT Balloon at Harvard Stadium (November 20, 1982). In the second quarter of the annual Harvard-Yale game, a balloon propelled by a buried hydraulic pump suddenly rose from the ground in a cloud of smoke. Written on the side of the weather balloon was "MIT"—the neighboring university where the pranksters attended school.

5. Run for the Hoses (April 20, 1976). Temperatures during the running of the 1976 Boston Marathon reached a torrid 100 degrees. The press bus, leading the runners, implored homeowners to grab their garden hoses and douse the runners as they passed. In response, residents of eight separate towns answered the call and soaked the runners, including Georgetown student Jack Fultz, who survived the heat to win that year's Boston Marathon.

4. Celtics vs. Lakers Heated (June 8, 1984). The Celtics-Lakers played Game 5 of the 1984 NBA Finals in the Boston Garden, where thermometers registered high temperatures of 97 degrees. The Celtics and Larry Bird flourished in the heat, while a beaten and aging Lakers team sucked for oxygen in the Celtics 121-103 victory.

3. Beanpot Blizzard (February 6, 1978). In the first round of the annual college hockey tournament, a historical blizzard hit Boston. During the second game between Boston College and Boston University, a state of emergency was called by the Governor and public transportation was discontinued. Many fans and Boston Garden employees were left stranded and forced to take up residence in skyboxes and locker rooms for upwards of five days.

2. Imposter Wins the Boston Marathon (April 21, 1980). As soon as Rosie Ruiz crossed the Boylston Street finish line ahead of all the other female contestants, race officials and journalists grew suspicious. The winner wasn't built like a runner, didn't understand basic running terminology and no one had seen her on the course. Eventually, officials stripped her of her title, charging that she had only run part of the course. She never gave the champion's medal back.

1. Stanley Steamer Cup Game (May 24, 1988). In Game Four of the 1988 Stanley Cup, temperatures in the Boston Garden registered 88 degrees. The Edmonton Oilers were leading the series 3-0, but the Bruins were gaining momentum. With the game tied at 3-3 in the second period, the humidity first caused fog to blanket the ice and then disrupted power. The Boston Garden lights were extinguished. The game was cancelled and the series returned to Edmonton. On their home ice, the Oilers completed the sweep of the Bruins.

When you think of Mount Rushmore, it's about the people who made this nation what it is today. So we apply that to our New England Patriots and come up with the four faces that you think of when you think Patriots football.

Honorable Mentions. Andre Tippett; Mike Haynes; Drew Bledsoe; Bill Parcells; Tedy Bruschi; Gino Cappelletti.

4. John Hannah. When doing this list, the first three on it came easy. But the last one was a tossup. But when I thought about the Pats player most regarded for his success and legacy, I went with Hannah. Regarded by many as the best offensive lineman in the history of football, his career lasted from 1973-85 and people still reference him today when talking about the all-time best big boys up front. "Hog" is an interesting character. He'll tell you what's on his mind, which has helped him cross over to a new generation of Pats fans. He's in the Pro Football Hall of Fame, which is where the other three on this list will end up someday.

3. Tom Brady. The one thing that Brady will fight as history moves forward is having played under Bill Belichick. BB will always be remembered as a genius and will get most, if not all, of the credit for the success of the Patriots. The team didn't fall apart in 2008 when Brady was injured and that will hurt his lifetime legacy. But let's not mistake how great Brady is. He may . . . may . . . go down as the best QB of all time, but definitely as one of the top three. He's good and he's on this monument, but history will show that he'll always be overshadowed by Belichick.

2. Bill Belichick. He's passed Bill Parcells in the high-speed lane because of his success with this franchise. He's come up with the 21st-century formula for a dynasty and has produced three Vince Lombardi Trophies and four Super Bowl appearances for New England. He's been as successful a drafter as there's been over a 10-year period in the NFL. He has come up with a way of doing things that's not popular because of his demand for secrecy, but you can't deny its effectiveness.

1. Robert Kraft. I think his face would be first on this monument. Without him, this franchise would be in St. Louis right now. Combine that with the fact he hired Bill Belichick, who then drafted Tom Brady, and that Kraft sunk his own money into Gillette Stadium . . . his face has to be first. I think all Pats fans would shudder to think what this franchise would be like without him at the top.

Best Things to Eat While Watching a Sporting Event :: AG

Food and sports go together like air and breathing. Beavis and Butthead. Gresh and Zo. Charlie Sheen and porn stars. This may be just one man's opinion, but to me these are the must-haves if you're going to do it right. Oh, and Tom Brady's favorite will start things out.

11. Popcorn (Tom Brady's Favorite). As long as Giselle isn't feeding it to him on national television like Cameron Diaz did to A-Rod, very few complaints here or anywhere.

10. Candy. Yes, candy, because ice cream, even on a stick, is too messy. Even if you do not have children, it's a guarantee that when the game gets into the fourth quarter, after having eaten most of the real food, you'll need something different to stimulate those taste buds to get you to the end of the game. Kit Kats are a personal favorite as well as Skittles. Do not go with Sour Patch kids or anything that's made for a six-year-old, unless you have a six-year-old there. Grown-ups will scoff at the real kiddy candies and they can ruin a great spread.

9. Veggie Tray. GO ahead and laugh. But tell me this: isn't there always one wife/girlfriend/straphanger/somebody who bitches about there being nothing healthy? Now that you see I'm right, it also helps the early arrivers munch on something other than what you have planned for the game itself. If people stay away and wait, fine, so be it. But you'll score big points if you have a small one of these.

8. Soda. A must. I'm a Pepsi guy. But this can include Gatorade. It can be used for mixed drinks or maybe even as a treat for some kids so they leave you alone to watch the game. Mountain Dew is a personal favorite. Plus, you know someone will drink too much booze too fast and will switch. At least give them something with flavor.

7. Some Sort of Chicken Poppers. BBQ Chicken, Buffalo Chicken, Teriyaki Chicken—all kinds of chicken to choose from. Put them in the oven and 20 minutes later there's a new finger food to chow on. And kids love 'em as much as I do. Anytizers are amazing in this role.

6. Hot Dogs. In New England, we use the split-top buns. I'm not a fan of these unless I have some coleslaw to plop on top of my dog. These are easy, satis-fying and, if you have a good brand, absolutely delicious. There are only two ways to make a good hot dog—grilling or steaming. Like you'd get in a gas station at 3 a.m. If you make them on a stove top in a pan or microwave them, you can't be my friend.

5. Soft Pretzels. Go to a supermarket and get the box of frozen pretzels where you cook them in an oven or toaster oven for about four minutes and see the smiles you get. My wife knows that these are a must for me . . . in the rare event I let her do the grocery shopping. I love these things and they take you back to when you were a kid and begged for one walking by the pretzel place in the mall.

4. Chips and (Begrudgingly) Dip. They're not my favorite (except Doritos), but I recognize that if you're going to have veggies out, you better have chips and dip. The problem nowadays is that you have too many chip choices. And it's not just brands, its flavors as well. You can't make everyone happy with chips and dip, BUT if you have none, you'll hear it even worse. A nice alternative is Pirate's Booty.

3. Alcohol. Not just beer, hooch as well. Wine for ladies. Beer for men. And hard stuff for real men! I'm a hard liquor guy. Jamison and ginger ale with lime. And lemons and limes are a must. Moderation is the key. Drink heavy early and lighter later. Unless you're the neighbor, then drink all you want, just don't puke in my house or you'll get an ass kicking.

2. Nachos. If it weren't for my wife, I'd never put them on this list. Betsey and her friend Mandy always, always, always get nachos when we go out, so I had to learn to make a ghetto version of them at home. I hate beans, most cheeses and jalapenos, so you can see why I had to be forced into putting this on the list. I'm the only guy on the planet who thinks beer and nachos is beneath me. And I don't care who thinks it's wrong. Sorry, honey.

1. Pizza or Pizza Rolls. If I'm at an event, I try at least one piece of pizza. Every person reading this knows what pizza places in his or her neighborhood suck, because you try them all. The home go-to is the Jeno's pizza rolls. Easy to cook in the oven or toaster oven and just effing awesome. If you've never had pizza rolls, you don't know what you're missing.

My co-author Michael and I created a Facebook page on which we asked for fans input to be used in this book. We promoted the page via my radio show, heard Monday through Friday from 10 a.m. to 2 p.m. on 98.5 The Sports Hub. We had a bunch of folks post comments for this list, including: Marc Cappello, Michael Hennessey, Alex Stewart, Benny from Luxe, Rob McMahan, Kevin Kelly, Andrew Henry, Mike Pignataro, Charod Williams, Mike Babchik, Nick Kostos, Mandy Soderi and Bill Liberis. Without their input, I never would have realized that there were so many fat guys in Boston sports history!

10. Curt Schilling. He was one of the best big-game pitchers of all time who didn't look like he should've been. He flat-out had a guuter (GRESHABULARY: *guuter—where a man's gut continues down towards his junk; for a female, it looks like they have their ass on backwards*). Schilling looked like a bartender, but pitched here like a Hall of Famer.

9. Bill Parcells. My radio partner Scott Zolak told me stories about how Parcells used to bust his balls because Scott was prone to putting on weight very easily. Parcells would joke during stretching and Zo would fire back, "This from a guy who does Dunkin' Donuts commercials." Parcells loved it. He's on the list of people you wouldn't want to see naked.

8. Thomas Hamilton. He only had a short stint with the Celtics in the mid-1990s, but when a bad, shorthanded team signs you and has to wait to play you because you're 7-2 and 330 pounds, you're a fat guy. He played 11 games and scored a total of 25 points . . . yet why do I have a funny feeling that Tommy Heinsohn felt he had an up side and was bullish on him?

7. John Bagley. How the hell do you become a fat point guard? Yet that's exactly what Bagley was. He was listed at 6-0, 185 pounds. But when you looked at him, you knew it was a lie. He played sporadically because of injuries . . . coincidence? Just Google a picture and you'll see why he's on this list.

6. David Ortiz. One of the best fat guy hitters in baseball history. I do think being fat goes with the position of being a DH, and Ortiz did nothing to debunk the myth. Seeing him at the plate, you wondered if he could get around on the inside fastball, but he could, and did it consistently. Then he'd run and you'd be brought right back to the reality that he was a slow-moving fat man who could rake.

5. Ted Washington. Acquired by the Patriots from the Chicago Bears in 2003, he may have been the best 3-4 nose tackle ever. At 6-5 and 350 pounds, he was immovable in the middle of any defense on the seven teams he played for in the NFL. He was the guy who paved the way for another fat guy on this list who occupies the middle of the Pats defense today. I'm a big dude. "Big Ted" is just a mammoth human being. He used that size to perfection and made life hell for a lot of centers in the NFL.

4. Mo Vaughn. I loved Mo. He was nimble, had good feet, could move around that first base bag with relative ease. A true power hitter, he won an MVP as a Red Sox and loved the nightlife. He's even bigger now. But part of that is because of the $70 million he made being a fat baseball player.

3. Vince Wilfork. At the end of the day, he may replace Ted Washington as the quintessential 3-4 nose tackle. He's listed at 330 pounds and that's total bull-shit. I love the guy. His family is great and he truly is the defensive leader of the Pats. His body type is perfect for the position. Guys at that spot don't run, they waddle. But when his big butt gets moving, look out. If he ever went all King Kong Bundy on a QB the way Tony Siragusa used to, "It's curtains!" (I'm stealing a Gorilla Monsoon line since I made a KKB reference.)

2. George Scott. He's the ultimate dichotomy—a fat guy who played first base but won eight Gold Gloves! Fat guys aren't supposed to move like that. He was a very good player and when Red Sox fans of the 1970s and '80s think of fat athletes, "Boomer" is at the top of the list. The player modern fans think of is No. 1.

1. Rich Garces. "El Guapo" was a cult hero for a time in Boston. He bounced around the bigs with the Twins, Marlins and Cubs before spending seven seasons in Boston. The Sox asked him to lose weight, which he did, and he wasn't the same pitcher. Some felt it changed his mechanics, as he'd been a fat guy the whole time he was a major leaguer. When he'd get a big strikeout, people loved how he'd pump his chubby arm with a balled-up fist. He was a genuinely nice guy (jolly) and IMHO did a nice job in the role he was asked to fill here. Mention the name "El Guapo" to a Sox fan and see the reaction you get. Priceless!!

Same as with the Patriots Mount Rushmore, the first three on this list are easy, YOU try and pick a fourth. It's near impossible. But I did it and I think you'll be surprised who my No. 4 is. . . .

Honorable Mentions. Bob Cousy, point guard for numerous championships, part of dynasty No. 1 under Red Auerbach, still around the team once in a while as a broadcaster; John Havlicek, jammed between Russell and Bird is Havlicek—great scorer, great rebounder, great player ("Havlicek steals it. Havlicek steals the ball" from Johnny Most will ring forever with C's fans).

4. Tommy Heinsohn. Maybe not the best player in Celtics history, but I'd ask this simple question: how many current C's fans can go two sentences without mentioning his name? He and Mike Gorman are an institution on the broadcast side of things and he won titles as a player and as a coach. He did the NBA Finals when they first came into national prominence in the 1980s on CBS, and if he wanted to play the TV game again on a national level, it's a phone call away. Fans of the team from the 1950s to the 2010s know him.

3. Red Auerbach. He turned the C's into a dynasty, thrice. And they weren't so bad in between. As a coach and front office executive, Auerbach had an amazing ability to set a standard for winning that was contagious, inspiring and demanding. His players went to the greatest of lengths for a man who never played in the pros. No small feat regardless of the era. He was a master of the draft and is the man who made this organization what it is today. There will never be another like him.

2. Bill Russell. This Celtic legend is regarded as the greatest center who ever lived. He has more championship rings from the college and pro ranks than can fit on a pair of hands. He was the first black coach in NBA history and endured playing in a time when being an elite black athlete drew racist rants and taunts. He broke down barriers, even if he felt uncomfortable doing so. He helped racially change this city's mindset and we're all the better for it. He took on all comers on the court and beat them all. If it weren't for a certain hick, he'd be first on this list.

1. Larry Bird. The "Hick from French Lick" is one of the three best players in NBA history. His battles with Dr. J, Magic Johnson, Dominique Wilkins, Michael Jordan and Isiah Thomas are the stuff of NBA legend. Race was a factor in reverse with all those rivalries. He was the NBA's version of "The Great White Hope." He pulled no punches and won championships. I'll never forget watching an NBA video where Magic Johnson says if you give Larry Bird a chance at the end of the game, he'll beat you every time. Lots of C's fans feel that way.

These are the best comebacks of TB 12's great career as Patriots QB. I didn't use the Super Bowl ones on this list because I was looking for real comebacks where he had to lead the team. There are just so many to choose from, it's almost surreal. And we have Brady's choice for best win to start things off.

11. At New York, December 2, 2001 (Brady's Favorite). We all know what happened in this Jets game at the old Foxboro Stadium. Bledsoe out; Brady in. The Pats were down 13-0 at the half and came back to win 17-16. It was their seventh win in 10 games and pushed them to 7-5, throwing them into the AFC East race. Tom was 20 of 28 for 213 yards in that game. Afterwards he told the media: "With each win, each week, we get confidence. Last year, the team was 5-11, now we're 7-5. This can jumpstart our season." It did, right to the Super Bowl.

10. At Pittsburgh, September 25, 2005. With the Patriots down 13-10 with 14:19 in the fourth quarter, Brady went 12 for 12 passing for 167 yards to set up another Adam Vinatieri field goal with 0:01 left for a 23-20 win. He led two different seven-play drives for scores and this game notched his 50th career win. It also snapped the Steelers 16-game-winning streak.

9. Vs. Buffalo, September 14, 2009. Brady's first regular-season game back from the 2008 knee injury that ended his season. The Pats were overwhelming favorites, but found themselves down 24-13 with 5:32 to go in the fourth quarter. Brady was masterful in his final two drives, going 12 for 14 for 112 yards and two touchdowns. He was aided by the fumbled kickoff return by Buffalo's Leodis McKelvin with the Pats down 24-19. And three plays later the Pats had the lead, 25-24. The king was back.

8. At Indianapolis, November 4, 2007. The Pats were 20-10 with 9:42 to go after a Peyton Manning one-yard TD run, and that's when Brady started to do his thing. He led them on a seven-play drive to make it 20-17. Then after the defense forced a punt, Brady and the boys went on a three-play drive that ended with Brady connecting with Kevin Faulk for the game-winner.

7. Vs. Miami, December 29, 2002. The Pats were down 21-7 at the half with a shot at the AFC East Division crown. Down 24-13 with 4:59 left in the fourth quarter, Brady led a 10-play, 68-yard drive (while in pain, by the way) that ended with a catch by Christian Fauria for the two-point conversion that made it 24-21. After a Dolphins punt, the Pats set up Vinatieri with a four-play, nine-yard drive and the game was tied at 24. The offense then set up Adam for the game-winner after winning the toss. Having Brady out there showed us that the Pats would make comebacks as a team with TB leading the way and controlling the huddle.

6. At Baltimore, December 3, 2007. This Monday night game was the closest call the Patriots had during their undefeated regular season. The Pats were down 24-17 early in the fourth quarter, then got a FG to make it 24-20 with 8:46 to go. With 3:30 to go and still down four, the Pats got the ball and went on one of the craziest drives in their history. With 1:53 to go, the Ravens got a stop on a Kevin Faulk catch on third-and-10 and then inexplicably called a timeout, giving the Pats time to gather. Then the Pats got stopped on fourth-and-one, but a false start was called on Russ Hochstein and the Pats converted the subsequent fourth-and-six on a Samari Rolle illegal contact penalty. Then on fourth-and-five with 0:55 to go, the Ravens got nailed for another defensive penalty (which caused their sideline to go nuts). The next play, Brady connected with Jabar Gaffney for the TD, after which the Ravens Bart Scott got called for unsportsmanlike conduct. The Pats were 12-0 and on their way.

5. Vs. Baltimore (Again), October 17, 2010. The Ravens returned to Gillette after kicking our ass in the playoffs the year before. Down 20-10 early in the fourth quarter, Brady led an eight-play, 60-yard drive that ended with a TD pass to Deion Branch. After a defensive stop, Brady led the Pats on a 13-play, 80-yard drive that ate up over six minutes on the clock and resulted in the game-tying field goal. Brady was 16 for 24 for 156 yards with one touchdown and an interception in the fourth quarter. The teams battled deep into overtime, where TB led New England to the game-winning FG with 2:00 left on the clock. This added even more heat to the Pats-Ravens rivalry.

4. Vs. San Diego, October 14, 2001. They say you always remember your first. Brady was named AFC Offensive Player of the Week after this performance. He completed 13 of 19 passes for 130 yards and two touchdowns during the fourth quarter comeback and the game-winning drive in overtime. Brady hit my boy Jermaine Wiggins with the game-tying TD. And to make it even better, TB outdueled Doug Flutie, who is one of the all-time jackasses on the planet. TB on the day was 33 of 54 for 364 yards and two touchdowns.

3. At Denver, November 3, 2003. The Pats were down 24-23 with 2:49 on the clock when long snapper Lonnie Paxton, nearly backed up into his own end zone, snapped the ball off the goalpost for a safety to make it 26-23. The Pats defense forced a three-and-out after the free kick, leaving Brady with the ball and just over two minutes on the clock. He led them on a surgical, six-play, 58-yard drive and connected with David Givens with 0:35 on the clock for the improbable 30-26 win. Not only was Brady great, but the strategy of Bill Belichick worked to perfection in a game that will never be forgotten.

2. At San Diego, January 14, 2007. This was actually one of Tom's worst post-season games. He was 27 for 51 for 280 yards and two touchdowns and three interceptions, including one that should've sealed the Chargers win. Down 21-13 with 6:25 to go, Brady threw an interception to Marlon McCree, who ran with the ball instead of falling down. He was stripped by Troy Brown and the Pats regained possession. So with 6:16 on the clock, a new set of downs and the ball at the Chargers 32-yard line, Brady went four of five to lead the Pats on a five-play 32-yard TD drive and to a two-point conversion that tied the game at 21. SD goes three-and-out, then Brady leads the Pats to a Stephen Gostkowski field goal with 1:14 to go and the 24-21 win. He made mistakes, but overcame them and went 6 for 9 on those final two drives.

1. Vs. Oakland, January 19, 2002. The "Tuck Rule" game. For Pats fans, it's "The Snow Bowl." Just out of field-goal range and down 13-10 with just under two minutes to go, Brady was sacked by Charles Woodson on a corner blitz and the "fumble" was recovered by Greg Biekert. But referee Walt Coleman ruled that Brady was trying to tuck the ball back to his body when he realized he was going to be sacked. Therefore, under a rule instituted in 1999, it was not a fumble. The Pats got the ball back and moved to the Raiders 29 and Adam Vinatieri hit a line-drive 45-yard field goal through the snow to tie the game. It was the greatest kick I've ever seen. In overtime, Brady went eight of eight for 45 yards on a 15-play, 61-yard drive that set up Adam for the game-winner. No one will forget long snapper Lonnie Paxton doing snow angels in the end zone after the kick went through the uprights. Yes, there was some divine intervention, but Brady played great in the snow. IMHO, still a horseshit call.

The essence of sports is competition. Two protagonists are pitted against each other to determine superiority. The unknown denominators in the equation are the officials of the competition. The below list represents events in which officials impacted the event (rightly or wrongly) and in the process injected themselves into Boston sports lore.

15. Don "Fat Pig" Koharski (May 6, 1988). Following a Bruins 6-1 win over the Devils in Game 3 of the 1988 Conference Finals, New Jersey Coach Jim Schoenfeld was enraged and waited for referee Don Koharski outside the locker rooms after the game. When the two met, Koharski fell. This provoked the Devils coach to yell, "Go eat another donut, you fat pig!" Schoenfeld was subsequently suspended. The Devils appealed the suspension, causing NHL officials to boycott the following game.

14. Larry Bird Four-Pointer Waved Off (March 12, 1985). In the midst of the greatest individual shooting night in NBA history, officials waved off a Larry Bird three-pointer and foul because they wanted attention also. Bird ended up with 60 points that night in New Orleans, but had to share the stage with officials who refused to be ignored.

13. "And the German Judge. . . ." (February 25, 1994). After a tumultuous pre-Olympic buildup for Nancy Kerrigan, which included a premeditated attack on her knee by Tonya Harding's white-trash camp, Kerrigan skated a gem in Lillehammer, Norway. Sadly, the (East) German judge, Jan Hoffman, chose Oksana Baiul after the Russian skater spontaneously threw in a late triple jump to sway perceptions of her technically deficient performance.

12. Tim Tschida and "Knobby" (October 17, 1999). Umpire Tim Tschida made multiple bad calls during the 1999 ALCS—none worse than his incompetent ruling on Yankee Chuck Knoblauch's "non-tag" of Jose Offerman. The gross injustice infuriated Fenway fans, who littered the field in disgust. After the game, Tschida admitted his mistake but also referred to the Yankee second baseman as "Knobby." This spoke volumes about his affection for the pin-stripes.

11. Lenny Wirtz Needs Attention (March 26, 1992). UMass and John Calipari were on the verge of upsetting the mighty Kentucky Wildcats and their slick coach, Rick Pitino. Unfortunately, official Lenny Wirtz turned away from the play and called a technical foul on Coach Calipari for being out of the coach's box. The technical changed the momentum of the game and UMass lost in the Sweet Sixteen.

10. Hockey East's Gross Injustice (March 7, 2003). Two players doing everything to win collided in a sad accident of competition. Joe Exter, a goalie from Merrimack, slid head first 50 feet out of his crease in an all-out effort for a loose puck. His head hit the knee of Boston College forward Patrick Eaves. Thankfully, a badly injured Exter recovered and Eaves was ultimately hit with an absurd five-game postseason suspension.

9. Cooney Helps Clemens (October 9, 1990). Like that scene in *Hoosiers* when Coach Norman Dale begs the official to throw him out of the game so Shooter will coach, Roger Clemens is forever indebted to umpire Terry Cooney for tossing him from Game 4 of the ALCS. With his Ninja Turtle shoelaces and eye black, "The Rocket" should have been wearing Depends when he saw Dave Stewart warming up in the bullpen. In 1.2 innings, Clemens had already given up three runs when he implored Cooney to toss him out, which Cooney mercifully did.

8. Judges Choose Flash Over Substance (April 6, 1987). The Hagler-Leonard fight was the most-anticipated middleweight fight in boxing history. When it was over, judges Dave Moretti and Jose Guerra rewarded Leonard and his flashy flurries over Hagler, who relentlessly stalked the running pretender the entire bout.

7. A Fraud Gets Caught (October 19, 2004). In the eighth inning of Game 6 of the ALCS, Alex Rodriguez hit a little roller to Red Sox pitcher Bronson Arroyo. When Arroyo tried to tag the Yankee with lip gloss, A-Rod knocked the ball out of Arroyo's glove with his purse. A-Rod was called safe, Jeter scored, A-Rod ended up on second base and Yankee Stadium was rocking—the rally was on. Amazingly, the umpires, including Red Sox nemesis Joe West, gathered, reversed the call and called the cheating Yankee out for interference. The rest is beautiful history.

6. Skate in the Crease (April 26, 1998). In Game 3 of the NHL Conference Quarterfinals between the Bruins and Washington Capitals, P.J. Axelsson scored in overtime to give the Bruins a 2-1 lead over the Washington Capitals. That was until referee Paul Devorski decided to look at the goal on replay. During the review, he detected the toe of Bruin Tim Taylor's skate in the crease and disallowed the goal. The Capitals won in double overtime and eventually eliminated the Bruins from the postseason.

5. Richie Powers Spoils Fun (June 4, 1976). In what would have been one of the greatest endings in Boston sports history, a hobbled John Havlicek hit a running, leaning bank shot at the end of the second overtime of Game 5 of the 1976 NBA Finals against the Phoenix Suns. The Garden crowd had already rushed the floor in celebration when stick-in-the-mud referee Richie Powers ordered time put back on the clock. A fan punched the official in disagreement and the Suns tied the game with the additional time. The Celtics did win in the third overtime.

4. Larry Barnett Allows Interference (October 14, 1975). On the biggest stage at the biggest moment, home plate umpire Larry Barnett failed to protect Red Sox catcher Carlton Fisk from an interfering Ed Armbrister. The non-call led to a Cincinnati Reds 6-5 victory in Game 3 of the World Series. From that point forward, the balance of the World Series was changed, solely by the umpire's incompetent interpretation and application of the game's rules.

3. Too Many Men on the Ice (May 10, 1979). One momentary loss of focus in the closing minutes of Game 7 of the 1979 NHL Semifinals and the Bruins paid a brutal price. Too many black sweaters on the Forum ice in Montreal compelled referee Bob Myers to whistle the infraction on the Bruins—the rest is part of Bruins infamy.

2. Official Robs Patriots (December 18, 1976). With the upstart Patriots on the verge of upsetting the mighty Raiders in Oakland, official Ben Dreith decided to inject himself into the game. It was one of three things: complete incompetence, complete ego or a partnership in NFL fraud.

1. I Love the Tuck Rule (January 19, 2002). Hey Raider fans! Yah, you dopes with the black face paint and Mad Max shoulder pads! It's in the rulebook, so live with it. Anyways, Charles Woodson illegally hit Brady in the head while he was tucking. I vote for referee Fred Coleman for Patriots Hall of Fame.

This one was tough to get down to just four choices, with so many great figures from the "Old Time Hockey" era. I think two are easy for this list, after that it's up in the air.

Honorable Mentions. Johnny Bucyk; Milt Schmidt; Harry Sinden.

4. Eddie Shore. The four-time MVP was the biggest star on the Bruins in the 1930s. He was immortalized in the movie *Slap Shot* in a reference to "Old Time Hockey" by Paul Newman and the Hanson brothers. Never a big goal scorer or assist man, Shore won MVPs because of the way he played defense and moved the puck. He was physical, even though he stood only 5-11 and weighed under 200 pounds. His number is in the rafters because he earned it laying the early foundation for what the Boston Bruins would become.

3. Phil Esposito. For some perspective on how amazing a goal scorer he was, consider that Espo scored 76 goals in the 1970-71 season; in 1971, Reggie Smith led the Red Sox with 96 RBI. The next season Espo scored 66 goals; that next season, Reggie Smith led the Sox with 74 RBI. Just amazing. He had seasons of 152, 133, 130, 145 and 127 points. The trade with Chicago goes down as one of the biggest ripoffs in hockey history. He's gone on to run organizations in the NHL and is so respected that the next guy on this list changed his number for him. One of the best goal scorers of all time.

2. Ray Bourque. The Bruins have the market cornered on defenseman legends. The five-time Norris Trophy winner was almost the 1990 Hart Trophy winner for MVP. In the mind of team management, he was the perfect Bruin, as he never really got into a heated contract dispute with the team. Some fans view this as noble, some think he was taken for a ride by a cheap, manipulating owner. Many fans view him as the quintessential Bruin. He was in the playoffs every year but two. He won a Stanley Cup, just not in Boston. But he'll always be a Boston Bruin, no matter where he won his title.

1. Bobby Orr. His plus/minus in the 1970-71 season was +124, which is just stupid. He is by FAR the best scoring defenseman of all time and has been voted the best hockey player ever behind Gordie Howe and Wayne Gretzky. The specter of #4 still looms large in Bruins history simply because we can't watch the B's today and think of a D-man who scores 40 goals. He won two Stanley Cups and the picture of him flying through the air to win one of those Cups is maybe the greatest sports photo of all time. Just like Orr is the best defenseman of all time.

Most Memorable Moments as Owner of the Bruins :: by Jeremy Jacobs

Note: Jeremy Jacobs has been owner of the Boston Bruins since the mid-1970s. He is also chairman of the National Hockey League Board of Governors. As an avid fan of the team and the sport, he recounts some of his most special moments as an owner of the legendary team.

8. Winter Classic at Fenway Park. It was destined to be a monumental day. Bruins at legendary Fenway—an original six team playing at one of the most hallowed sports grounds in the world. Walking down on the field with Bruins players and legends. It was a magical day and we won.

7. Bruins Sweep Montreal Canadiens in First Round of 2009 Playoffs. The fans were amazing during the games. Best fans in the league. The play was incredibly exciting.

6. Game 1 of Stanley Cup Finals on May 15, 1990. Despite the special place that was the old Boston Garden, it was not without its issues. We regularly had problems with power. In fact, the lights went out during overtime play in Game 1 of the 1990 Stanley Cup Finals between the Bruins and Oilers. Edmonton won the game 3-2 in triple overtime and went on to win the series in five games. I only wish the lights going out for us had been good luck. It was the longest overtime in NHL history. While the game didn't go our way, I have never been in a more charged environment. I just wish we had won.

5. Bobby Orr's #4 Jersey Retired by the Bruins on January 9, 1979. At the ceremony, the crowd at the Boston Garden gave him the most amazing applause. It lasted so long that most of the night's program had to be scrapped. The crowd did not allow Orr to say his thank you speech until he put on a Bruins jersey. Great player and friend. Only regret is that he didn't finish his career as a Bruin. He should have.

4. Phil Esposito Night, December 3, 1987. Phil had always worn #7, the same number that Raymond Bourque wore. In a show of respect, Bourque skated up to Esposito and removed his #7 jersey, revealing a #77 jersey underneath— giving up the #7 to Phil to raise the jersey to the rafters. Two great Bruins. Incredible show of what it means to be a Bruin.

3. Normand Leveille Skate, September 26, 1995. During the closing ceremony of the old Boston Garden, we invited former Bruins left wing Normand Leveille back to the Garden to skate. Leveille had a very serious brain aneurysm years before and was gravely ill for many weeks. During the ceremony, Leveille came out on the ice skating with assistance from Bruins Captain Ray Bourque. The house erupted and by the time he was finished, there wasn't a dry eye in the house. Unbelievable strength and incredible spirit.

2. Stanley Cup Parade, 2011. Having won the Stanley Cup in Vancouver on Wednesday, June 15, we didn't have a real chance to celebrate the win until the Stanley Cup parade on Saturday. The crowds were immense and the fans were so excited to be part of this historic event in Bruins history. My entire family was there riding with Chara and Thomas in the lead Duck Boat. I have often said we are nothing without our fans. That day proved it.

1. Winning the Stanley Cup, 2011. Winning the Stanley Cup was one of the singularly most amazing experiences of my entire life. From the season opener in Prague to—107 games later—hoisting "The Cup" in Vancouver, I was so proud of this amazing group of players. We were the underdogs through the entire playoffs, with three Game 7 victories and getting the final win on the road. The jubilation on the ice after the win in Vancouver has to be one of the most emotional moments of my life. Words can't describe my emotions watching Zdeno hoist the Cup in the air and pass it to Recchi and on to Tim and to each player. Looking into the stands to see the fans who had trekked to Vancouver to be there to share in the moment. In the locker room with the pure jubilation. My entire family was in Vancouver, include my children and their spouses and grandkids. So many moments—I need a whole list just for the Stanley Cup most memorable moments.

Note: Jack Parker is one of the greatest coaches in college history. The head coach of the Boston University hockey team since 1973, Parker has over 850 wins and three Division I National Titles. Born in Somerville, Coach Parker attended Catholic Memorial High School, where he was MVP of the hockey team and then Boston University where he was captain in 1968. The man knows his movies, too. Here, he lists what he considers the finest films about sports.

Honorable Mentions. *Fear Strikes Out—The Jimmy Piersall Story; Chariots of Fire; The Fighter; On Any Given Sunday; The Pride of the Yankees—The Lou Gehrig Story.*

10. *Requiem for a Heavyweight.* The Playhouse 90 TV production with Jack Palance—fabulous acting job (better than the movie of the same name with Anthony Quinn).

9. *North Dallas 40.* Pro football player Nick Nolte explains why the real NFL is not so good. "We're not the team, they're the team. We're just the equipment."

8. *Hoosiers.* The underdog does it again. Gene Hackman is good and Dennis Hopper is great. Great scene when the coach (Hackman) measures the court and height of the basket in the big stadium to assure his team that even though they're playing in a big arena, the court is exactly the same as their high school gym back home.

7. *Seabiscuit.* A nice story, beautifully shot and a good history lesson about how hard times affected the nation. If a broken-down trainer and horse can recover and win, so can the country.

6. *Bang the Drum Slowly.* Great insight into how and when a team "comes together." Memorable last line, "From now on, I rag on nobody."

5. *Somebody Up There Likes Me.* Paul Newman stars in another well-shot fight movie. "What'd he ever give me except his wine breath and the back of his hand."

4. *Rocky.* What's better than rooting for the underdog? Great ending. "They'll be no re-match . . . I don't want one."

3. *When We Were Kings*. Ali being Ali—what could be better? "Everyone must've blinked at the same time."

2. *The Hustler*. Great inside peek at the seamy side of pool. "I'm shooting pool Fat Man, and when I miss, you can shoot."

1. *Raging Bull*. Robert De Niro gave one the best acting performances of all time. "He ain't pretty no more."

Boston's Most Wanted List :: AG and the Fans

Since I wrote four lists on the "Most Hated" people in the four major sports, I figured I'd ask the fans via our book's Facebook page to come up with the guys *they* hate the most. I usually clean up the writing, but this time I literally took the fans' postings right off the site and pasted them into the manuscript as is (with some cuts for space). I told the fans that if they did their part, they'd get some glory . . . and now they're about to. Each entry is headlined by the name of the fan making the contribution (not by the player getting hated on) and is listed in no particular order.

Fan Kevin Steele. Would have to be A-Rod just for overall douchery. George Steinbrenner for the overabundant arrogance. Peyton Manning for having the audacity to be mentioned in the same breath with the great Tom Brady. Have to go with Zo's guy LeBron James—not sure why he's so hated, he's never beaten the C's; I guess it's how he made "The Decision." The guy who should be higher is Kobe—unlike LeBron, he has beaten the C's, and he had the whole Colorado thing. Those are my recent day top 5.

Fan Chuck Gellman. Jack Hamilton. He beaned Tony Conigliaro and essentially ended one of the most promising careers in baseball history. Tony C. was being compared to guys in the Hall of Fame as a rookie.

Fan Nick Cabral. A-Rod—dude's such a clown, not entirely sure anybody in New York even likes the guy.

Fan Kevin Steele (again). My other five in no order: Rex Ryan; Eric Mangini because of Spygate; I almost forgot the goon Matt Cooke; maybe Manny for the way he acted at the end of his time in Boston; and Eli Manning just for being a punk and winning the Super Bowl against the Patriots.

Fan Ron McMahan. Ulf Samuelsson and Matt Cooke—cowards. Bill Laimbeer—spoiled rich kid . . . look it up. Peyton Manning—is all the crying necessary? Ken Linseman/Chris Nilan—hated 'em both until they played for the B's. The 2010 New York Jets with Antonio Cromartie and LaDainian Tomlinson.

Fan Josh Merrifield. Rob Deer. That D-BAG told me to piss off when I asked for his autograph; I WAS EIGHT! I ended up flipping him off.

Fan Jim Winfield. Ulf Samuelsson. Big ol' d-bag here!

Fan Kris Waterman. Ulf Samuelsson (ruined Neely's career), Matt Cooke, Peyton and Eli Manning, Aaron Boone, Bucky Dent, A-Rod, Bill Laimbeer, Kobe Bryant, LeBron James.

Fan Kevin Burge. Chris Nilan—I don't care who he was playing for, he was a punk just alone for what he did to Rick Middleton.

Fan Dolly Jo McPherson. Tiger Woods—total scum and all you sportscasters who still put him up on that pedestal need to get a clue. I don't enjoy hearing his name referenced when he's not even playing in the tournament. And, I don't need you to compare every shot the rest of the field hits to one that he hit last week. I have enough hatred for him to fill the other nine spots, sorry.

Fan Adam Almeida. Aaron Ward—do I really need to elaborate? The entire Lakers organization for countless NBA Finals and heart-grasping games. A-Rod for being such a dink 24/7. Steve Ott and Matt Cooke for being weaselly MFs! And Eric Mangini for being such a snot-nosed tattletail yet still yearns for Belichick's respect.

Fan Andrew Henry. Barry Bonds, Eric Mangini, the Manning Bros, Jack Tatum, LeBron James, A-Rod, Bill Romanowski, Scott Boras, Brett Favre, Roger Clemens, Kobe Bryant.

Fan Richard Cardente. The New York Yankees 1901-present and beyond. Bill Laimbeer. Al Davis. Don Shula. (P.S. don't include Rex Ryan. Don't give him the satisfaction of thinking he's one of the most hated around here.)

Fan Kevin Kelly. Johnny Damon (Benedict Arnold didn't just leave, he went to the enemy), Adam Vinatieri (same reason). Phil Jackson (thinks he's better than Red Auerbach). A-Rod (schmuck in general, Hamburger Helper gloves don't help). Matt Cooke (need I say more).

Fan Steve Lallier. A-Rod—just because he is the No. 1 boob overall. Matt Cooke—Marc Savard will never be close to what he was as a player after that cheap shot. LaDainian Tomlinson—because he whined like a girl when he played in SD and now is with the enemy, the Jets. Hal Gill—sucked as a Bruin and played very soft for his size and is now a Canadien. Phil Kessel—whined about Claude as a Bruin and is now whining in Toronto after getting traded and plays one-way hockey.

Exciting Plays :: MC

These are the moments that made you jump out of your seat and yell in disbelief. This list is more about the quality of the play and less about the impact of the play on a game. It is a series of snapshots of the greatness of sports. These are the moments that we watch and listen to again and again to be amazed by the talent and accomplishments of our athletes. (Note: This list does not include Flutie's Hail Mary pass or Orr's Stanley Cup winning goal—those plays have a home on another list.)

Honorable Mentions. Catch by Tom Waddle of Boston College against Penn State; end-to-end goal by Rosie Ruzicka; Jim Rice's home run over the Fenway flagpole; Tony Eason-to-Irving Fryar Hail Mary pass; Conner Henry dunk; Doug Flutie bootleg for Patriots; Coco Crisp's catch in center; Tedy Bruschi's interception and touchdown in the snow at Foxboro.

13. John Kennedy's Inside-the-Park Home Run (July 5, 1970). On a hot Sunday afternoon at Fenway, journeyman John Kennedy was pinch hitting for the Red Sox in the fifth inning. He proceeded to hit the ball to right field. The ball wrapped around the right-field wall. While the outfielder chased, Kennedy rounded the bases. The inside-the-park home run brought the crowd to its feet much like another John Kennedy had done so many times before in Boston.

12. Watson Blows Up Bailey (January 14, 2006). In the AFC Divisional Playoffs in Denver, the Patriots were on the Bronco's five-yard line, driving for a go-ahead touchdown. On third down, Tom Brady took the snap and was pressured up the middle. He rolled right and released the ball toward Troy Brown, but Champ Bailey intercepted the ball two yards deep in the end zone. With nothing but green in front of him, the speedy defensive back sprinted down the sideline. The Patriots 255-pound tight end Ben Watson ran 140 yards from the other side of the field and blew up Bailey as the Broncos CB geared down to score. The ball was knocked through the end zone for what should have been a game-saving touchback for the Pats. Sadly the refs decided to place the ball at the two-yard line for the Broncos, who won.

11. Stealing Home (April 26, 2009 and August 3, 1982). Both Jacoby Ellsbury and Billy Hatcher brought down the Fenway house with the most exciting play in baseball—the straight steal of home. Ellsbury's scored with a tumbling head-first slide against the Yankees on ESPN's *Sunday Night Baseball*. Hatcher touched the plate with a cool stand-up slide, then bounced right into the dugout.

10. Bob Windsor's Sacrifice for Victory (October 27, 1974). The Patriots were down to their last play and trailed the Minnesota Vikings 14-10. Jim Plunkett threw a pass to tight end Bob Windsor. With no time left on the clock, Windsor broke tackles and dragged Minnesota Vikings into the end zone for a game-winning score. Windsor hurt his knee on the play, ending his season.

9. Mugsey's Walk-Off Bunt (August 28, 1982). Trailing 5-0 to the Angels, the Red Sox rallied to force extra innings. With two outs in the bottom of the 10th inning and the bases loaded, slow-of-foot catcher Gary "Mugsey" Allenson laid down a perfect bunt to score Carney Lansford and cap off an exciting Saturday afternoon rally in the Fens.

8. Trot Nixon's Rocket off Rocket (May 28, 2000). This was baseball at its best. It was an ESPN Sunday-night duel between Pedro Martinez and Roger Clemens in Yankee Stadium. With the scored tied 0-0 in the ninth inning, Nixon took a Clemens fastball into the right-field bleachers and gave the Red Sox a victory over the hated team and pitcher.

7. Fred Lynn's Catch in Shea Stadium (July 27, 1975). With the Red Sox in first place, they came to Shea Stadium (Yankee Stadium was being renovated) and swept the Yankees in a Sunday doubleheader on two shutouts. The play of the day was a diving catch by Fred Lynn running toward the wall in left-center. Left fielder Jim Rice leapt over the prone Lynn, while a plane shadow passed over them.

6. Rondo Steal and Lay-In (May 22, 2010). To date, it is Rajon Rondo's signature play. In Game 3 of the NBA Eastern Conference Finals, Rondo and the Magic's Jason Williams competed for a loose ball. While Jason Williams counted his tattoos, Rondo dove to the floor, collected the ball, stood up, beat Williams off the dribble and laid the ball in. The series was over at that point.

5. Cam Neely's 360 (October 28, 1993). Bad leg and all, Cam Neely was in the midst of a historic run of 50 goals in 44 games. One highlight goal came against the Ottawa Senators. It featured a streaking Neely after he received a cross-ice pass from Cam Stewart. As he came to the right faceoff circle, Neely twice faked slap shots and then spun 360 degrees before he ripped a backhand into the far corner of the net.

4. Bobby Orr's Goal vs. Atlanta. This goal represents so much about the player. Orr started behind his own net and then used his amazing skating skills, changing speeds and cutting on sharp edges. When he arrived at the Flames crease, he was forced wide and had to wrap around the net. When he came out on the other side, he slipped a backhand shot magically under a diving defender. Instead of wildly celebrating, Orr then simply bent down and coasted with his stick, leaning on his thighs with great humility.

3. Round 9 of Micky Ward vs. Arturo Gatti (May 18, 2002). There are not many sporting moments that make me jump out of my seat, but Round 9 of the first Gatti-Ward fight was one of the most exciting rounds in boxing history. Jim Lampley's call matched the fight, "Ward nods as if to say, 'Come on! Come on! C'mon—let's fight!'"

2. Yastrzemski in Yankee Stadium (April 14, 1967). Red Sox rookie pitcher Billy Rohr made his debut appearance in Yankee Stadium against Hall of Fame pitcher Whitey Ford. Entering the ninth inning, Rohr had a no-hitter. Tom Tresh led off the inning, hitting a screaming line drive over left fielder Carl Yastrzemski's head. Ken Coleman's call said it all, "Yastrzemski is going hard way back, way back and he dives and makes a tremendous catch!!!" Rohr lost the no-hitter a couple of batters later, but pitched a shutout. The game served as an omen of the magical season ahead.

1. Larry Bird's Magic (May 5, 1981). In Game 1 of the NBA Finals against the Houston Rockets, Larry Bird took a jump shot from the right side of the top of the key. Immediately recognizing that the shot was astray, Bird calculated the direction of the rebound. With the information processed, he ran to the baseline, gathered the rebound while falling out of bounds and—in the same motion—switched the ball from his right hand to his left hand and rolled a 12-footer through the hoop for an amazing basket. Red Auerbach called the play the greatest in NBA history.

Bruins Are Stanley Cup Champions! :: MC

For years, the people of Bruins Nation have thirsted for the Cup. Stories of past championships back in the early 70s were starting to fade into folklore. However, the 2011 Bruins team rekindled the pounding heart of Bruins Nation by battling through great adversity to earn the team's sixth Stanley Cup Championship. In 2011, Boston realized the four-leaf clover of championships over the past decade. Boston is now officially Titletown! Here are some of the things we'll never forget.

10. Since 1972. Prior to the magical run of 2011 the Bruins have been to the Stanley Cup Finals five times since the last championship in 1972. Over that period, Bruins Nation has dealt with the mismanagement of the lockout roster, too-many-men-on-the-ice penalties, Dave Lewis's moustache, Cam Neely and Kevin Stevens getting benched, the uneven trade of Joe Thornton and the 3-0 collapse against the Flyers. However, all is forgiven. They gave Boston back its Cup!

9. Top Hits, Punches and the Bird. The site of a pent-up Shawn Thornton sniffing ammonia before Game 3 in full froth signaled the end of the Canucks. For 25 playoff games, the Bruins made Boston proud. They honored their obligation of representing the city by hitting everything that moved, winning battles in the corner and sacrificing their bodies to block shots. From Andrew Ference flipping off the condescending Montreal fans to Brad Marchand making Daniel Sedin into a bobblehead with seven lefts to the face to Tim Thomas leveling Henrik Sedin, they made us proud to be Bruins fans.

8. Goals. Sure the power play was anemic, but that just made the challenge that much more exciting. The Bruins outscored opponents by 28 goals including David Krejci's twelve goals (four game winners) and Nathan Horton's two overtime goals (three game winners). However, the goal of the postseason was scored by Brad Marchand when he outworked and out-willed all five Canucks including Ryan Kessler for a shorthanded gem in Game 3 of the Finals.

7. The Brass. I have to pump the tires of the Bruins' brass—from Julien to Chiarelli to Neely to the Jacobs family. How fragile one's job-security is when you are responsible for a professional sports franchise. If the Bruins lost in the Montreal series, Peter Chiarelli and Claude Julien would have been fired. Instead, midseason acquisitions by the Bruins' GM of Chris Kelly and Rich Peverley gave the coach perfect pieces for the championship puzzle. The coach then pulled all the right strings pairing up Chara and Seidenberg, using the fourth line for energy and impact, and never panicking all the way to a Duckboat parade.

6. Tim Thomas. The Bruins' goalie who so many could identify with for being overlooked, undervalued, and under-appreciated. All Thomas did was submit the greatest postseason goaltending performance in NHL history. He stole games, stopped breakaways, dove with hockey stick extended and was the author of the best body check of the playoffs. His clutch performance puts him shoulder to shoulder with Yaz, Brady, Havlicek and Vinatieri.

5. Chara and Seidenberg. Has a pair of defenseman ever played better in NHL postseason history? They held Thelma and Louise Sedin (who combined for 198 points in the regular season) to two goals and three assists. They took the body, cleared rebounds, moved the puck. Despite the fact that they faced the other teams' best forwards the two Bruins' defenders combined for a plus-28 in the playoffs.

4. Punks, Villains, Cheapshot Artists. After 25 games of up and down action, we were bound to add some new names to our most hated list. The Montreal Diving Team was led by a flopping P.K. Subban. Philadelphia had the usual suspects, no more than Daniel Carcillo. Tampa was led by a Claude Lemeiux-like Steve Downie. But the worst was left for last where the Bruins had to deal with a biting Alexandre Burrows, a gutless Maxim Lapierre, a blindsiding Aaron Rome and a cheapshot artist in Jannik Hansen. They all had one thing in common in the end, though—they were LOSERS!

3. Statistics.
- In game two of the Tampa series, rookie Tyler Seguin unveiled future brilliance with four points in one period tying an NHL record
- Mark Recchi became the oldest player ever to score in the Stanley Cup Finals at age 43
- Chara and Seidenberg averaged 27:39 and 27:38 respectively in ice time for the 25 playoff games
- Tim Thomas: four shutouts, 798 saves, first-ever shutout by the visiting goalie in a Finals Game 7

2. Randomocity.

- The Bruins lost the first game in three of the four series
- The Finals series was over when Roberto Luongo complained about Tim Thomas not saying anything nice about him
- How cool was it when Bobby Orr was waving the Nathan Horton flag?
- Players like Campbell, Paille, Kelly and Peverley provided the necessary intangibles to maintain momentum, energy and grit to grind out a seven-game series
- You knew it was a big game when Rene Rancourt added a third pump of the fist after the national anthem
- When Chara raised the Cup, it was over eight feet high

1. Fans, Celebration and Parade. There are no more loyal fans than those who support the Bruins. To those who never wavered in their passion, I congratulate you. The parade was the biggest in Boston sports history. From Southie to Cape Cod to Portland to Providence, this is a Bruins town!

My Top 5 Moments in 2011 :: by Dave Goucher

Dave Goucher gave us his Top 10 career moments back on page 204. Here now are his Top 5 moments from the amazing Stanley Cup run in 2011.

5. 2011 Bruins-Canadiens, Game 5. The Bruins had dropped the first two games of the series at home, but found a way to pull even with two victories in Montreal. Tim Thomas, after a shaky first two games, had found his groove, and never was this more evident than in Game 5. In double overtime, Travis Moen and Brian Gionta broke in on a 2-on-1 rush and it looked certain that Gionta would score. But Thomas flashed out his left pad to save the game. Nearly halfway through the second overtime, Nathan Horton put home the rebound of an Andrew Ference shot, scoring what was, at the moment, the biggest goal of his career. But he would soon top that more than once.

4. 2011 Bruins-Canadiens, Game 7. The pressure on the Bruins to win was enormous. Their season had ended with a Game 7 loss three years in a row, including crushing home losses to Carolina in overtime and Philadelphia, losing a 3-0 lead in the series and a 3-0 lead in the seventh game. Speculation was rampant, if the Bruins failed to get out of the first round, that significant changes were around the corner, from coaches to players to perhaps management. The back-story for me was that I had called five previous Game 7's for "my team" either in the minors or in Boston, and they'd lost them all. As a franchise, the Bruins hadn't won a Game 7 in 17 years, and they'd never won a series after dropping the first two games. But the B's got off to an early 2-0 lead early. The first thing I thought of was the year before, when a 3-0 Game 7 lead against the Flyers wasn't enough. And before I knew it, the Canadiens tied the game in the second period. But when Chris Kelly scored in the third it appeared the Bruins were on their way. Not so fast. A terrible penalty call on Patrice Bergeron with 2:37 left led to P. K. Subban tying the game. I had a bad feeling heading into OT. But there was Nathan Horton again, scoring his second OT goal to win the series. Finally a Game 7 victory was theirs, setting up a grudge match and eventual sweep of Philadelphia.

3. 2011 Bruins-Lightning, Game 7. The afternoon of the game my next door neighbor/college roommate, Kyle D'Arcy, stopped by the house to wish me good luck and remind me this was the biggest game I'd ever call. Half an hour later, his son Jack, all of eight-years-old, said, "Dave, just wanted to wish you good luck considering this is the biggest game of your career and everything." I started laughing out loud. Shortly thereafter I got a text from someone else that read, "no pressure tonight, it's just most of the country that will be listening." Great. Another friend asked me for a shout out and B's assistant coach Doug Houda asked me to say hello to his brother, Tom, who would be working the mines in British Columbia. When the game started to unfold, it felt like the teams were playing overtime the entire night. I was convinced the team that scored first would win. And who else but Nathan Horton delivered, scoring the only goal of the game with 7:33 left. He became the first player in NHL history to score two Game 7 winners in the same playoff year, and the Bruins were in the Stanley Cup Final for the first time in 21 years.

2. 2011 Bruins Championship Parade. Not every moment I remember most is from the broadcast booth, and never in my life have I experienced anything like being on a duck boat in the Bruins' rolling rally parade. The noise level was indescribable, with over 1.5 million people lining the streets of the city. There were fans hanging out of windows and climbing up trees and waving from rooftops. I remember seeing a fan wearing a Richard Nixon mask and giving him the "double V" for victory sign. I expected the throng of people to thin out at some point but it never did. The city had witnessed six of these parades in the previous decade, but never had so many people turned out to celebrate a championship. And to be right in the middle of that cauldron of noise and emotion is something I will never forget.

1. 2011 Bruins-Canucks, Game 7. The home team had won the first six games, with the Bruins dominating on home ice 17-3. But they'd managed to score just two goals in Vancouver. It was a long two days waiting for Game 7. The morning of the game was sunny and mild, so I grabbed a coffee and went down by the water, thinking of the magnitude of the game I was about to call. The Bruins and their fans had been waiting 39 years for a Stanley Cup. The Patriots, Red Sox and Celtics had all won titles over the last decade and enjoyed their own parades on duck boats through the city. My mind started to gravitate towards that. If the B's won, they'd have a celebration of their own. And to me, the Cup would be back home again, where it belonged. That was about as much thought as I gave to what I might say. The last thing I wanted to do was script something. The game was a mismatch, a 4-0 Bruins win led by two goals apiece from Patrice Bergeron and Brad Marchand. And Tim Thomas wrapped up the Conn Smythe trophy with a shutout, allowing a staggering eight goals in seven games in the Finals. It set off a wild celebration throughout New England, and I ended up saying, "Get the duck boats ready, after 39 long years the Cup is back home, the Bruins are 2011 Stanley Cup champions!" I wanted it to be short, sweet and memorable and I wanted to capture the moment. Hopefully I did that.

Top 100 Boston-Area Athletes of All Time

This is the mother of all lists. And when you see all these great athletes' names together and consider their accomplishments, you will see why Boston is the mother of all sports towns. Obviously, compiling and ranking the Top 100 Boston athletes of all time is a nearly impossible task (although not nearly as impossible as taking four in a row from the Yankees in the ALCS after being down 3-0), but we did it. In choosing rankings, we considered things like the sport involved, years of service, consistency, clutch performance, local connections, historic significance, and other factors. This is our best shot at the Top 100. Feel free to take your best shot at us.

100. Chris McCarron. The jockey from Dorchester won 7,141 races including six Triple Crown events and five Breeder Cup classics.

99. K.C. Jones. An eight-time world champion as a player, he also won two as a coach. The Celtics retired his number.

98. Frank Brimsek. Because of him, the Bruins traded Tiny Thompson to Detroit. Good goalie for many years.

97. Matt Light. I never thought he'd be a three-time Pro Bowler and around for four Super Bowls. A very nice career for a very nice guy.

96. Uta Pippig. First woman to win the Boston Marathon three years in a row. She won the marathon in 1996 while burdened with significant physical issues which sent her to the hospital after crossing the finish line. I don't care where you're from; that's impressive.

95. Mike Vrabel. Picked off the scrap heap from Pittsburgh, he came here and was a leading sacker for the Pats during their Super Bowl years of the 2000s. Will be a coach some day.

94. Johnny Damon. A part of the "Idiots" that lost to the Yankees in the 2003 ALCS, but came back and won the World Series the next year. Played a nice center field, then went to the Yankees after the Sox thought he was done.

93. Dick Radatz. The two-time All-Star was a closer well before the role became en vogue. Was funny as hell as a talking head on sports radio as well.

92. Mike Greenwell. Robbed of the 1988 MVP because Jose Canseco had a steroid-fueled 40-homer, 40-steal season. Good player, not a great one.

91. Rick Middleton. "Nifty" had moves like no other Bruins forward. He finished with 402 goals.

90. Vince Wilfork. Minded the middle of the Patriots defense for two Super Bowl wins and a multiple Pro Bowler. He has a chance to move up this list with more stellar play and leadership.

89. John L. Sullivan. Bare knuckles champion and the first athlete to earn over one million dollars. A bad ass and rich to boot.

88. Deion Branch. Super Bowl XXXIX MVP who left town over WHAT ELSE, money. Traded to Seattle and after the Pats let Randy Moss go in 2011, they traded back for him.

87. Jason Varitek. Next to Carlton Fisk, the best catcher the Sox have ever had. I don't know what he'll be remembered for more—being a great game caller or fighting with A-Rod in Fenway.

86. Irving Fryar. Could've been one of the greats if drugs, alcohol, and stupidity didn't get in the way. Went to Miami and Philly, found himself, and had a nice career.

85. Dustin Pedroia. Rookie of the Year who then won the MVP the following season. On his way to climbing this list and chasing Bobby Doerr for the best second baseman in Red Sox history.

84. Wes Welker. Traded for by the Patriots in the 2007 offseason, he went on to catch over 350 balls in three seasons with Randy Moss by his side.

83. Tim Wakefield. The knuckleballer for the Red Sox has done it all—start, close, relieve. A valuable member of the Sox for many years who may not have always loved his role, but went and performed anyway.

82. Fernie Flaman. Had two stints with the Bruins, serving as captain in his second tour of duty. He had the third most penalty minutes in NHL history at the time of his retirement.

81. Steve Nelson. Patriots Hall of Fame linebacker in the 1970s and '80s who manned the middle. Went on to be a successful coach at Curry College.

80. Tiny Thompson. Four-time Vezina winner with the Bruins in the 1930s. Also won a Stanley Cup in 1929.

79. Jim Nance. The only AFL player to rush for more than 1,400 yards in a season.

78. Nick Buoniconti. The Springfield native was traded to the Miami Dolphins during the Boston Patriots AFL days and never looked back, leading Miami's "No Name Defense" to a perfect season in 1972.

77. Jo Jo White. The Celtics guard was the 1976 NBA Finals MVP and a two-time world champion. His son is a successful actor now.

76. Rodney Harrison. Safety who signed from San Diego. Harrison was the Woody Woodpecker of the Pats last two Super Bowl wins. He's an instigator whose issues with HGH didn't hurt his public persona.

75. Paul Silas. More than 10,000 points and 10,000 rebounds in his NBA career. Is now a subservient NBA head coach.

74. Jonathan Papelbon. Sox closer for half-a-decade. Was the perfect bulldog out of the bullpen who has averaged around 35 saves a season. May not be able to spell his own name, but the way he's been able to throw strikes for the Sox, who cares?

73. Richard Seymour. The first top selection for Bill Belichick, he was a stud for many years with the Pats until they traded him to Oakland in 2009 because he and BB didn't get along.

72. Terry O'Reilly. Took over the captaincy of the Bruins from Wayne Cashman and was known as "Taz"—as in the Tazmanian Devil. Coached the Bruins to the Stanley Cup Finals in the late 1980s as well.

71. Johnny Pesky. Fans know him now as a funny old man who hits fungoes in spring training. But look at his numbers from his playing days—they were awesome! He hit for some pop, drove in runs, hit for well over .300 and then got called to war. He came back and was good, but not great like he was before. If you don't know Pesky the player, look it up—you'll be impressed with old "Needle Nose."

70. Bruce Armstrong. A six-time Pro Bowler as a Patriot in the 1990s. Was the captain of the team for most of his stay. Is regarded as a selfish leader who shouldn't have been captain.

69. Francis Ouimet. The Brookline caddy shocked the world by winning the U.S. Open as an amateur in 1913 at The Country Club.

68. Curtis Martin. Was almost a Pro Football Hall of Famer in 2011. Gave the Pats that lead running back they needed while rebuilding the franchise in the early 1990s.

67. Joe Cronin. Hit .300 or better and drove in 100 or more runs eight times in a career spanning from 1926 to 1945. Had his number retired by the Red Sox.

66. Drew Bledsoe. Gave the Patriots their first real franchise quarterback. And yes, he was replaced by Tom Brady, but was a big part of the rebirth of the New England Patriots in 1993.

65. Cedric Maxwell. An NBA Finals MVP in 1981. Was a very underrated part of the C's run in the 1980s. Now a Celtics radio color analyst.

64. Dit Clapper. First to play 20 seasons (1927-47) in the NHL. Played both winger and defenseman and was named an All-Star at both positions.

63. Dennis Johnson. DJ came to Boston in 1983 to match up against bigger guards and play great defense. And that's what he did, plus so much more.

62. Troy Brown. Had a 100-catch season and a knack for making the big play. The play he'll be remembered for most came in the 2005 playoffs against San Diego when he saved the season with an interception-reversing strip of Marlon McCree.

61. Mo Vaughn. The "Hit Dog" was an MVP with the Red Sox, winning it over Albert Belle. He bounced for the cash and serenity of the West Coast, signing with Anaheim and collecting a lot of money for not a lot of production. A big man who could move and play good defense at first.

60. Steve Grogan. The quarterback with the neck harness might be the toughest player to ever pull on the Patriots jersey. He led the Pats to 75 wins, ran for 35 touchdowns and threw for 182 more.

59. Brad Park. This New York Rangers defenseman was traded to the one place he may have been hated the most: Boston. And he excelled as a Bruin. He was the prototypical example of "hate him with them, love him with us." Part of Don Cherry's Lunchpail Gang.

58. Ray Allen. He is a part of a much-needed Celtics resurgence and is the leading three-point shooter in NBA history. He, Garnett and Pierce became the Celtics new Big Three and they didn't disappoint, winning a championship in their first season together.

57. Ed Macauley. A seven-time All-Star, six times with the Celtics. He was traded for what ended up being Bill Russell. Good value, Red.

56. Curt Schilling. "The Bloody Sock Game" in the 2004 ALCS against the New York Yankees will go down as one of the gutsiest big-game performances in sports history. If for nothing else, he'll be remembered for that.

55. Randy Moss. Played 52 games as a Patriot, scored 50 touchdowns. Enough said.

54. Nomar Garciaparra. Will be remembered as being part of the great shortstop debate in the late 1990s. He was traded in 2004 and missed out on the Sox winning the World Series.

53. Tedy Bruschi. Middle linebacker and clutch defender for New England's four Super Bowl appearances in the 2000s. A local hero after coming back from a stroke to play again.

52. Fred Lynn. Won the Rookie of the Year and the MVP in 1975. Was viewed as perfect for Fenway but was traded to Anaheim over, you guessed it, money.

51. Robert Parish. "The Chief" was the center for the great 1980s Celtics teams and remains a very underrated player in Celtics history. He matched up against Kareem, Moses Malone and Ralph Sampson, as well as other NBA big men. If I had that responsibility I'd probably smoke weed like he did too.

50. Johnny Kelley. The patriarch of the Boston Marathon won twice and came in second seven times. He finished the race 61 times.

49. Johnny Bucyk. "The Chief" is a Bruins legend. He was revered as a player, beloved as a broadcaster and is now a part of the organization's front office. His play may not warrant him getting such a high spot, but his longevity buys him some spots. As do his 545 goals.

48. Bill Sharman. Played in the 1950s in the early Auerbach era and formed what some consider as the best backcourt duo of all time with Bob Cousy. Who am I to question that?

47. Clarence DeMar. The seven-time winner of the Boston Marathon was known as "Mr. DeMarathon."

46. Doug Flutie. The most exciting college player in New England sports history. The diminutive QB carried Boston College with jump passes, scrambling and Houdini-like escapes from would-be tacklers. He was so much more than a Hail Mary pass.

45. Stanley Morgan. The four-time Pro Bowl receiver had his best season in 1986 with over 1,400 yards and 10 touchdowns. He was a dynamic player and will always be underrated because he played on some bad teams.

44. Harry Agganis. "The Golden Greek" might have gone on to establish himself as the greatest athlete to ever come from Massachusetts. A two-sport superstar from Lynn Classic, then Boston University, he signed a contract with the Red Sox. Sadly, he perished in 1955 just as he was approaching his prime.

43. Tris Speaker. Started his career in Boston and was a part of the "Million-Dollar Outfield." Won World Series titles in 1912 and 1915.

42. Dwight Evans. Arguably the best right fielder in Red Sox history he was an eight-time Gold Glove winner and hit just under 400 homers. Was as consistent as the day is long. And a gentleman to boot.

41. Ben Coates. I remember hearing a certain quarterback who played with Coates say, "I didn't care if he's triple teamed. I'd throw him the ball and he'd catch it." New England's tight end throughout the 1990s, Coates finally won a Super Bowl during his last season in 2000 with Baltimore. He's got a great chance to end up in Canton, Ohio. A 100-catch season for a tight end in the 1990s! Amazing.

40. Kevin Garnett. He may only spend five years as a Celtic, but his impact can't be denied. We will always compare those who come after him when it comes to intensity and the ability to want to play defense. He'll go down as one of the best of all time in the NBA. But you need more than five years of service with the Celtics to move past some of the legends of the organization on this list.

39. Tommy Heinsohn. Legendary Celtics player, coach and now broadcaster. You can't think about the Celts and not think of Tommy.

38. Jimmie Foxx. A three-time MVP in the 1930s and the second major leaguer to hit 500 home runs following Babe Ruth. Works for me.

37. Gerry Cheevers. One of, if not the best goalie in Bruins history. A contract dispute took him to the WHA in 1972, but as a Bruin there was no doubt he'd be getting the call for ANY big game. Even after returning from the WHA, he was damn good, just not as durable.

36. Andre Tippett. I must say I was surprised when he was elected to the Pro Football Hall of Fame. He and Lawrence Taylor were regarded as the best outside linebackers of their day, but when compared, LT wins hands down. That doesn't mean Tippett doesn't deserve his due. He could flat-out get to the quarterback.

35. Wade Boggs. Like Ted Williams, he had the ability to see the ball in a way others couldn't. He used the wall to slap many a double in his day and when the Sox made renovations to Fenway, he knew how it would affect every hitter in the league, and how it would affect him in particular. He may be the one guy who went to the Yankees and doesn't have it held against him.

34. Luis Tiant. A two-time All-Star with the Red Sox, had his best season in 1974 when he won 22 games. But he will be remembered for his windup delivery and great disposition.

33. Ty Law. Mike Haynes is in the Hall. When Ty makes it, I'll probably move him up past Haynes. His pick in Super Bowl XXXVI should've made him MVP, but it went to Brady. He locked up Marvin Harrison and was a pain in the ass of Peyton Manning because he was just that good.

32. David Ortiz. He will forever be remembered for his walk off in Game 4 of the 2004 ALCS, but he was more than that. The face of the Red Sox World Series teams will forever be remembered for clutch hitting and being "Big Papi."

31. Adam Vinatieri. The best clutch kicker in the history of football. He's as important to the legacies of Tom Brady and Bill Belichick as they are to his. I'd never seen an athlete as clutch as Larry Bird, until Adam. And he's won another Super Bowl with Indianapolis. But that won't be held against him.

30. Gino Cappelletti. The 1963 AFL MVP and longtime Patriots radio analyst was the best player for the Boston Patriots—hands down. He's the AFL's all-time leading scorer as a kicker and wide receiver. He should be in the Pro Football Hall of Fame.

29. Mike Haynes. He only played six years in New England, but is a Pro Football Hall of Famer at cornerback. He gained national glory with the Raiders, but when he was here, the Pats knew at least a quarter of the field was handled.

28. Manny Ramirez. Steroids have tainted this man's legacy, but for almost 10 years he just raked for the Red Sox. He was an automatic 40 homer/120 RBI guy. Put him in at cleanup and that's what he did. And his antics off the field, good and bad, will never be forgotten.

27. Bobby Doerr. The best second baseman in Red Sox history. He will be challenged someday by Dustin Pedroia, but for now it's all this nine-time All-Star and Baseball Hall of Famer.

26. Milt Schmidt. After Eddie Shore, the Bruins next great star. As part of the Kraut Line, he dominated the NHL before heading off to fight in World War II.

25. Carlton Fisk. Behind only Mike Piazza and Johnny Bench in career home runs for a catcher, no one will forget his shot off the foul pole in the 1975 World Series. He called a great game and unfortunately was driven out of town to Chicago. But he's a New England boy and will always be one of us.

24. Jim Rice. For a 10-year period, maybe the most feared hitter in baseball. He made it into the Hall of Fame on his last year of eligibility. Steroids helped his case to get in to the Hall, not because he used them, but because we remember when hitting almost 400 career home runs meant something.

23. Paul Pierce. He has a spot on the Top 10 Celtics of all time. He can get his shot, play defense, and has surprising lift. His game isn't pretty, but it's pretty effective. And he gets extra credit for dealing with years of losing before getting that elusive championship.

22. Roger Clemens. Tied with Cy Young for career wins as a Red Sox, he would've gone down as the best right-handed pitcher of his generation if not for the steroid scandal. And as we watched him make a dogged but poor effort to try to clear his name, we came to realize that his competitiveness is his greatest strength, and also his greatest weakness.

21. Kevin McHale. The reason he ranks this high is because he played his whole career in Boston. Garnett may go down as a better player, but I'll always remember Garnett as a player for the Minnesota Timberwolves. This Minnesota Golden Gopher was a part of the 1980s Celtics team that helped establish the NBA on a national and then international stage.

20. Cy Young. The co-winningest pitcher in Red Sox history. He threw 275 complete games as a member of the Sox with 192 wins. Pretty amazing, no matter the era. And I don't mean ERA.

19. Eddie Shore. Boston's first blueline superstar. He won four MVPs, the most by any defenseman. He could move the puck and was the Bruins first big star. Immortalized when brought up by Paul Newman and the Hanson brothers in the movie *Slap Shot*.

18. Sam Jones. A 10-time NBA champion who scored over 15,000 points. Was a five-time NBA All-Star. Only Russell has more titles as a Celtic.

17. Bill Rodgers. One of the greatest runners in history. Here's all you need to know: he won 22 marathons in his career and out of 59 marathons, ran 28 of them in 2:15 or under. Ridiculous.

16. Dave Cowens. The Celtics big man of the 1970s was as solid and steady a player as the city has ever seen. A seven-time All-Star, a two-time NBA champion and a league MVP.

15. Cam Neely. The big Bruins forward could score as well as fight. He was the perfect Bruin. He'd drop a biscuit in the basket and then drop his gloves to some fool. Kiss Boston's collective ass, Ulf Samuelsson, for shortening Neely's career.

14. Marvelous Marvin Hagler. We forget about him because the longtime Brockton resident now lives in Italy. But all you need to say is Hagler-Hearns or Hagler-Leonard and you're immediately taken back to Atlantic City or Las Vegas for 1980s mega-middleweight fights that actually meant something. And so what if he was born in Jersey.

13. Phil Esposito. One of the greatest goal scorers in the history of the NHL. He led the Bruins to two Stanley Cups after coming over from Chicago in 1967. He had the ability to raise the level of the guys around him. Johnny Bucyk had his best goal-scoring season playing with Espo.

12. John Havlicek. In many ways forgotten by today's Celtics fans, he was a part of Boston lore from 1962 to 1978 and Larry Bird picked up right where he left off. An NBA Finals MVP and the man who "stole the ball" in the 1965 NBA East Finals which led to the great Johnny Most "Havlicek steals the ball" call that is one of the best in NBA history.

11. John Hannah. Even today when discussing the best offensive lineman of all time, fans still mention "Hog." He was a real road grader and was lucky enough to finally play in a Super Bowl in his last season. For just about any player, that would solidify a career. But this 10-time All-Pro didn't really need the help. He was already on his way to the Hall of Fame.

10. Ray Bourque. Another in a long line of world-class Bruins defensemen. He was nowhere the scorer that Orr was (who was?). But the guy knew how to play the puck and understood the game, seeing it two moves ahead. It's a shame he had to go to Colorado to win a Stanley Cup, but still one of the best Bruins ever.

9. Pedro Martinez. The best pitcher in Red Sox history. His 1999 and 2000 seasons are the two best consecutive seasons a pitcher has ever had in Major League Baseball. Fun, petulant, however you feel about him, he's a champion and one of the best of all time.

8. Rocky Marciano. I know people may have to look up his stellar career, but the former heavyweight champ dominated boxing in the 1950s and was a bona fide crossover star in television and film.

7. Carl Yastrzemski. The last Triple Crown winner in baseball back in 1967, Yaz patrolled left field at Fenway and was able to make the move to first base and hang on a few more years as DH. If it weren't for Ted Williams, he might be regarded as the best hitter in Sox history.

6. Bob Cousy. The "local yokel" from Holy Cross is regarded by some as the best point guard ever. He and Russell made a formidable inside-out duo and Cousy became great friends with the man who gave him a real chance in the NBA—Red Auerbach. He knew Red so well he called him by his given name, "Arnold." That tells you something.

5. Larry Bird. His battles with Magic Johnson and Isiah Thomas are legendary. And he was a three-time world champion to boot. Maybe the best clutch player ever in this city.

4. Tom Brady. Has the chance to eventually take the top spot on this list. I know people will be screaming "Larry Bird." But I think Brady has surpassed him because TB12 is the franchise player for the region's most popular franchise. Not many cities have a three-time Super Bowl champion quarterback.

3. Ted Williams. The best hitter who ever lived. He's the last man to hit over .400 and we may never see that done again. After Babe Ruth, he's the Red Sox player you think of next.

2. Bill Russell. The guy won 11 championships and did it against greats like Wilt Chamberlain. He's the greatest center who ever lived and was THE reason the Celtics became a dynasty, the first time around.

1. Bobby Orr. As we've noted, maybe Boston's biggest sports icon. He's done it all, including winning two Stanley Cups. In this city, that's what matters most. Hockey rinks across New England exist because of the popularity of Bobby Orr.